The Life of Buddhism

The Life of Buddhism

Edited by
Frank E. Reynolds and
Jason A. Carbine

MOTILAL BANARSIDASS PUBLISHERS
PRIVATE LIMITED ● DELHI

First Indian Edition: Delhi, 2005

(Published by arrangement with the University of California Press)

ISBN: 81-208-2007-X (Cloth)
ISBN: 81-208-2042-8 (Paper)

MOTILAL BANARSIDASS

41 U.A. Bungalow Road, Jawahar Nagar, Delhi 110 007
8 Mahalaxmi Chamber, 22 Bhulabhai Desai Road, Mumbai 400 026
236, 9th Main III Block, Jayanagar, Bangalore 560 011
120 Royapettah High Road, Mylapore, Chennai 600 004
Sanas Plaza, 1302 Baji Rao Road, Pune 411 002
8 Camac Street, Kolkata 700 017
Ashok Rajpath, Patna 800 004
Chowk, Varanasi 221 001

FOR SALE IN SOUTH ASIA ONLY

Printed in India
BY JAINENDRA PRAKASH JAIN AT SHRI JAINENDRA PRESS,
A-45 NARAINA, PHASE-I, NEW DELHI 110 028
AND PUBLISHED BY NARENDRA PRAKASH JAIN FOR
MOTILAL BANARSIDASS PUBLISHERS PRIVATE LIMITED,
BUNGALOW ROAD, DELHI 110 007

Contents

Note to the Reader

Each of the essays in this collection is preceded by a brief introduction. These introductions contextualize the Buddhist practice being discussed in terms of important structures and dynamics of the Buddhist tradition as a whole. These individual introductions are also intended to augment the general introduction that follows.

In most cases, the main body of each essay has been lightly edited to suit and facilitate the purposes of this collection. The basic format and style of each essay has been left intact, but we have made minor adjustments that make each of them more suitable to the beginning student of Buddhism by omitting diacritics (a policy that we have also followed in our own introductory segments), by clarifying important references with parenthetical notes, by removing overabundant non-English vocabulary, and by slightly rewording certain sentences. However, we have generally abided by the transliteration conventions adopted by the authors of the individual essays.

The main body of one essay, that taken from William LaFleur's *Liquid Life,* has been more substantially changed. We have added two paragraphs of our own to assist certain transitions. We have footnoted these paragraphs in the essay itself.

With the permission of the original publishers and individual authors, we have edited the original footnotes, removing information more appropriate for the advanced or specialized student and altering certain footnotes for clarity. We have also occasionally added our own footnotes, which are labeled "editors' note."

At the end of this collection, we have provided a lightly annotated bibliography, which highlights secondary sources and primary materials that are vital for the more advanced study of Buddhist history and culture. This bibliography does not include the books and journals from which our excerpts have been taken. However, the student should consider these books and journals to be important as well, and we strongly encourage seriously interested readers to engage each essay in its original form and content. The relevant bibliographic information for each essay is provided in the first footnote of every chapter.

We would like to thank AMS Press, the *History of Religions* journal, Cambridge University Press, Princeton University Press, the *Journal of the International Association of Buddhist Studies,* Shambhala Publications, Norwegian University Press, the Siam Society and Charles Keyes, Harvard University Press, Cornell University Press, the *Journal of the Pali Text Society* and Richard Gombrich, and Doubleday for permission to use the essays that have been included in this collection.

Dan Arnold contributed to the footnotes included in chapter 8 and to the development of the annotated bibliography. Ingrid Klass provided important assistance, both by proofreading the entire text and taking the primary responsibility for structuring and compiling the index. We would especially like to thank our typist, Rosemary Carbine, for her patience, for her energy, and for the many helpful suggestions she made as the project proceeded. Finally, we have greatly appreciated the crucial financial support that has been made available by Dean Clark Gilpin of the University of Chicago Divinity School.

General Introduction

This book brings together a carefully selected set of fifteen essays that provide a distinctive kind of introduction to the "life of Buddhism." These essays deal not with the development of Buddhism through history but rather with the presence of Buddhism in a number of relatively contemporary contexts. They highlight not what Buddhist texts say and what Buddhist adherents believe but rather what Buddhist practitioners actually do.

Our choice of essays has been guided by two intentions. First, we have endeavored to provide a geoculturally diverse and balanced collection. Among the fifteen essays, two countries—Japan and Thailand—provide the locale for three essays each. Tibet, Myanma(r)/Burma, and Sri Lanka provide the locale for two essays each.[1] The remaining three essays concern Buddhist practices in China, Korea, and the United States.

Second, we have sought to bring together a group of essays that offer concise depictions and analyses of particular practices that are intrinsic to the structure and dynamics of Buddhist life. These include such diverse items as temple architecture and iconography, consecration of sacred objects, distinctive patterns of monastic and lay behavior, communal and more personalized rituals, meditative practices, devotional expressions, and pilgrimages. They also include the construction of religio-political and religio-social hierarchies, the differentiation of

---

1. Myanma, Myanmar, and Burma are names used by different individuals and groups to refer to the same country. Each of these names appears at specific points in the introduction and in the essays that follow.

gender roles, the management of asocial behavior within society, individual life stories, and confrontations with the harsh realities of dying and death.

To creatively engage this collage of essays, a certain amount of historical background and perspective is needed. To that end, this introduction will provide basic information about the history and structure of Buddhism not included in the essays themselves. We will discuss Buddhism's early and later development in India and its expansion into other areas of Asia and beyond. In the process, we will offer brief characterizations of the three major variants of the tradition. These are the Hinayana/Theravada branch, which has become dominant in Sri Lanka and much of mainland Southeast Asia; the Mahayana branch, which has become dominant in the Buddhist communities of East Asia; and the Esoteric branch, which has become established in Tibet and has also retained a significant presence in Japan. We will also consider the possibility of a fourth but relatively recent variant of the Buddhist tradition, a North American branch.

Early Buddhism: Buddha, Dharma, Samgha

Buddhism originated in northeastern India sometime between the late sixth and early fourth centuries B.C.E.[2] Though we know very little about the details of the earliest tradition, it is clear that it coalesced into a pattern quite common in that area at that particular time. This pattern centered on a wandering mendicant who renounced the lay life and acted as a teacher or master. It involved a religious message and mode of practice that the mendicant-teacher transmitted to those who would listen. And it included a community that venerated the mendicant-teacher and sought to live in accordance with the message that he taught and the mode of practice that he advocated.

Buddhism was the most successful of the several new religions that emerged in this context.[3] Its founder/teacher came to be known as

2. The disagreement between scholars who prefer the early date and those who prefer the late date remains unresolved.

3. Among the similar religious groups that developed in northeastern India at about this time, the only one that had a degree of success that in any way paralleled the success achieved by Buddhism was the Jain tradition founded by Mahavira. Jainism has persisted up to the present time in India but has not become established in any significant way outside the Indian subcontinent.

Sakyamuni and as the Gautama Buddha.[4] He was called Sakyamuni be-cause he was considered to be the great sage (*muni*) of the Sakya people. He was called the Gautama Buddha because he was a member of the Gautama clan and because his followers recognized him as one who had attained the highest religious goal of enlightenment, or Buddhahood.

Though the early Buddhists recognized a plurality of Buddhas (pri-marily several Buddhas of the past), their attention was focused on Gautama.[5] As a Buddha he came to be perceived as a *mahapurusa* (great person) who combined in a very distinctive way the powers, virtues, and attractions of a fully perfected *yogin* (meditative saint) on the one hand and of a *cakravartin* (a universal and righteous monarch) on the other. Early Buddhists believed that Gautama's supreme attainment as Buddha was associated with many previous lives of preparation and with the pos-session of marvelous, supranormal powers and abilities. Further, these early Buddhists also held that his attainment was associated with in-tense meditative practices, culminating in a personal and dramatic expe-rience of enlightenment that took place under a great bodhi tree located at a sacred site that came to be known as Bodh Gaya. They understood that Gautama had made a profound meditational effort and that he had, by this effort, conquered the forces, especially desire, that cause rebirth and suffering.[6] For these early Buddhists, Gautama had attained a pen-etrating insight into the structure and dynamics of reality and achieved a clear view of how life ought to be lived.

The early Buddhist community's memories of the Buddha's min-istry often highlighted his ability to generate, simply by the evocative power of his preaching and presence, profound religious transforma-tions among those he encountered. They attributed to him an ability and willingness to use his marvelous and miraculous powers to convince those with whom he came into contact. And they conveyed an appealing image of a mentor with an uncanny ability to adjust his message both to the needs and to the capacities of his interlocutors.

These memories also included an important account that focused on

4. In the general introduction and in the introductions to the particular essays, we will generally use Sanskrit rather than Pali versions of Buddhist names and terms. Excep-tions will be made in certain instances in which the Pali version is obviously more appro-priate to the context.

5. In this introduction, and in the essays that follow, any reference to "the Buddha" is a reference to Gautama. When other Buddhas are intended, this will be indicated in the text.

6. These forces are often symbolized in Buddhist art and myth by the god Mara and his seductive daughters.

the events surrounding the Buddha's passing away. The most famous version is contained in the Pali Mahaparinibbana Sutta in which the Buddha is depicted as a great person who took the initiative to extend his life and influence beyond the point of his earthly demise. In anticipation of his approaching death, he assigned to his renunciant followers the responsibility for the preservation and propagation of his teachings (sometimes referred to in the later tradition as his *dharmakaya*, or dharma body). He then assigned to his lay followers the responsibility for preserving and caring for his relics (sometimes referred to in the later tradition as his *rupakaya*, or form body).

The exact character of the dharma (teaching, truth) that the early Buddhists perceived and remembered in the Buddha's words has been very much in dispute, both within later Buddhist communities and among modern scholars. There is, however, at least one formulation that most knowledgeable Buddhists and most modern interpreters have recognized as a viable summary. This formulation is that of the four noble truths, a series of teachings that is both doctrinally and practically oriented.

The four noble truths can be stated as follows: (1) All existence (including all sentient life) is constituted by composite entities that are impermanent and subject to dissolution. Further, this impermanence and dissolution is part and parcel of a virtually endless process of birth, death, and rebirth. This process is called samsara, and dissatisfaction and suffering are intrinsic to it. (2) Desire is the primary driving force of samsara and the dissatisfying experiences that are embedded in it. Desire— above all the desire for self-preservation and self-existence—engenders mental and physical activities that lead to karmic retribution. The law of karma ensures that all deeds produce appropriate fruits that condition one's present life, one's future lives, and/or both. (3) Release from samsara and the desire that fuels it can be achieved. Buddhists have come to designate this state of release as nirvana. (4) The method for achieving nirvana is practicing the noble eightfold path. This path consists of right understanding, right thought, right speech, right action, right livelihood, right effort, right mindfulness, and right concentration. It is also identified as the middle way, since each of its facets stresses a mode of "right" activity that avoids an overly self-indulgent or an overly ascetic quest for ultimate happiness.

As the noble eightfold path is understood in the context of the four noble truths, it is a form of practice that leads ultimately to the attainment of nirvana. However, early Buddhists also emphasized that ordinary individuals, by following the basic components of the noble eightfold path, could gain more pleasurable conditions in this life and in future lives, in this world and in the world of the gods.

Much like the details of the early Buddhist understandings of the dharma, the details of the structure and dynamics of community life that characterized early Buddhism are shrouded in later sectarian controversies and scholarly debates. However, it is possible to affirm with confidence that the early Buddhist community included a group of wandering mendicant renouncers (both monks and nuns) and a network of lay supporters (both male and female) with whom the renouncers had varying degrees of contact and affiliation. It is also possible to identify two very distinctive and closely correlated developments that made a crucial contribution to the success that Buddhism ultimately achieved.

The first of these developments began very early, probably within the lifetime of the Buddha himself. In a process that occurred gradually, the Buddha's renunciant followers were organized into a truly monastic order that encouraged long-term residence in settled monastic communities. This order, which came to be known as the samgha, was regulated by rules and procedures attributed to the Buddha himself. There were, of course, many Buddhist renunciants who continued to pursue a life of wandering mendicancy. However, the majority—both male and female—soon acquired affiliations with local monastic establishments.[7]

The second directly correlated development was the emergence of an increasingly close relationship between members of the samgha and members of the laity. This development was both a cause and an effect of the increasingly settled and localized character of samgha life, and it was maintained through a carefully formulated division of responsibilities. Though there were always areas, sometimes very large, of overlap between the activities of the renunciants and those of the laity, a general distinction can be highlighted. Monks took primary responsibility for exemplifying and embodying the virtues and powers of renunciatory practice. Their task was to provide the laity with access to such virtue and power by maintaining and communicating the values of dharmic insight and scholarship and by offering themselves as charismatic repositories of the Buddha's presence. As their contribution, the members of the laity took primary responsibility for the material support of the religion (including but not limited to the support of the renunciants) as well as for the establishment and maintenance of dharmic order and well-being in secular society.

---

7. As far as we know, the Buddhist samgha was the first fully formed monastic community that developed anywhere in the world.

Indian Developments: Hinayana, Mahayana, Esoteric

Within the first century or two after the Buddha's death, the religion that he founded acquired a distinctive identity and spread well beyond the confines of its original homeland in northeastern India. In the middle years of the third century B.C.E., a major breakthrough occurred when King Asoka (ca. 270–30) became a public supporter. Asoka ruled over the first truly pan-Indian empire, and his words and actions—inscribed and reported on stone pillars scattered throughout his empire—greatly aided the Buddhist cause. After his death, he became the protagonist in many widespread Buddhist legends. These legends provided images of Buddhist kingship that had a major impact on the complex and often very close relationship that persisted between Buddhist communities and royal authority.

Buddhism remained one of the major religions in India from the time of Asoka until about the thirteenth century C.E. During this period, Buddhism also spread out from the subcontinent and became a great pan-Asian religion that held sway in many royal and intellectual centers in many different regions. Yet despite the fact that Buddhism was expanding and becoming adapted to its many new geocultural environments, India retained a very important role. It was recognized as Buddhism's place of origin, where the holy sites associated with the life of the Buddha could be visited. And it was also recognized as a primary locus of Buddhist creativity. In fact, it was in post-Asokan India that the three major branches of the Buddhist tradition originated and took on many of their most basic characteristics.

Tendencies that later developed into the first two major branches of Buddhism were present from very early on. However, these tendencies did not generate separate and distinctive traditions until well after Asoka's reign. It was sometime around the advent of the Common Era when a definite though still fluid division began to emerge. One group of renouncers and lay supporters retained a very strong continuity with the mainstream monastic schools that had developed during the first several centuries following the Buddha's death. This group came to be known as the adherents of the Hinayana, or Lesser Vehicle.[8] A second

---

8. Though the name Hinayana is obviously a pejorative term coined by the opposition, there is no viable substitute. Some scholars have used the term Sravakayana (the Vehicle of the Disciples), but this has never been widely accepted. Many others have employed the term Theravada, but this kind of usage invites serious confusion. As we shall see below,

group of renouncers and lay supporters adopted a more innovative approach to recapture what they took to be the true intention of the Buddha and his message. They identified themselves as the adherents of the Mahayana, or Great Vehicle. Variations within both groups, as well as changes that occurred over the course of time, make generalizations difficult. However, several important differences can be identified.

The adherents of the Hinayana schools were characterized by a strong focus on the central significance of the Gautama Buddha. The most important stories that they told were about him, including stories about his previous lives and his relics. Many of the most significant meditations that they practiced involved remembering his person and deeds. And a wide variety of rituals that they performed—especially the veneration of his relics and images—evoked a sense of his continuing power and presence. It is true that most Hinayana schools took serious account of Maitreya, the Buddha of the Future. In fact, various forms of Hinayana practice grew up around the expectation of the day when, far in the future, Maitreya would descend from his present abode in the Tusita heaven to reestablish the religion in all its purity. However, Maitreya's significant role within the Hinayana community never seriously challenged the primacy of Gautama.

The adherents of the various Hinayana schools also continued to recognize the authority and the completeness of two collections of the Buddha's teaching that had been passed down within the well-established monastic communities. One collection, the Sutra Pitaka, consisted primarily of sermons. The other collection, the Vinaya Pitaka, included the rules and procedures governing the samgha. In addition, most of the Hinayana schools developed their own collections of scholastic doctrinal formulations—formulations that characteristically made a clear ontological distinction between samsaric realities on the one hand and nirvana and Buddhahood on the other. These so-called Abhidharma collections came to serve as the third of the Three Baskets (the Tripitaka) that most Hinayana schools recognized as the full and authentic rendition of the Buddha's teaching. With the passage of time, the Hinayanists developed commentaries and other textual genres that enabled them to extend and adapt their understandings and practices in light of changing conditions. However, adherents of the Hinayana traditions maintained

---

Theravada is the self-designation that has been adopted by one particular school among the many that are encompassed within the broader Hinayana rubric. According to the ancient tradition, around the beginning of the Common Era eighteen different schools were considered to be within the Hinayana orbit.

their distinctively conservative ethos through their continued recognition of the ultimate authority of the words of the Gautama Buddha as they were remembered in the Tripitaka.

The Hinayana understanding of the ultimate goal of the religious life was also quite conservative. Though the possibility of attaining Buddhahood was never theoretically denied, the goal on which Hinayanists focused was the attainment of the status of an arhat. The arhat was a fully perfected renunciatory saint who achieved nirvana by practicing the path set forth by Gautama in the sutras and in the vinaya regulations. Non-Hinayanists often criticized the attainment of arhatship as a selfish and therefore inappropriate goal; but Hinayanists consistently maintained that the quest for arhatship transformed one into a rich "field of merit" that others could use to facilitate their own spiritual progress.

For the most part, the adherents of the Mahayana branch of the Buddhist community did not reject the tradition of their Hinayana co-religionists. Rather, they incorporated the Hinayana heritage into a more diverse and encompassing orientation. Though evaluations of the Hinayana approach (and particular versions of that approach) varied greatly among them, Mahayanists generally asserted that Hinayanists adhered to a lesser vehicle that had real but limited value.[9]

For Mahayana adherents, Gautama retained a key role as the founder of the Buddhist tradition. However, within the Mahayana perspective the immediate importance and relevance of many other Buddhas were recognized. These included many great celestial Buddhas who were accessible to Buddhist practitioners and thus played a significant role in the life of the Buddhist community. In addition, the Mahayanists recognized the existence and importance of a significant number of great celestial bodhisattvas who were given a status virtually equivalent to the status of fully realized Buddhas. These great bodhisattvas were beings who had—according to the Mahayana accounts—progressed virtually to the end of the path that leads to Buddhahood. Yet they had resisted entrance into nirvana so that they could continue their work for the salvation of all sentient beings.

9. The context within which the Mahayana tradition emerged remains obscure. Some scholars have suggested that the place to look is the component of the renunciant community that maintained the practice of wandering rather than settled living (the so-called forest monks) and/or the communities of monks and laypeople that gathered around the early Buddhist stupas (funerary mounds that often housed relics of the Buddha). Others have focused on the mainstream monastic schools that had the closest affinity to the kind of orientation that became fully differentiated in the Mahayana context.

The emergence of a clearly differentiated Mahayana branch of Buddhism was also marked by the appearance of a new kind of sutra attributed to Gautama. Unlike the sutras that made up the Sutra Pitaka recognized by the Hinayana schools, these new Mahayana sutras were purportedly preached at special times to special audiences that included only the most intimate and adept earthly disciples. These new Mahayana sutras were very diverse, not only in terms of the different Buddhas and bodhisattvas that they featured but also in terms of the various doctrinal positions that could be deduced from them.

Despite their great diversity, Mahayana sutras tended to assume or affirm that the characteristics of the great Buddhas and bodhisattvas were, in one way or another, congruent with the characteristics of the entire universe or the cosmos itself. This affirmation was closely correlated with the Mahayana doctrinal emphasis that samsara and nirvana were not ontologically separate realities. In fact, for the enlightened, samsara and nirvana were identical in that both were ultimately characterized by voidness or emptiness.

The emphasis on the immanence of the great Buddhas and bodhisattvas and the correlated emphasis on the absence of an ontological difference between samsara and nirvana both contributed to another distinctive aspect of the Mahayana tradition: Mahayana teachers tended to recognize many sources and methods of spiritual assistance for all people, but especially for persons of relatively low spiritual attainment.

The new Mahayana sutras, in addition to presenting significant Buddhological and doctrinal innovations, also set forth a new religious goal. While the Hinayanists considered this goal to be quite unrealistic and presumptuous, Mahayanists considered it to be much superior to the Hinayana goal of attaining arhatship. This new Mahayana goal was that of becoming a fully enlightened Buddha. Thus, all truly serious Mahayana adherents—renunciants and members of the laity alike—were expected to take up the practice of the bodhisattva path that focused on the attainment of Buddhahood. In some Mahayana contexts this was dramatized and ritualized through the taking of bodhisattva vows that involved a specific affirmation of the intention to work for the salvation of all sentient beings.

Many of the elements and tendencies that became primary characteristics of the third major branch of Indian Buddhism, the Esoteric tradition, were present from the early years of Buddhist history. These elements and tendencies were maintained within a variety of Buddhist contexts, especially among forest monks. But it was not until the fourth to sixth centuries C.E. that a clearly differentiated Esoteric pattern began to emerge on the fringes of the Mahayana community. During the centuries that followed, the Esoteric branch became an important component in many forms of Buddhist monastic and social life, both inside and outside India. In India, the Esoteric tradition came to be known by several names including Vajrayana, Mantrayana, and Tantrayana.

Within the Esoteric context, Mahayana Buddhology was both affirmed and extended by the inclusion of new Buddhas and other important figures, including some who were feminine and some who appeared in fierce or threatening guises. Mahayana doctrine was basically accepted but was given a distinctive twist through the particular emphasis placed on the claim that samsaric reality consisted of illusions that were directly generated by various dichotomies and oppositions. Among the dichotomies and oppositions that Esoteric practitioners sought to overcome were those between male and female, good and evil, and samsara and nirvana.

However, the crucial innovation that marked the differentiation of the Esoteric tradition from the Mahayana tradition was the appearance of a new genre of Buddhist texts called tantras as well as the use of meditative techniques and ritual practices associated with these texts. These tantras and their associated techniques and practices were taken to constitute an essential component of the message of the Gautama Buddha that neither the Hinayana nor the Mahayana traditions had seen fit to properly maintain. Further, the tantric meditative techniques and ritual practices were believed to be especially effective in cultivating spiritual and magical power and often involved activities that required the violation of the traditional rules of Buddhist ethics including—in some cases—sexual ethics.[10] Some were extremely sophisticated and complex and were intended to facilitate the rapid achievement of very advanced mystical goals and even Buddhahood itself. Others were aimed at the achievement of very mundane, this-worldly objectives.[11]

The Esoteric tantras and practices were closely associated with the extension and intensification of the relationship—significant in all Buddhist traditions—between a spiritually accomplished master and his dis-

10. Scholars continue to disagree about the extent to which sexual references in tantric texts should be interpreted metaphorically and the extent to which they were intended to be taken literally.

11. Though it is possible to distinguish between more spiritual goals and more mundane goals, it is important to recognize that in most Buddhist approaches the two are closely related. This is especially true in the Esoteric context, in which the acquisition of magical power is given special prominence.

ciples. In the Esoteric context, those who were recognized as masters were considered to have reached extraordinary levels of spiritual attainment and to have at their disposal enormous resources of spiritual and magical power. These resources were seen as crucial because many if not most tantras were intentionally written so that they were very difficult to comprehend. In fact, many were written so that only a person who had reached a very high level of spiritual attainment and insight could uncover and transmit their meanings. Highly personalized guidance, often by a master who was viewed as a "living Buddha," was considered a necessary prerequisite for the effective understanding and practice of what could otherwise be quite dangerous studies and activities. This need for proper guidance by the spiritual master was thus believed to be applicable for all practitioners, regardless of the spiritual or mundane objective at hand.

From the scant information that is available, it seems that the Hinayana, Mahayana, and Esoteric branches of Buddhism continued to co-exist in India right up to the early years of the thirteenth century. At that time, the last major strongholds of Indian Buddhism succumbed to the combined force of Hindu competition and Muslim invasion. After the thirteenth century a few pockets of Buddhist presence were left in various parts of the subcontinent; and in recent years there has been an interesting new Buddhist movement that has attracted a significant number of converts from the lowest echelons of Hindu society.[12] However, the major Buddhist communities that have persisted to the twentieth century have been Buddhist communities in other areas of Asia.

Sri Lanka and Southeast Asia

As Indian Buddhism spread throughout Asia, it took on distinctive forms in different geographical and cultural regions. The Sri Lanka/mainland Southeast Asia form persists in the areas now called Sri Lanka, Myanmar, Thailand, Cambodia, and Laos. It is closely identified with a particular Hinayana tradition known as the Theravada, or "Way of the Elders." The East Asian form endures in China, Korea, Japan, and Vietnam. It is

12. This new Buddhist movement was brought into being through the conversion, in 1956, of Dr. B. R. Ambedkar, who was an important leader of the so-called scheduled castes. Many of his followers converted with him, and during the last four to five decades, the group has grown to include well over a million adherents (some responsible estimates go as high as two million).

closely identified with Mahayana Buddhism and an East Asian version of the Esoteric tradition that continues to coexist with it in the Shingon and Tendai schools in Japan. The Tibetan form is currently practiced in the areas now identified as Tibet, Mongolia, Nepal, Bhutan, and in pockets of India. This Tibetan form is closely identified with a rather different version of the Esoteric tradition often referred to as Vajrayana, or the Thunderbolt Vehicle.[13]

The expansion of Indian Buddhism into Sri Lanka and mainland Southeast Asia began very early. An inscription of King Asoka asserts that he commissioned Buddhist emissaries to travel to many areas of the Indian subcontinent as well as to areas of Sri Lanka and Southeast Asia. There is strong evidence that these emissaries did arrive in Sri Lanka and that a Buddhist community was established in the capital city of Anuradhapura. In Southeast Asia, the situation is less clear. However, there are long-standing local traditions claiming that Asokan emissaries did arrive in southern Myanmar and that they did succeed in establishing a Buddhist community among the local inhabitants.

In Sri Lanka there has been a more or less continuous development of the Buddhist community that was established at the time of the Asokan mission. In Southeast Asia the beginnings of a more or less continuous Buddhist history are associated with archaeological remains in southern Myanmar that date from the third to fourth centuries C.E. From the time that these Buddhist communities in Sri Lanka and Southeast Asia were first established through the end of the first millennium C.E., they maintained close relations with one another and with their counterparts in India. They continued to use the classical Indian languages Sanskrit and Pali (related to Sanskrit) for religious purposes. And these communities came to include practitioners of Hinayana, Mahayana, and Esoteric traditions.

Despite close similarities with the Indian Buddhist community, the Buddhist communities that developed in Sri Lanka and mainland Southeast Asia produced their own particular characteristics and emphases. Perhaps the most distinctive development during the first millennium C.E. was the clear emergence within the Hinayana tradition of a Theravada school that used Pali as its sacred language. In Sri Lanka, the Theravadins had their major center at the great Mahavihara monastery originally founded in Anuradhapura at the time of Asoka. They created and

---

13. The reader should understand that the boundary between these religio-cultural forms of Buddhism are often blurred and do not correspond in any exact way with the boundaries of contemporary political units.

preserved a written Pali version of the Tripitaka, and they produced an extensive tradition of commentaries on virtually all of the Tripitaka texts.[14] In addition, they became engaged in an ongoing series of complicated interactions with Sinhalese kings from whom they often (though not always) received royal support. Although our knowledge of the contemporaneous Buddhist developments in mainland Southeast Asia is much more fragmentary, it is clear that a parallel Theravada tradition was established, primarily among the Mon peoples who lived in southern Myanmar and central Thailand.

During the early centuries of the second millennium C.E.—as Buddhism in India collapsed and virtually disappeared—Buddhists in Sri Lanka and mainland Southeast Asia set out on their own independent course, embarking on a process of transforming the received tradition and adapting it to its new situation. This process, spearheaded by reform-minded kings, resulted in the reconstitution of the Theravada tradition and in the eventual establishment of that tradition as the dominant religious force in both these areas. This newly reconstituted Theravada tradition included a number of strands that were often in tension with one another. It included an "orthodox" component that was conservative and tended to receive special support from kings who desired to exercise greater control over the religion. It included a new emphasis on the use of vernacular languages and on the closely correlated extension of Buddhism beyond the royal courts and great monasteries into the countryside and into the lives of ordinary villagers. It also included many elements that it had inherited from the Hinayana, Mahayana, and Esoteric traditions that had previously coexisted with it.

This new Theravada tradition achieved a dominant position in Sri Lanka and Myanmar in the eleventh through the thirteenth centuries, and it soon spread into other areas of mainland Southeast Asia. In the thirteenth, fourteenth, and fifteenth centuries, it became firmly established in the religious landscape of Thailand, Cambodia, and Laos. In Thailand, it was adopted by the Thai people, who were in the process of imposing their control over an older Mon population that had been Buddhist for some time. In Cambodia, it gradually displaced the Hindu and Mahayana traditions that had prevailed in the previously great kingdom of Angkor. In Laos, it was entrenched in an area populated by a

---

14. Many modern scholars have accepted as historically accurate not only the Theravada account that tells of the writing down of the Tripitaka in the first century B.C.E. but also the Theravada claim that this was the first time that the Tripitaka tradition (previously memorized and transmitted orally) had been committed to writing.

people closely related to the Thai. All these developments also affected the Theravada ethos itself by giving it a flavor associated with local histories and local cultural characteristics.

During the modern period, the Theravada tradition has been seriously challenged by colonialism, by modern modes of thought, and by postcolonial traumas such as violent ethnic conflict (Sri Lanka), military/ socialist rule (Myanmar), rapid capitalist development (Thailand), and radical communist revolution (Cambodia and Laos). But in each of these five countries where they constitute a majority of the population, the Theravadins have adapted more or less successfully to changing conditions.[15] Despite the differences in the challenges that have been faced and the kinds of adaptations that have been made, many of the basic characteristics of the Theravada ethos have not been compromised. All across the Theravada world the religious primacy of the Gautama Buddha is still affirmed, the authority of the Pali textual tradition is still widely recognized, and the use of Pali as a sacred and transcultural language is still retained.

Central and Eastern Asia

The transmission of Indian Buddhism to Central and Eastern Asia began in a serious way before the beginning of the Common Era. Already in Asokan times an important Buddhist community had been established in northwestern India in the area now called Pakistan. This area was at the Indian end of trade routes that extended northward into Central Asia and then eastward all the way to China. Many of the merchants who traveled along these long and arduous routes were Buddhists, and many Buddhist monks joined them on their journeys. Gradually Buddhist communities developed in the various kingdoms that had grown up at various points along the way. By the second half of the first century C.E., there is evidence that Buddhists had already established a presence as far east as China.

During the next eight centuries (roughly from 65 C.E. to 840 C.E.)

---

15. The countries where this generalization is most problematic are Cambodia and Laos. The communist governments that took power in these countries in the mid 1970s instituted policies designed to downgrade or eliminate Buddhist influence. At first these communist governments (particularly the genocidal Pol Pot regime, which ruled Cambodia from 1975 to 1979) seemed to be succeeding. However, Buddhism has persisted in both countries and in recent years seems to be regaining at least some of the ground that it lost.

the development of Buddhism in China was both highly impressive and extremely complex. In the early years, Buddhism was closely associated with the indigenous Taoist tradition and in some contexts appears to have been viewed as a Taoist sect. However, with the collapse of the great Hán empire (206 B.C.E. to 220 C.E.), Buddhism began to attract increasing interest. Vast arrays of Buddhist texts were translated from Sanskrit into Chinese—a task that was made extremely challenging by the radical difference between the two languages. By the fourth, fifth, and sixth centuries, as Buddhist ideas became more effectively interpreted in Chinese terms, Chinese Buddhists began to compose Buddhist texts of their own and to develop distinctively Chinese Mahayanist "schools." These schools included some that were characterized by complex systems of Mahayana philosophy, such as the T'ien-t'ai and the Hua-yen. They also included some that involved an emphasis on particular forms of Mahayana practice, such as the Pure Land school, which focused on devotion, and the Ch'an school, which was especially concerned with meditation. In the late sixth century, when China was once again unified as it had been under the Han, Buddhism became a favored religion of the court.

Two major developments took place in Chinese Buddhism during the period that stretched between the high-water mark of Buddhist creativity and influence (roughly 850 C.E.) and the serious intrusion of modernity (roughly 1850 C.E.). The first development was a reconfiguration of the Chinese Buddhist community. During this reconfiguration, the more philosophically oriented schools tended to gradually disappear from the scene, while the more popular and practice-oriented Pure Land and Ch'an schools emerged with the strongest sense of identity. The second development was the gradual intermingling of Buddhism with the traditions of the Confucians and the Taoists and with Chinese popular religion. This intermingling created both philosophical systems and religious practices that incorporated important Buddhist elements but could not be identified with Buddhism as such.

Chinese Buddhism, in addition to generating its own very distinctive Buddhist traditions, also passed on those traditions to other areas of East Asia. Though Buddhism reached Vietnam at about the same time that it became established in the Chinese heartland, Vietnamese Buddhists have been—throughout their long history—deeply influenced by Buddhist texts and practices that originated in China. Korean Buddhists, who received their traditions directly from China in the late fourth century and possibly earlier, also cultivated a creative interaction with their Chinese co-religionists that lasted throughout the entire premodern period.

At a somewhat later date (the middle centuries of the first millennium C.E.), Chinese Buddhism was transmitted to Japan, at first via Korea and soon thereafter through direct contacts. In Japan, Chinese Buddhism was gradually transformed into a tradition displaying many characteristics that were very distinctively Japanese. In the Nara (710–84) and Heian (794–1185) periods, several of the schools that had already developed in China were established and adapted in Japan. In the case of the Esoteric Shingon (Chinese Chen-yen) and the primarily Mahayana Tendai (Chinese T'ien-t'ai) schools, texts and practices were brought from China by two Japanese monks, Kukai and Saicho. These monks were subsequently venerated and in some contexts virtually deified by their Japanese followers.[16] Several of these Japanese schools, including Shingon and Tendai, have persisted up to the present time.

The Buddhist schools that became the most popular in Japan emerged in the context of a major transformation that occurred in the twelfth and thirteenth centuries. During this period several charismatic monks established new sects that attracted many adherents and deeply influenced subsequent developments in Japanese culture, society, and politics. These still-influential sects include two important Zen (Chinese Ch'an) sects founded by Eisai (Rinzai) and Dogen (Soto); major Pure Land sects founded by Honen (the Jodoshu or Jodo sect) and Shinran (the Jodo Shinshu or Shin sect); and an often militantly nationalistic sect founded by and named after Nichiren.

During the modern period, Buddhism has fared quite differently in various parts of East Asia. In mainland China, Vietnam, and North Korea, local Buddhist communities remained basically intact through the colonial period; and in some areas—most notably China—they engaged in serious efforts to bring about modernist reforms. However, the last several decades in China, North Korea, and Vietnam have witnessed the rise of communist governments that have severely oppressed Buddhist practitioners and institutions. Local Buddhist communities have managed to survive in many of these areas; but they have been so severely weakened that their future remains very clouded indeed.

In Japan, South Korea, and Taiwan the challenges that Buddhists have faced have been quite different both in kind and in severity. Japanese Buddhist communities suffered serious repression during the late nineteenth and early twentieth centuries. At that time, the Meiji government

---

16. The T'ien-t'ai/Tendai school is generally considered to be a Mahayana school, but in Japan it has come to include a number of important Esoteric elements as well.

sought to restore the power and rule of the emperor, to mobilize the nation, and to achieve rapid modernization. In the process, it promoted Shinto as the state religion. (Shinto is an indigenous religion of Japan predating the arrival of Buddhism.) With the passage of time the situation improved, and the established Buddhist sects were once again allowed to carry on with their activities. Then, after World War II, a number of Japanese-initiated, Buddhist-oriented "new religions" such as Reiyukai and Soka Gakkai gained large numbers of converts and became significant forces in many aspects of Japanese life. In Taiwan and South Korea, local Buddhists have encountered stiff challenges from Christian competitors, but they have managed to keep their traditions fairly well intact and to introduce significant innovations as well.

Tibet and Neighboring Areas

The first discernible phase of the transmission of Indian Buddhism to the isolated Himalayan plateau of Tibet occurred during the period from 620 to 866 C.E. At that time, the first great Tibetan empire was established and ruled by the Yarlung dynasty. King Songsten Gampo, who was the founder of this dynasty, took two closely related actions that set the process in motion. He became a staunch supporter of Buddhism (which by that time had become the dominant religious and intellectual tradition across much of Asia), and he sent emissaries to India who developed a script used to commit the Tibetan language to writing. In the two centuries that followed, the Buddhist cause in Tibet was significantly advanced through the support of subsequent rulers and also through the activities of Buddhist practitioners from India. The most famous of these was a monk named Padmasambhava, who has been remembered as the patron saint of Tibetan Buddhism, as the great miracle worker who quelled the local demons, and as the founder of an important Esoteric sect (Nyingma Pa) that has played a major role throughout Tibetan Buddhist history.

The demise of the Yarlung dynasty in the mid ninth century constituted a setback for the Buddhist cause in Tibet. Yet the process of transmission and transformation continued until the early thirteenth century, when the final collapse of Buddhism in India coincided with the establishment of a Buddhist theocracy in Tibet. This continuing process of transmission and transformation involved a massive amount of translation through which an amazing number of Buddhist texts of all kinds

(Hinayana, Mahayana, and Esoteric) were rendered from Sanskrit into Tibetan. It also involved a major reform movement that was nurtured by Indian monks and that led to the formation of several new Esoteric/ Vajrayana sects. These included the Sakya Pa, the Kadam Pa, and the Kagyu Pa sects, which rejected some of the more unconventional practices associated with Padmasambhava and the Nyingma Pa tradition. On the religio-political front, this process involved the forging of an alliance between the powerful Mongol forces, which were in the process of conquering much of Asia, and the Sakya Pa monks, who, in the thirteenth century, assumed responsibility for governing a significant area of the Tibetan plateau. The Sakya Pa theocracy ruled Tibet from 1216 to 1354, when it was replaced by a secular regime.

Between the thirteenth and the mid twentieth centuries, Tibetan Buddhists maintained their religious dominance in Tibet, continued the process of establishing their version of Buddhism among the Mongols, and extended their Buddhist tradition to surrounding Himalayan areas as well. In the specifically religious arena the major development was a fifteenth-century reform that led to the establishment of the Geluk Pa monastic sect. This sect was renowned for its scholarship and was more stringent than the other Tibetan sects in its observance of the traditional monastic discipline and in its insistence on Mahayana doctrinal training as a preparation for and accompaniment to tantric techniques and practices. Further, during this medieval period, the Tibetans developed a unique leadership system based on a very distinctive theory of reincarnation. Soon after a religious leader died he was considered to be reborn as an infant who was identified by the community as the reincarnation of the deceased leader. This child was appropriately trained and then, at the proper time, assumed the leadership role that his predecessor had held.

In the religio-political sphere the main development during the late medieval period occurred in the mid seventeenth century when a Mongol army led by Gushri Khan conquered Tibet. After his military victories, Gushri Khan turned the administration of the country over to a Tibetan leader of the Geluk Pa sect who had previously served as his personal religious advisor. This Geluk Pa monk was the Dalai Lama, who was recognized as the fifth in a series of Dalai Lamas who were taken to be the successive reincarnations of the bodhisattva Avalokitesvara. The Geluk Pa theocracy that was established at this time continued to rule the country until 1959, when the fourteenth Dalai Lama was forced by the Chinese invasion to flee from Tibet and to take refuge in India.

The Chinese invasion and the Chinese annexation of Tibet marked a radical turning point in the history of Tibetan Buddhism. Within Tibet itself the persecution of Buddhism that was perpetrated by the Chinese—particularly during the course of the great Cultural Revolution in the 1960s—was devastating. However, despite the physical and institutional destruction that has been wrought, much of the Tibetan population has remained steadfastly loyal to Buddhism. Buddhism has, in fact, become a rallying point for Tibetan resistance to Chinese control and oppression. Outside the country, the Dalai Lama has maintained leadership of a large diaspora community made up of Tibetan refugees who have settled primarily in India and in many parts of the Western world as well.

Expansion in the West

Having completed our historical discussion of the development of the distinctive Buddhist cultures that developed in the pan-Asian realm, there remains a concluding question worthy of consideration. That question is whether there has developed in the late nineteenth and twentieth centuries in North America a fourth branch of Buddhist culture that should be considered as at least a junior partner alongside the other three.[17] Buddhist immigrants from each of the three Buddhist cultural areas that we have already discussed have established a strong Buddhist presence in both Canada and the United States. A steadily increasing number of North Americans who do not have an Asian background, including members of the artistic and intellectual elites, have taken up the practice of Buddhism. A great many Buddhist texts (including Hinayana, Mahayana, and Esoteric texts) have been translated into English. Original Buddhist materials are now being written by North American practitioners who publish their work in English; and in many Buddhist communities in Canada and the United States, English has become the primary language not only for religious instruction but for liturgical purposes as well. Perhaps the most important fact is that distinctively North American emphases have begun to emerge in the areas of doctrine, practice, and community life. These emphases

17. It could be argued that the relevant area should be expanded to include other regions in the so-called Western world, particularly the United Kingdom, France, and Australia. However, focusing on North America (more specifically on the United States and Canada) makes it possible to characterize distinctive elements with greater specificity.

include, for example, a strong ecumenical concern, a special interest in interreligious dialogue, a heavy focus on certain meditational practices, and a deep commitment to social activist causes. Taken together these various developments demonstrate that the question concerning the emergence of a distinctively North American tradition of Buddhism is both relevant and important, and they also suggest that in the not-too-distant future an affirmative answer may be justified.

PART I

Temples, Sacred Objects, and Associated Rituals

Figure 1. Higashi Hongwanji Temple in Kyoto, Japan. Photograph by Don Farber.

CHAPTER I

Temples and Monastic Complexes (Japan)

Temples and monastic complexes have long formed a fundamental component of Buddhist religious expression and practice. They have contained highly segregated halls for monastic living, meditation, and study. They have also contained other halls, edifices, artistic representations, and images for devotional expression of a more inclusive character. Buddhist temples and monasteries have served as a primary locus for collective rites and ceremonies. Among the most important of these rites and ceremonies are monastic legal proceedings (such as higher and lower ordinations) and procedures in which the laity takes moral precepts (for example, not to kill, lie, and steal). Others include annual community fairs and celebrations, especially those surrounding the lives and deeds of Buddha(s) and bodhisattvas. Finally, there are also daily prayers and petitions to the Buddha(s), bodhisattvas, and hosts of other supernaturally powerful beings that seek to draw upon the powers of these beings to assuage a range of day-to-day problems and concerns. These problems and concerns include, among others, illness, financial troubles, disruptions in the natural world such as droughts and floods, and anxieties concerning personal relationships and the stability of the social and political order.

Buddhist temples and monastic complexes (and the monks who live in them, manage their upkeep, and oversee their daily and annual rites and ceremonies) have traditionally been focal points for significant and often elaborate acts of lay piety and generosity. These acts have been

The essay in this chapter was taken from James Bissett Pratt, *The Pilgrimage of Buddhism and a Buddhist Pilgrimage* (New York: Macmillan, 1928), 503–12. Courtesy of AMS Press.

crucial to the survival and social prestige of Buddhist temples and monastic complexes by providing them with the material and cultural resources to develop as centers of religious, artistic, and cultural creativity.

At least two basic features of the Buddhist tradition as a whole motivate laypeople to give to temples and monastic complexes. First, temples and monastic complexes provide access to potentially efficacious sacred power and authority. Such sacred power and authority may consist of supernatural blessing and protection, provided by Buddhas, bodhisattvas, gods, goddesses, and other supernatural beings. Or they may more simply manifest in wise counsel given by a well-known or respected monk.

Second, and closely related, temples and monastic complexes provide an important context for the generation of a specific type of spiritual quality, "merit." Making merit, a rather ubiquitous concern in most Buddhist practices, helps one attain a better rebirth and also, ultimately, to attain a state of rebirth and/or mind necessary for liberation from the cycle of rebirth.

Generating merit may occur in various ways. For instance, practitioners may simply listen to sermons and stories of the Buddha's life, thereby becoming mentally calmed. Or they may provide the financial and material resources for temples, monasteries, and the monks associated with them. Significantly, Buddhist temples, monastic complexes, and their respective monks are depicted as the most efficacious sources for the cultivation of merit. This is not surprising, since these institutions and individuals are the primary loci for the maintenance and propagation of Buddhism itself.

Thus, it is appropriate to begin our survey of the life of Buddhism with a descriptive account of Buddhist temples and the activities associated with them. The setting of this first essay is Japan in the first quarter of the twentieth century, and the observer is, at times, overly romantic. However, his descriptions convey the kind of complexity and diversity that has been (and still remains) characteristic of sacred sites and activities throughout the Buddhist world.

A VIEW OF TEMPLE LIFE AND PRACTICE

James Bissett Pratt

If the pilgrim to Japan makes Kyoto his first stop, his attention immediately upon alighting from the train will be called to the great roofs of the Higashi Hongwanji, the immense temple of the Shin sect near the station. The majority of Buddhist temples in Japan follow the Chinese custom of facing south; but there are exceptions aplenty, and this is one of them. Like many Shin temples, it faces the east. Three monumental portals pierce the front wall of the sacred enclosure, the central one a gigantic gateway with a high double roof, rich with elaborate carving.

Passing through the portals, one finds oneself in a spacious court. A small shrine is at one's left, with a kind of pavilion before it in which a few old or weary people are always to be found, resting in the shade and chatting pleasantly with their neighbors. Beyond this is the southern gateway and a bell tower. A fountain is playing in the court, made in the form of a huge lotus bud, and in another place there is a large bowl with running water, roofed over for the protection of pilgrims who often wash here before worshiping. One sees also a few large bronze lanterns.

But at first these things are hardly noticed, for one's eyes turn irresistibly toward the two great halls on the western side of the court. The northern and larger of these is the *hondo,* or founder's hall, with a double roof, and the smaller Amida-do, to the south, with a single roof, is connected with the larger building by a covered corridor.[1] Along this corridor are piled several huge coils of rope, many inches in thickness and made of human hair, donated for the purpose by zealous Buddhist women at the time of the building of the temple. It was with these ropes that the great beams of the temple were carried and hoisted into place. The roofs of both the main halls are too high and steep to give that sense of perfect proportion which the earliest Japanese temples possess; but the curve of the roofs and the tilt of the eaves, rather less pronounced than those of Chinese temples, are exceedingly graceful. And what the exterior lacks in beauty, as compared with the few extant specimens of early Japanese architecture, is more than atoned for by the impressiveness of the interior.

To one whose acquaintance with Buddhist temples is confined to China and Korea, these great Shin temple interiors will come as a revelation. Here no confusion of tawdry decoration and cheap votives, no burning of paper money or even of incense, no dirty floors or fantastic Lohan images;[2] just a great, cathedral-like open space (in this case 42 by 66 feet) covered with matting and immaculately clean, a rail dividing the hall into two unequal parts, and behind it a rich but not confusing al-

1. Editors' note: Amida is a Buddha who is especially prominent in Pure Land traditions.

2. Editors' note: Lohans are the semidivinized saints of the Chinese Buddhist pantheon.

tar, and a single image, executed in exquisite taste. The standing Amida in the Amida-do is particularly beautiful and reminds one at once of the Madonna in some Italian cathedral. The worshipers, as well as the building, present a striking contrast to those one has become accustomed to in China. As I have said, there is here no burning of paper money, no fortune-telling, but just little groups of silent, earnest worshipers, coming in, kneeling a few moments before the shrine in earnest prayer, and silently departing. The whole atmosphere of the place is unmistakably religious; and he who cannot worship his God (whatever that may mean to him) in this shrine of Amida must, I think, be somehow lacking in spiritual susceptibility.

The Higashi Hongwanji Temple of Kyoto is typical of nearly all the large temples of the Shin sect and fairly representative of many Jodo temples as well. It can hardly be said to represent all Japanese Buddhist temples, for the Buddhist temples of Japan have no such regularity of plan as that one finds in most Chinese temples. So far as I know there is only one Japanese temple laid out on the regular Chinese plan—the large headquarters of the Obaku division of the Zen sect at Uji, built in 1650 by Chinese Buddhists and kept for many years after its founding in the hands of Chinese monks.[3] Some of the larger Zen and Shingon temples, while not following at all strictly the Chinese pattern, follow the general scheme of having a large portal, with guardian gods, and back of it, in a spacious enclosure, a succession of two or three large temple-halls, with the buildings for the monks at the rear and on the sides. This, however, is not very common, and, as I have said, there is no regular plan for either the exterior or the interior of a Japanese temple.

Yet certain things are fairly constant. Most constant of all, perhaps, is the universal cleanliness and excellent repair—a characteristic of nearly every temple I have visited in Japan. Nearly all Buddhist temples have a court or enclosure, though I have seen one or two without anything of the kind. The enclosure is usually entered through a roofed gateway in which are often enshrined the gigantic and terrible Ni-O—the two Devas, Indra and Brahma.[4] These are genuine objects of popular worship, as the many little "spit-balls" of paper sticking to the wire netting in front of the gods clearly show.[5] In place of the Ni-O one may

3. Editors' note: Readers should be aware that more recent scholarship has shown that this temple was actually founded and built in 1665, or shortly thereafter.

4. Editors' note: Indra and Brahma are originally Indian deities shared with Hinduism.

5. It is a popular belief that one may tell whether or not one's prayer to the Ni-O will be answered by chewing a bit of paper, making it into a "spit-ball," and throwing it at the wire grating. If it sticks, the prayer has been heard.

find the Kings of the Four Quarters, so familiar in Chinese and Korean contexts.[6]

Sometimes the temple enclosure is entered through a torii (of the more artistic and less archaic variety),[7] borrowed, of course, from Shinto in the days before the rise of the Meiji government, when the two religions were practically one.[8] Sometimes just within the gateway is a tiny Shinto shrine, especially in the temples of the Shingon and Nichiren sects. There may also be a pagoda (reliquary), with two, three or five stories. In some temple grounds, especially in those of the Shingon sect, one will find a *sotoba* or stone monument made up of five parts, symbolizing the five material elements. The lowest part is a cube or another solid shape with six faces (each face being a parallelogram) signifying earth; the second a sphere signifying water; the third a cone with broken apex, signifying fire; the fourth a crescent signifying air or wind; and the uppermost a ball ending in a tip or flame-like point, signifying ether. A few temples have, in some part of their grounds, a peculiar cylindrical metal column known as a *sorinto*. The upper part of the shaft is surrounded with nine metal rings and usually surmounted with a lotus carrying a pointed ball, like that on the summit of the sotoba.

The court or enclosure of a Buddhist temple is one of the loveliest things in Japan. The stone lanterns, the ancient pine trees, the wonderfully wrought brazen dragons that spout water in a fountain, the stone Jizo (a bodhisattva), wrapped about with votive cloths presented by devout worshipers whose little children have gone to the far land where now only Jizo can help them, the bell tower, the façade of the temple itself with perhaps half a dozen smaller structures standing about it, the lotus pond with its gold fish, the many pigeons that fly about the court, owing their living to the kindness of the pilgrims, and most of all, the glad looks of the worshipers who have come in their best kimonos to do homage to the Buddha, and the joyous faces of the many children almost invariably found here, make it a scene not to be forgotten. For the temple courts are the playgrounds of Japan. They do not merely happen

---

6. Editors' note: The Kings of the Four Quarters are considered to be defenders of the dharma; they are found in South Asian contexts as well.

7. There are two forms of torii, one with straight cross beams and of rather ponderous appearance, the other much more graceful, with cross beams that have swaying lines and an upward tilt at the ends. The straight and ponderous kind is thought to be the more ancient form, while the graceful type is by far the more popular. The archaic style of torii is found only at a few Shinto shrines (never at Buddhist temples) and is always the token of a self-conscious effort to revert to pure Shinto uncontaminated with Buddhist or Chinese influence.

8. Editors' note: See the general introduction.

to be playgrounds. The children are desired. Many temple courts are provided with swings and various simple games; and the children love the place and learn thus early to associate religion with delight. A very large proportion of the men and women of Japan must look back upon some Buddhist temple as the scene of their happiest hours.

Besides the children there are tired mothers with their babies on their backs, and weary people of various ages. Some have come here with their grandchildren to watch them play, some have come for an hour's chat with old friends, in the shade of a great tree or beside the fountain; some, still in the midst of life's work, have fled here for a moment's refreshment and worship, spent in part before the calm image of Amida in the shrine, in part out here in the fresh air of the courtyard filled with the cooing of doves and the shouts of children.

Many of the tenderest memories and most significant moments of life thus cluster round the Buddhist temple. Not only the children but at times people of all ages find the temple court a kind of playground. Many a temple has a monthly fair, when for a whole night the sacred enclosure is luminous with colored lanterns and filled with booths at which you can buy all sorts of pretty things, and the air is musical with the notes of the temple gong, the chanting of priests, and the voices of young people.

But the temple enters also and of course into the solemn hours. Here the funeral service is held, and the memorial service for the dead. Here the tablets of many of the departed are preserved and sometimes a portion of their ashes,[9] and around many a Buddhist temple lies the ancient "churchyard" as we should call it—its gray stones clustering about the sacred walls, just as they so often do in New England—and Old England.

The main hall of the temple, in some of the Buddhist sects, is not infrequently closed. But except at night the temple enclosure, and at least one of its shrines, central or subordinate, is always open, and worshipers enter and depart during any hour of daylight. If one is tempted to criticize the enormous amount of capital that has been expended on Buddhist temples in Japan, saying that all this money might have been invested in more profitable ways, this answer may be at least given that hardly anything in Japan is in more constant use than her temples.

---

9. In the Shi-Tenno temple at Osaka the ashes of the dead are sometimes mixed with clay and made into small Buddha images, which are deposited in one of the shrines, a rather striking symbolization of the hope that the departed one has "become Buddha."

The temple proper—the building itself as well as all the subordinate buildings belonging to it—is, like everything else in Japan, made of wood—of wood and paper. Frequently portions of the roof and ends of the overhanging beams are elaborately carved. There is usually no great front door, as in Chinese temples, but just many sliding screens, mostly of paper. A familiar figure just outside the door of many of the larger temples is Binzuru, one of the sixteen Rakans (semidivinized saints), who, the story goes, once looked after a woman too curiously and thereafter was forbidden to enter the sacred building. This punishment (or was it his sin?) seems to have resulted in making him more popular than all his brethren. Tradition has endowed him—or his image—with a miraculous power of healing. The worshiper who is ill has only to rub his hand upon the part of Binzuru's image corresponding to the diseased part of his own body and then to rub his hand upon the infirm member; if he does this with sufficient faith he will be healed. So firmly planted is this belief in large numbers of temple visitors, that the legs and arms of most Binzuru images are half rubbed away. The Binzuru at the Asakusa temple in Tokyo has healed so many parts of so many ailing bodies that there is hardly anything left of the poor fellow. The government at times has had to lock up the Binzuru images to prevent the spread of disease through their miraculous touch.

The other Rakans are seldom seen. There are two or three temples in Kyoto, and one in Nagoya where they are carved in the round though of smaller size and less fantastic in shape than in China, and so far as I know they never (except at Obakusan) occupy the position in the central temple which Chinese custom assigns them. Usually one sees them, if at all, represented not in carving but painted upon vertical scrolls, hung up in the exhibition rooms of the temple, or (quite as often) in some museum. For the Rakans in Japan are of antiquarian and artistic interest chiefly and (except for Binzuru) form no part of the real life of the religion.

The interior of the temple is arranged in various ways with little that is absolutely uniform. There is, of course, always a central shrine or throne—more commonly a shrine with doors that may be, and often are, closed. Within this shrine (or on the throne if there be one) usually sits or stands an image of one of the Buddhas, Bodhisattvas, or founders, although a tablet may be substituted for the image, bearing a name upon it, or (as in some Shin temples) the sacred formula Namu Amida Butsu. As I have indicated, the shrine is quite frequently closed and the image may be shown only at certain times of the day or, it may be, only at intervals of many years. In front of the shrine stands the altar, a long and narrow table which usually contains a large incense burner in the middle, two candlesticks, one on each side, and at each end a spray of lotus leaves gracefully carved of wood and gilded. The candlesticks may be of brass or lacquer; the incense burner is usually of bronze, though it may be of lacquer or of porcelain. Usually the altar contains little or nothing else besides these five things, though at times one finds it crowded with offerings of food, flowers, and candles, as in China. Among the votives frequently placed on or near the altar (sometimes in the shrine itself), the Shinto mirror is not uncommon. In the larger temples there are usually two subordinate shrines at the right and left of the central shrine and further back—close up against the rear wall. These are usually sacred to Kwannon or Jizo, or Fudo or Monju, or to the founder of the sect or some distinguished abbot; or one of them may be devoted wholly to the tablets of the dead.

Besides the shrines and altars I have mentioned, a Buddhist temple may contain all sorts of things; and in fact its irregularity of plan and the almost endless variety which it may present constitute a large part of its unfailing fascination. In a large and popular city temple like that of the Shi-Tenno in Osaka there are any number of little side shrines to all sorts of Buddhist and Shinto nobility (if I may use the phrase), with votives of every kind from the odd to the pathetic—from pictures of mothers with breasts spouting streams of milk, to little kimonos that once belonged to children now dead, and presented by their parents to Jizo in the hope that somehow he may clothe them. Many Buddhist temples have long rows of show apartments which are in fact museums and in which are to be seen some of the choicest specimens of Japanese painting at its best.

All monastic temples of course possess dormitories and a refectory, and most of them have offices as well. The larger temples thus form a maze of buildings, with hundreds of occupants. Sometimes one finds a round or octagonal building erected to house the Buddhist scriptures. Occasionally these round library buildings are so constructed as to revolve when sufficient force is applied—the idea being that by whirling the building and its contents around several times one may in economical manner acquire the merit of reading all the books. The idea may seem superstitious, but it is probably true.

One rather interesting feature—unique so far as I know—is to be found in the great Zenko temple (of the Tendai sect) in Nagano, up among the central mountains. A steep dark stairway in the main hall leads down into a passage running beneath the central shrine. One gropes one's way in absolute darkness, turns two corners, and under the holy of holies one's hand (guided by a long depression on the wall) comes into contact with a key, the touch of which has some miraculous quality. Then one pushes on past two more corners in the same Stygian darkness and clambers up another stairway into the light. It is indeed an act of faith; and faith, let us hope, never goes without some reward.

But I fear that my attempt at description, overloaded as it probably is with detail, has failed to transmit to the reader any suggestion of the charm possessed and exhaled by the Buddhist temples of Japan. It is upon the temple that the people lavish their greatest care. Nothing is too good or rich for it. Their own houses are often tiny shells, but the house of the Buddha is lofty and full of that restrained beauty for which the Japanese have so sensitive a feeling. In all their lovely villages and towns the temple is the loveliest thing of all.

But to see the temple at its best one must desert the towns and cities altogether and thread one's way up some ravine or climb to the forest solitudes of some mountain side, where, far from the haunts of men, the Buddha and a few of his chosen monks dwell apart in a monastic shrine whose curving roofs and ancient thatch and lichen-covered lanterns and images seem to be as much Nature's own as the peaks and glades that surround them. Up some deep gorge you make your way, as at Komoro, among the central rib of mountains near Samayama, following a rushing stream whose many waterfalls shout the praises of the Kami and the Buddhas, greeted now and then by an ancient image of Dengyo Daishi (the semidivinized founder of the Japanese Tendai tradition who is also known as Saicho) partly covered over with ivy; and further along you climb a crag commanding a wide panorama where you find a shrine with ancient images, at the feet of which space opens below you for a dizzying distance.[10] The little path beyond it leads you past a few gray stone figures, and on to the Tendai temple, at the top, where in unbroken calm Shaka (i.e., the Buddha Sakyamuni) in his golden shrine grants peace alike to monks and pilgrims.

Sometimes an entire mountain top of many square miles extent is given up to temples—*is* in fact one great temple enclosure. Notable especially is Hiei-san, the mountain near Kyoto, once covered with over three thousand monasteries of the Tendai sect, until Nobunaga's fires

---

10. Editors' note: Kami are the divinities and divine spirits who are ubiquitous in the Shinto context.

and his soldiery brought destruction to nearly all.[11] Early in Tokugawa (1600–1868) times some of them were rebuilt on the old foundations, and though the glory of Tendai on Hiei-san never returned, the forest glades and the summit and sides of the mountain have still many a noble shrine to the Buddha and his great Japanese disciple.

Impressive these woodland temples are and captivating to the eye and to the imagination quite beyond any power of words to express. Down long avenues of giant cryptomerias you tramp, and suddenly through the trees a vista of forest aisle opens up ahead with a gateway and the swaying lines of a temple roof at the end of it. The Japanese nightingale among the leaves heralds your approach with his unforgettable song, strangely tentative in its beginning, and prolonged into a trill of unimaginable sweetness. But the temples are silent and the woods are silent with a silence that seems musical, and that speaks of awe and reverence and centuries of meditation.

Behind one of these forest temples lie the ashes of Dengyo Daishi, and before the central shrine burn two lamps whose fire, tradition says, goes back to him—well over a thousand years ago. Through the woods comes the boom of some distant temple bell. And occasionally through a forest window on the mountain slope you catch a vista of Lake Biwa, in the valley below you, stretching off far to the northeastward, and other mountains beyond it, and the rest of the world out there—the busy, struggling world out there, while you and the monks and the ashes of Dengyo Daishi and the fire which he lighted are still here in the shadow of the great cryptomerias, where the monks chant their praises to the Buddha at dawn and evening, and where a day seems as a thousand years, and a thousand years as a day.

---

11. Editors' note: The reference appears to be to Japanese feudal lord/warrior Oda Nobunaga (1534–1582). Among other moves, Nobunaga took strong measures against Tendai monks and their properties on Mount Hiei to consolidate his power and rule.

Figure 2. A Burmese Buddhist image with text in background. Photograph by Dale Eldred.

CHAPTER 2

Image Consecrations (Thailand)

The preceding excerpt dealing with temples and monastic complexes clearly depicts the presence and importance of images of Buddhas, bodhisattvas, and other deities and divinized figures. The spiritual or supernatural power and efficacy represented, embodied, or actualized in such images allows them to mediate memories, blessings, and protection to the Buddhist community and to Buddhist devotees who offer their veneration.

Though images of Buddhas and bodhisattvas generally have very distinctive aesthetic qualities, their aesthetic form does not fully account for the sacred power that they are believed to possess. In many cases, especially when images are considered to be particularly efficacious, they have been imbued with sacrality through a sophisticated process of ritual consecration.

Buddhist processes of consecrating images vary a great deal from one region to another and depend to a considerable degree on the sacred figure whose image is being consecrated. However, Buddhist traditions generally retain the lengthiest and most sophisticated consecrations for Buddha and/or bodhisattva images. Such consecrations often involve, among other elements, preaching, recitation of key Buddhist texts, and, as with virtually all Buddhist rituals officiated by members of the monastic community, the presentation of lay gifts to the sangha. The following excerpt presents an account of the particular ritual process employed in

The essay in this chapter was taken from Donald K. Swearer, "Hypostasizing the Buddha: Buddha Image Consecration in Northern Thailand," *History of Religions* 34 (1995): 271–79. Courtesy of the University of Chicago Press.

northern Thailand in the consecration of images of the Gautama Buddha. (In the following essay, since he is dealing with a Theravada tradition, the author uses the Pali forms of Buddhist terms. For example, he uses Gotama rather than Gautama, dhamma rather than dharma, nibbana rather than nirvana, and so forth.)

CREATING AND DISSEMINATING THE SACRED

Donald K. Swearer

Buddha image consecration ceremonies in northern Thailand can be held at any time of the year. Generally speaking, however, they occur after the end of the monastic rains retreat (*vassa*) and prior to the *Visakha Puja,* the celebration of the Buddha's birth, enlightenment, and death. Consequently, even though there is no stipulated season for the consecration of a Buddha image, the ceremonies tend to occur more frequently between November and May. Although Buddha image consecration ceremonies in northern Thailand may be held at almost any time of the year, to the best of my knowledge they always take place within the precincts of a monastery (Thai: *wat*). I have never heard of a Buddha image consecration ritual's being held in a home, which is the common practice in Burma for a home shrine image. Northern Thai consecration rituals may vary considerably in specific details: the length, the specific texts chanted and preached, the number of images or other sacred objects (e.g., amulets) being consecrated, the number of monks involved, the number and status of lay sponsors, and the building in the monastery compound where the ceremony is conducted. Although image consecrations may occur at virtually any time of the year and can extend over more than one day, the northern Thai consecration ritual takes place during the night with the climax occurring just before sunrise. The timing of the ceremony homologizes the event with the episode of the Buddha's enlightenment, which progressed through the watches of the night and culminated at sunrise. Furthermore, although the rituals may vary greatly in specific details, they contain four basic components: chanting, preaching, meditation, and presentation of gifts to the *sangha.*

Consecration rituals usually take place within a specifically constructed sacred enclosure inside the *vihara,* the image hall where most public meetings are held. A royal fence (*rajavati*) demarcates the perimeter. A string strung from the principal *vihara* image (previously consecrated) intersects over the *rajavati* to form a virtual ceiling of 108 small squares. This is the same sacred thread (Thai: *sai sincana*, or water-pouring thread) held by monks as they chant during all types of religious services. It plays a crucial role in transferring or conducting sacred power from a particular source, especially a Buddha image, to animate or inanimate objects and is essential in making holy water, that is, water sacralized through the chanting of mantras (formulaic sacred words or sounds). Numerous distinctive objects are situated in and around the *rajavati*, including four clay jars filled with water, four nine-tiered umbrellas, stalks of bamboo and sugarcane, bunches of coconuts, pedestal tables, piled high with small cone-shaped banana leaf containers of fragrant flowers and incense, betel nuts and betel leaves, and husked and unhusked rice. Also to be found are a table with a monk's bowl and other monastic requisites and a stand with emblems of the eight royal requisites (sword, spear, umbrella, banner, etc.). The images to be consecrated are placed in the center of the *rajavati* on small beds of grass, eyes covered with beeswax and heads hidden by white cloth.

The extent and variety of objects suggest different but interrelated levels of meaning. Several symbolize the story of Prince Siddhattha's renunciation of his royal status in quest of a higher enlightenment. (According to the classical Buddha biography, Siddhattha was the given name of the person who came to be known as the Gotama Buddha.) The emblematic requisites of both kingship and monkhood denote Siddhattha's mythic journey from his royal household to the attainment of Buddhahood. The grass on which the images rest represents the gifts of eight tufts of coarse kusha grass given to the Buddha prior to his enlightenment by the Brahman Sotthiya; the grass magically became a crystal throne.

The central event of the Gotama Buddha story is Prince Siddhattha's enlightenment, or attainment of Buddhahood. The crucial referent for the Buddha image consecration ritual is the description of the course of the attainment of enlightenment through the watches of the night. The beeswax closing the eyes and the white cloth covering the head suggest the Buddha prior to his enlightenment. Mouth, nose, and ears may also be sealed with beeswax, perhaps to guarantee that none of the power being charged into the image will escape. Such a sealing off of the image would also appear to safeguard the sacralization process as well as to protect those present at the ceremony from the intensity of the energy being generated within the image. Three small mirrors mounted on a cruciform stand facing the images symbolize the Buddha's attainment of the three knowledges (i.e., enlightenment): knowledge of the recollection of his past lives; knowledge of the coming into being and passing away of all beings; and knowledge of the destruction of mental intoxication. Reversing the mirrors at the conclusion of the ritual represents the completion of Prince Siddhattha's spiritual journey and the attainment of omniscience.

The structure of the *rajavati,* furthermore, suggests a second level of meaning imbedded in the ritual. The ceiling of 108 squares is referred to as a magical cosmos. It resembles a geometric mandala (sacred circle) touching the earth through the conduits of sacred cord hanging from its perimeter. The objects at the entrances represent objects basic to traditional village existence—sugarcane, bamboo, coconuts, bananas— elements used in ceremonies to ward off evil and engender good. The clay jars filled with water, various candles, and a peacock fan represent the four constitutive elements, or *dhatu*—earth, water, fire, air. The *rajavati* also fuses the polarity between the religious and royal realms, so central in the sacred biography of the Buddha. The royal fence establishes the horizontal perimeter of the sacred enclosure within which the images are consecrated. Yet, reminiscent of Siddhattha's journey beyond the walls of the royal city, when the "training" of the images is complete, the *rajavati* no longer serves a useful function and is dismantled.

The evening's events begin around 7:30 P.M. with monks and assembled laity paying respects to the Buddha, taking the precepts, and asking forgiveness for transgressions. Lighting a victory candle constructed of a wick of 108 strands (the combined cosmic powers of the Buddha, Dhamma, and Sangha) and made to the height of the chief sponsor, initiates the consecration ritual proper. The officiating monk chants: "By the power of the Omniscient Buddha, the supermundane Dhamma, and the highest virtue-attaining Sangha may all suffering, calamities, and dangers vanish. May all beings live without injury." The chief sponsor then lights a large candle invoking the Buddha Vipassin, the first of the last six Buddhas preceding Gotama, and two candles on either side symbolizing the *lokiya* (mundane) and *lokuttara* (transmundane) dimensions of the Buddha-dhamma.

The evening's main activities alternate among chanting, preaching, and meditation. Chanting includes *paritta* (protection) *suttas* from the standard Theravada repertoire as well as texts unique to the northern Thai ritual context. In most image consecration rituals throughout Thailand, the Pali *Buddha Abhiseka* will be chanted. At that time nine or more monks sit in meditation around the *rajavati* with the *sai sincana* cord extending from alms bowls placed in front of them to the Buddha images and amulets being consecrated. The monks invited to meditate for this occasion are often renowned for their attainment of extraordinary powers associated with trance states (*jhana*). By recalling or recollecting these attainments during their meditation, the monks transfer them to the image. At the same time many of the lay congregants sit in meditation, some having encircled their heads with *sai sincana* cords hanging down from the linked squares forming a ceiling over the images. While the assembly meditates, bronze Buddha images reflect the flickering light of burning candles, and the hall reverberates with the cadence of monks chanting the story of the Buddha's enlightenment. In such a numinous, liminal environment, the transformation of material object into living reality seems palpably true. By this sustained, focused act of attention, the image as ritual object becomes sacred. Furthermore, this act of commemoration of recollection (*buddhanussati*) calls forth a profound sense of communal identity linking the assembled congregants and the Buddha.

In northern Thailand monks frequently preach the *Buddha Abhiseka* in northern Thai as well as chant the text in Pali. Other northern Thai sermons will invariably include the Buddha's First Enlightenment (*Pathama Sambodhi*) as well as one or two other traditional favorites of this occasion, such as Siddhattha's Renunciation. As we would expect, all of the sermons recount the life of the Buddha, especially the events of his renunciation and training, his conquest of Mara, and the night of his enlightenment. In addition to recounting the Buddha story, the texts also impart the seminal teachings of the Buddha's *dhamma*, for example the Four Noble Truths, the Eightfold Noble Path, Dependent Coarising, and so on. The most dramatic teaching event occurs at the end of the ceremony. At sunrise, when the images have been duly consecrated, the monks chant the *Dhammacakkappavattana Sutta* (Discourse on the Turning of the Wheel of Law) in reenactment of the Buddha's first discourse to the five ascetics.

Prior to the conclusion of the ceremony several other important events take place: the cloth and beeswax coverings are removed from the heads of the images, the images are fanned with a long-handled peacock fan, they are presented with forty-nine bowls of milk and honey-sweetened rice, and, finally, images and congregants are blessed with holy water.

The removal of the headcoverings symbolizes the completion of the training of the image or, as it were, the Buddha'a attainment of enlightenment. Coincidentally, of course, the assembled congregants have also been "trained." The fanning of the images and the presentation of sweetened rice reenact two events in the legendary life of the Buddha: the god Sakka's act of respectful veneration toward the Buddha after his enlightenment and the offering of sweetened rice presented to the Buddha under the Bodhi tree by the young woman Sujata. Fanning the image also "cools" the heat generated by the transformation of a material object into a living reality. The sweetened rice is cooked in the early morning hours over a wood fire stirred by young, pre-pubescent girls and then divided into forty-nine bowls symbolizing the seven days the Buddha spent at each of seven sites after his enlightenment.

Much of the *Buddhabhiseka* ritual has mimetic or performative significance. As the very presence of the absent Buddha, the image must be coded with the right story much as an alias is coded with the life story of the person the alias represents, or the actor becomes the role she or he plays, or, from a somewhat different perspective, as we are our particular stories. That is, in being the Buddha, the image is the Buddha's story. Since a crucial component of the Buddha's story is the Buddha's teaching (*dhamma*), the image and the congregants are instructed in the *dhamma*. Furthermore, the chants, sermons, and monk meditators infuse into the images the powers of higher meditative states of consciousness. What is said, in particular what is chanted, and what is done, both in terms of meditation and various ritual movements, are intended to accomplish something, to make something happen, to be efficacious. The image becomes a living representative of the person, career, and power of the Buddha as well as the person, story, and power of charismatic monks.

It will be instructive to look briefly at the two principal texts preached during the consecration ritual. One, the *Pathama Sambodhi*, rehearses the Buddha's attainment of thirty perfections from his birth as Prince Vessantra, through his incarnation in Tusita Heaven, his descent into the womb of Mahamaya, his appearance as Prince Siddhattha, his passage through the four sights (old age, suffering, death, mendicancy), his renunciation, his temptation by Mara, attainment of enlightenment, the forty-nine days after his enlightenment, and the preaching of the *Dhammacakkappavattana Sutta*. Virtually a quarter of the text focuses on the Buddha's attack by and defeat of Mara:

Mara's forces numbering several hundred thousand were fearsome. With Mara in the lead they came in a procession eighty-five miles in length and breadth and sixty-three miles in height. The divine beings—Indra, Brahma, Yama, the Nagas, and the Garudas—were apprehensive but waited for the Great Being to defend himself and attack the forces of Mara.

Then by their magical powers Mara's army assumed awesome forms that aroused great fear. They carried spears and swords, bows and arrows, and raised a deafening cry. They surrounded the Great Being and then launched their attack, but no harm came to the Blessed One due to his great merit.

Then Mara mounted Girinandamekkha, an enormous elephant 1,500 miles tall. Mara himself, standing on the elephant's neck, was four miles tall. By his magic power he generated a thousand hands, each holding a weapon, and charged the Great Being intent on killing him.

The spears and arrows Mara's army hurled at the Buddha were transformed into flowers and fell as an offering at the feet of the Blessed One. Mara's forces then looked up and saw the Buddha sitting like a lion-king on a lotus in the midst of a wheel, unafraid of the army arrayed before him.

The Blessed One reflected, "I embarked on the mendicant path and became a Buddha. I attained the thirty perfections through perseverance. In a previous life I was Prince Vessantara. The generous sacrifice of my wife and children caused the divine beings Indra and Brahma to bless my great gift (*dana*) with celestial waters. From that time such a blessing is witness to my enlightenment. I gained this diamond throne through the store of my great merit."

The text's conclusion transfers the Buddha's conquest of evil and subsequent attainments to the assembled congregants.

All people who listen to the sermon called the *Pathma Sambodhi* about the Buddha's way to and attainment of his final supreme enlightenment and who follow its teachings will attain three kinds of happiness of which the deathless state of Nibbana is the highest. Whether you copy the text on your own or hire someone to do it, give it as a *puja* offering or just listen to it, you will receive a blessing (*anisamsa*) and will be reborn in heaven or as a human being greatly beloved by both divine and human beings.

Anisamsa texts constitute an important genre of northern Thai Buddhist literature since the majority of Buddhist rituals are classified as meritoriously efficacious (Pali: *punna;* Thai: *tham pun*). Although merit-making rituals can be justifiably interpreted—as this text suggests—in "magical," consequentialist terms, when contextualized as the conclusion to the *Pathma Sambodhi,* a principal text of the *Buddhabhiseka* ritual, the *anisamsa* fits into the "actualizing" intent of the ritual. That is, within the ritual context the blessing follows from the actualization of the Buddha in the experience of the congregants.

The *Buddha Abhiseka* text, which is chanted and/or preached, only briefly summarizes the Buddha's birth and enlightenment quest.[1] The

1. This translation of the *Buddha Abhiseka* is based on a version currently preached during the Buddha image consecration at monasteries throughout the Chiang Mai val-

bulk of the text focuses on the Buddha's various supernatural or jhanic attainments, for example: psychic powers; realization of the states of stream-enterer to *arahatta-phalanana* (these are four states that involve ascending degrees of realization of supramundane reality); attainment of the three knowledges; and transcendence of rebirth.

The Blessed One (*Tathagata*) reached the supermundane state through perseverance and effort. As one in whom the passions are extinct, the *Tathagata* burned up all demerit, and through his wisdom realized the *dhamma* of cause and not-cause. During the first watch of the night all of the *Tathagata's* doubts disappeared.

At that time the Buddha was able to recall his previous lives. His heart was pure. Devoid of defilements, he overcame the eight worldly factors.[2] In the middle watch he was able to see the death and birth of all beings through the divine eye superior to all human and divine beings.

In the last few pages these attainments are infused into the image:

The Buddha, filled with boundless compassion, practiced the thirty perfections for many eons, finally reaching enlightenment. I pay homage to that Buddha. May all his qualities be invested in this image. May the Buddha's boundless omniscience be invested in this image until the religion ceases to exist. . . .

May the Buddha's boundless virtue acquired during his activities immediately after his enlightenment be stored in this image forever. May the knowledge contained in the seven books of the *Abhidhamma* perceived by the Buddha in the seven weeks after his enlightenment be consecrated in this image for the rest of the lifetime of the religion. May the power acquired by the Buddha during the seven days under the Ajapala tree, the seven days at the Mucalinda pond, etc., be invested in this Buddha image for 5,000 rainretreats. The Buddha then returned to Ajapalanigrodha where he preached the 84,000 verses of the *dhamma*. May they also be stored in this Buddha image. May the Mahabrahma (great god) who requested that the Buddha preach come into this image.

The Buddha image consecration ritual concludes at sunrise. The image has been instructed in the life story of the Buddha and empowered with his supernormal attainments. The presence of the Buddha principle represented by previous Buddhas has been invoked in symbolic action as well as chant. Assembled monks and laity "feed" the image with forty-

---

ley. The text is a redaction edited by Bunkhit Wacharasat, a major publisher of sermons presented to the sangha on various auspicious, merit-making occasions.

2. The eight worldly factors are gain and loss, fame and obscurity, blame and praise, happiness and pain.

nine small bowls of milk and honey-sweetened rice. As dawn breaks, the monks chant the verses of the Buddha's victory over the realm of samsaric grasping, his enlightened penetration of the truth of dependent coarising, and the *Dhammacakkappavattana Sutta*. Monks remove the headcoverings from the images and respectfully fan them with a peacock feather fan. Finally, the laity feed the monks as they earlier "fed" the Buddha. The *sangha* sprinkle consecrated water (*abhiseka*) on images and people and chant a final blessing: "Just as overflowing rivers make the ocean full, so *dana* given from this world reaches the dead. May all of your wishes be successful. May all your wishes be as complete as the full moon and the bright, shining diamond."

The Buddha image consecration ceremony establishes a common thread of meaning inherent in most Buddhist rituals, and in doing so it connects the founder with the past and present, the dead and the living. Three terms applied to the northern Thai ceremony illustrate this generalized significance: "eye opening," "training the image," and "consecration" (*abhiseka*). To open the eye of a Buddha image is to enliven it, to bring it to life, to make it present, to instill it with power. To train the image is to instruct it in the life history and teachings of the person the image represents. Within the context of Buddhist ritual and ceremonial practice, to *abhiseka* means to consecrate by means of pouring water or lustrating. At its deepest level, not only to make sacred in the sense of purify but to re-create and make new as represented by the life-giving force of water. To *abhiseka*, then, is to focus and disseminate power, the power of the sacred, the holy, indeed, the power of life. An *abhisek*-ed image or an amulet, be it of the Buddha, a king, or a holy monk, is a locus of such power. But *abhiseka* also permeates all aspects of life, much as water itself does: a teenager pouring water on the heads or hands of relatives at Thai New Year, a monk using a bamboo whisk to sprinkle water in blessing on an assembled congregation, a lay practitioner anointing a *cetiya* enshrining sacred relics at a monastery's annual celebration. Beyond the images or the rituals themselves, *abhiseka* expresses a weltanschauung: on one level, a belief in the magical power or potent efficacy of particular material objects such as Buddha images and amulets, but on another, and one too often overlooked, a sense of reality that unifies and makes meaningful an otherwise arbitrary and chaotic world.

Figure 3. The procession of the Buddha's tooth relic in Sri Lanka. Photograph by John Ross Carter.

CHAPTER 3

State Rituals and Ceremonies (Myanma)

From a very early stage in its history, Buddhism has been involved in a variety of interactions with the political orders with which it has coexisted. These interactions have ranged from highly positive and relatively symbiotic relationships to situations in which the Buddhist tradition and the political order in question have acted quite decisively to subvert each other.

One relatively positive interaction between sangha and state occurred within two centuries after the death of the Gautama Buddha (in the middle of the third century B.C.E.). At that time, a great Indian monarch named Asoka became a strong supporter of Buddhism and used his authority to influence the composition and orientation of the sangha. Asoka encouraged the spread of the religion in innovative ways that simultaneously attempted to promote social harmony on a large scale and to legitimate his rule. In almost all the Asian areas where Buddhism has spread, it has—at various times—been linked with kings who have taken on a Buddhist identity and have sought to control and support Buddhist society (including both monastic and lay components) within their realm.

In carrying forward their efforts to control and support the sangha and laity, Buddhist kings have sought to demonstrate their piety through a variety of means. One of the most common and historically signifi-

The essay in this chapter was adapted from Juliane Schober, "Buddhist Just Rule and Burmese National Culture: State Patronage of the Chinese Tooth Relic in Myanma," *History of Religions* 36 (1997): 218–43. Courtesy of the University of Chicago Press. Copyright © 1997 by the University of Chicago. All rights reserved.

cant strategies has been the cultivation of a special relationship with, and veneration of, particularly potent embodiments of the Buddha's sacred power. In many cases this particular relationship has been centrally concerned with public rituals and ceremonies that crystallize around a bodily relic supposedly retrieved from the ashes after the Buddha's cremation. Perhaps the most famous example of such bodily relic–oriented ritual and ceremonial activity is that associated with the tooth relic presently housed in the Temple of the Tooth in Kandy, the highland city that once served as the capital of Sri Lanka. During much of the medieval period, this relic served as the palladium of the Sinhalese kings who ruled the island.

In the excerpt that follows, Juliane Schober describes a recent series of events in which another Buddhist tooth-relic tradition was employed by the present military government of Myanmar to legitimate and solidify its rule.

A TOOTH RELIC AND THE
LEGITIMATION OF POWER

Juliane Schober

In early 1994, the military-dominated State Law and Order Restoration Council (SLORC) which then governed Myanma[1] enjoined millions of people in Burma to participate in a series of elaborate rituals so citizens and foreigners could pay homage to the Chinese Tooth Relic during its 45-day-long procession throughout the nation. This ritual veneration of the Buddha's relic exemplifies a modern transformation of an established mode in traditional, cosmological Buddhism. Participation in its economy of merit transforms a ritual community into a national community in which the state regulates access to merit, prestige, and power through complex hegemonic structures. This essay explores the ritual theater of the state to show how this Buddhist ritual process operates to obligate national elites in various domains, and ethnic groups in the periphery, to the hegemonic structures of the center. The analysis presented here draws on contemporary media texts and on anthropological fieldwork in various contexts of venerating the Sacred Tooth.

---

1. In this essay, I will use the names "Burma" and "Myanma" interchangeably. In 1997, a shake-up occurred and the name of the ruling group was changed to the State Peace and Development Council. However, this has generally been seen as a change in name rather than substance.

The rituals described here occurred in the context of a crisis of authority that has endured in Myanma since 1988 when the national constitution was abolished and a military regime assumed power. This crisis of authority intensified after 1990 when the SLORC refused to honor popular elections favoring a democratic multi-party system. Despite economic reforms that largely benefited the privileged, the experiences of the past decade have proven painful to many and have further exacerbated divisions within the national community. Particularly harsh have been the controls that SLORC has instituted over the Buddhist *sangha* and the severe punishments that have been imposed on monks who have criticized the regime.

As the state has continued to operate without a national constitution, the absence of secular mechanisms for legitimating political power structures has led to a renewed emphasis on traditional religious means of legitimation, albeit within modern contexts. In the absence of a secular, constitutional legitimation of state powers, the SLORC regime has relied increasingly on its patronage of Buddhist relics and symbols. It has lavishly sponsored the veneration of the *rupakaya* of the Buddha as a populist strategy for legitimation, and as a venue for implementing its vision of a national ideology and community. (The *rupakaya* is the "form body" or material body of the Buddha that is identified with his relics, with stupas or pagodas which are funerary monuments that usually contain a relic, with images, and with other similar kinds of sacred objects.)[2]

The elaborate and expensive ritual theater that the government has undertaken has been aimed at multiple audiences and has deftly deployed Buddhist symbols that have great resonance in Burmese history, culture, and politics. But despite the use of traditional cosmological and mythological motifs, the needs that the state-sponsored veneration of the Buddha's relic have been designed to address have emerged out of the pragmatics of modern politics. This state-sponsored veneration has been generated in order to legitimate political hegemonies, to mobilize large and diverse numbers of people, and to promote the political and cultural integration of an imagined national community. The ritual "progress" (*dethasari*) of the Sacred Tooth in Burma can therefore be seen as a vehicle for negotiating hegemonic visions of a modern nation, the moral authority of political elites, national community, history, and culture.

---

2. In the Theravada tradition the two bodies of the Buddha that persist after his death are his *dhammakaya* (body of teachings) for which the monks assume primary responsibility and the *rupakaya* for which the laity is expected to show special care.

Setting the Stage

The ritual journey (*dethasari*) of the Chinese Tooth Relic from Beijing, China, to Yangon, Myanma, and upcountry between April 20 and June 5, 1994, constituted a culmination within a broader cult of national veneration of stupas, images, relics, and similar sacred objects, and of an extended series of state-sponsored rituals featuring political functionaries and their subordinates in public settings throughout the nation. A series of state-sponsored rituals that dramatized SLORC's religious authority preceded the arrival of the Sacred Tooth in Burma. The weeks leading up to the culminating ritual journey were marked by Myanma's 1994 New Year celebrations in which SLORC functionaries assumed public roles in various ritual contexts. The *New Light of Myanma* (NLM), a major government-run daily paper, described SLORC elites as rightful patrons who deserved popular respect. It also depicted state officials as jovial recipients of water absolutions (*abhiseka*) from state employees in public settings orchestrated for this purpose by ministries and state offices in the capital and in urban centers throughout the nation. Large public gatherings and merriment celebrated the auspiciousness of the Burmese New Year with traditional songs and dances. Following this initial ritual affirmation of political hegemony, political elites performed water absolutions at *rupakaya* sites, including pagodas, Buddha images, and Bodhi Trees throughout the nation. These rituals were symbolic assertions of SLORC's role as rightful patron of *rupakaya* and restorer of royal sources of merit in Myanma's history and culture.

The Sacred Tooth's procession similarly created fields of merit that mapped a universal Buddhist cosmology onto the territory of a modern nation. It placed SLORC in a lineage of past kings and obligated to it ritual clients comprised of military, technocratic, business, and ethnic elites. In preparing for the Tooth's arrival, SLORC planned a procession (*dethasari*) of cosmic proportions. The procession's splendor combined traditional Buddhist symbols of *devas* residing in the heavenly realms, and regalia of a just ruler (*dhammaraja*) with modern technology like Boeing 737 jet aircraft, luxury cars and buses. Complex preparations heralded its journey. Ministers and other highly placed officials attended multiple coordination meetings in order to develop a protocol for the "conveyance of the Sacred Tooth" that was modeled after Burmese traditional prescriptions for the royal procession. Their discussions considered such things as arrangements for the relic's itinerary; the artists' work to construct an encasement and throne upon which the relic would rest;

reports on the physical condition of the elephant that was to carry the sacred object in procession from the airport to its temporary residence at Kaba Aye, the famous Buddhist center in Yangon; the closure of traffic routes due to large-scale dress rehearsals prior to its arrival; and arrangements for security, crowd management, and health emergencies.

Extensive reports of preparations as well as of the actual ritual events appeared in government-run print, audio, and video media. Journalists, film makers, and other government mass media representatives participated in high-level planning sessions to ensure a public relations success. After the relic's arrival, daily radio broadcasts featured songs venerating the Tooth Relic. Rituals were televised routinely and a commemorative video was produced for sale to the public. The state's patronage of religion and especially of the Buddha's *rupakaya* was carefully featured alongside reports of modernization projects and in editorials explicating the state's vision of modernity and Buddhism.

The placement within the paper of the reports related to the Tooth Relic similarly pointed to the significance attributed to these rituals. A logo of the Sacred Tooth's encasement accompanied all coverage over the two-month period. It was often placed near or beneath government slogans praising the military's sacrifice and accomplishments in furthering national unity, peace, and prosperity. Clearly, the message was that the military—like the relic—was worthy of support and reverence by citizens.

The construction of SLORC's ritual community as national community, and of a national history associated with the state's vision of Buddhism, was clearly evident in editorials about the Tooth Relic's procession and its significance. The following comment in an editorial put out by the NLM is representative:

With the State Law and Order Restoration Council working overtime for the promotion, propagation, and perpetuation of the Sasana (the Buddhist religion), it is a great reward for the people of this land that the Tooth Relic has been brought on a *dethasari* journey for the benefit of all who would like to take the opportunity to pay homage.

The Progress of the Sacred Tooth

Traveling from Beijing aboard a special Air China flight that briefly stopped in Kunming, Yunnan (a province in Southern China that borders Myanma), the Buddha's Tooth Relic was accompanied by a delegation of eight Mahayana monks, three Tibetan lamas, four Yunnanese

Theravada monks, and eleven lay persons. This last group included Mr. Luo San Chinai, the Deputy Director of the Chinese Bureau of Religious Affairs, Lt. Gen. Myo Nyunt, a prominent SLORC leader who served as Minister of Religious Affairs and Chairman of the Buddha Tooth Relic Conveyance Work Committee, as well as officials from the religious and foreign affairs ministries. When the relic arrived at Yangon's International Airport, it was officially welcomed by Secretary-1 Lt. Gen. Khin Nyunt (also a prominent leader in SLORC), Myanma's chief justice, the attorney general, other ministers, senior members of the military, members of the State Maha Nayaka Council (the government-sponsored council that regulates affairs of the *sangha*), prominent nuns, leaders of Buddhist lay associations, the Chinese ambassador to Myanma, and representatives of the Chinese Lay Buddhist Association.

A cast of more than 5,000 members of the military, civil servants, actors in costumes of celestial *devas,* and traditional royal service men staged a grand and dramatic reception. Thousands of on-lookers lined the streets of the capital to watch as the procession passed by with its elephant-drawn carriage and festive emissaries. Its motorcade included the limousines of political and religious dignitaries. It also included dozens of buses with schoolchildren; university students; pagoda trustees; representatives from music, film, and literary guilds; members of the government-sponsored national grassroots organization, Union Solidarity Development Association (USDA); and leaders of Hindu and Chinese religious associations, the Red Cross, and the Fire Brigade. It proceeded past lavishly decorated portals constructed for the occasion along a road that led for several miles to the Maha Pasana Cave at the Kaba Aye in Yangon. At the Kaba Aye, the relic was enshrined and placed on public display around the clock.

Inside this artificial cave, which had also served as the site for U Nu's Sixth Buddhist Synod,[3] the relic was displayed in a special encasement placed on a lotus throne and flanked by two replicas and a gilded Emerald Buddha statue whose history is said to be linked to the Chinese Sacred Tooth during the first Burmese empire. SLORC chairman Lt. Gen. Than Shwe and other government ministers were the first to pay homage to the Sacred Tooth and donate money. Later that day, Secretary-1 Lt. Gen. Khin Nyunt and senior monks of the Burmese Maha Nayaka Council publicly venerated the relic, paid respects to the Chinese

3. In the mid-1950s, U Nu, the post-independence prime minister of Burma, sponsored an elaborate international synod to celebrate the 2,500-year anniversary of the founding of Buddhism.

monastic delegation and met with members of lay associations in charge of continuous chanting before the Sacred Tooth. The secretary also inspected donation procedures and the jewelry that had been donated. The next morning, the Sacred Tooth again received homage and offerings from Myanma's head of state, Lt. Gen. Than Shwe, his family, and senior politicians. Food was offered to the Chinese monks and the Sacred Tooth was then made available for public homage. Early each morning, cabinet ministers (in descending rank order), their families, and subordinates made offerings to the Sacred Tooth. For a six-week period, daily television, print, and photo coverage of these rituals featured government officials, public veneration, and tallies of donations that had been made.

Following two weeks of public homage in Yangon, an elaborate float and motorcade commenced a journey that conveyed the Tooth Relic north along a much traveled and historically significant route. The relic's ritual journey proceeded on SLORC's newly completed highway from Yangon to Mandalay, the last royal capital and economic center of upper Burma that links several ethnic regions to the nation's heartland. On its path, the procession stopped at sites of historic and contemporary significance. After five days, it arrived in Mandalay where its public display allowed both *sangha* and laity to gain merit. After nearly two weeks of public veneration there, the relic was carried south again to Thazi, a market town along the rail track, from where it was flown back to Yangon and again enshrined at the Maha Pasana Cave.

During the final two weeks of display, ritual veneration by the SLORC elite, organized collectives, and the public reached enormous proportions. This final period coincided with the Burmese celebration of the Buddha's birth, enlightenment, and *parinibbana* (passing away) on the full moon day of Kazon (May 24, 1994). On June 5, SLORC chairman Lt. Gen. Than Shwe, his family, and high-ranking ministers paid homage, made offerings, and gave donations. Traffic in Yangon was once more rerouted to accommodate a procession in which the Sacred Tooth, carried in its elephant carriage, was returned to Yangon International Airport. At the airport, amidst still more grand ritual theater, the relic was placed on board the plane that flew it back to the Chinese capital of Beijing.

Consecrations and Pilgrimages

The relic's ritual journey set into motion a number of secondary cycles of ritual merit that enhanced and extended its religious and political impact. These ritual cycles fall into two categories. The first includes repeated consecrations of the Tooth and ancillary sacred objects. The second involves pilgrimages to sites of the relic's temporary residence by various client groups fulfilling their obligations towards the center.

The consecrations extended the ritual presence of the Buddha's relics through the use of long-established patterns in Theravada and Burmese traditions. The lineage of the Buddha's relics, represented by the Sacred Tooth, was—in classical Theravada fashion—ritually extended through two replicas fashioned for the purpose of this journey and conveyed along with the "original." The consecrations also included a third sacred object, a Burmese gilded Emerald Buddha image that myth associates with King Anawratha, the famous monarch who established the first Burmese Empire in the eleventh century C.E. According to the legend, the king received the gilded emerald image as a consolation from the "Chinese" guardians of the Sacred Tooth Relic who refused to relinquish the relic itself.

In the course of its ritual journey in 1994, the Tooth Relic was consecrated five times. The consecrations, which were performed in a highly theatrical fashion, had as their officiants Chinese and Burmese members of the *sangha* and were sponsored by the political representatives of SLORC. The first consecration occurred prior to the departure of the Tooth Relic from Beijing and involved Mahayana monks, Tibetan lamas, and 150 Yunnanese monks. Subsequent Tooth Relic consecrations were performed in the presence of the two replicas and Anawratha's gilded Emerald Buddha statue shortly after its arrival in Yangon on April 30, 1994, and again immediately prior to its departure for its upcountry tour on May 5. Two additional consecrations were performed in the course of the relic's upcountry journey in Pyinmana on May 8 and then again in Mandalay on May 10.

The three ancillary sacred objects were displayed alongside the Tooth Relic at Kaba Aye's Maha Pasana Cave where they also received public veneration and were consecrated. The multiple consecrations of the relic itself and of its three associated sacred objects served to augment the number of sites where the Buddha's remains, or their substitutes, would reside in Myanma. With donations collected during the relic's visit to Burma, SLORC has since completed the construction of two separate religious pagodas, one in Yangon and one in Mandalay. These pagodas are dedicated to housing the two copies of the Sacred Tooth and Anawratha's Buddha image. Thus the legacy of the Sacred Tooth has been established both in the "center" and in the north.

The travels of the Sacred Tooth not only established new ritual fields of merit at crucial locations within the nation, but also engendered countless pilgrimages to the sites of its temporary residence. These pilgrimages were undertaken both by client groups within the boundaries of Burma itself and by transnational pilgrims. These pilgrimages mobilized large numbers of diverse social groups and formalized complex ritual patterns of patronage that obligated pilgrims to the elites of the SLORC-dominated state. Groups of pilgrims from relatively local origins included religious associations formed at the state's instigation. Other groups were constituted by classes of civil servants in government offices, neighborhood collectives, business people, and groups of professionals, such as medical specialists, and teachers and students from institutions of higher education. Pilgrims who journeyed from a greater distance tended to be leaders of ethnic minorities who resided in the more remote hill country. The ethnic groups represented included the Wa, Kachin, Palaung, Pa-O, the Shan, and the Lisu. Among these pilgrims were also Chinese (particularly Chinese with connections to Yunnan) and Indians (mostly Hindus) living in Burma. Each of these groups of pilgrims traveled to venerate the Buddha's remains and to donate significant amounts of money that they, their families, and their communities had collected to meet their obligations to participate in the state's ritual patronage.

Another cycle of pilgrimages was created by Buddhists from abroad who visited Myanma during this time period. The protocol for high-profile visitors prescribed the veneration of both the Sacred Tooth and other Burmese reliquaries. In addition to the Chinese Mahayana, Tibetan, and Yunnanese Theravada monks who accompanied the relic, lay and monastic delegations arrived from South Korea and Laos. Cultural exchanges featured Russian novices who received ordinations and attended Buddhist training courses in Burma. Burmese missionary monks living in Calcutta, Bodh Gaya (the site of the Buddha's Enlightenment in northern India), and Sri Lanka returned to Myanma to pay homage to the relic and accept honors awarded to them by the Maha Nayaka Council and the Ministry of Religious Affairs. Prominently featured was a pilgrimage group led by a Burmese monk living in Singapore who was affiliated with Theravada communities in Penang, Malaysia, and Los Angeles. Together with one hundred lay Buddhists—many of whom were Singapore citizens of Chinese descent—he toured many historically and religiously significant sites in Burma. A similarly grand tour was also arranged for the senior members of the Chinese monastic delegation.

Patterns of Patronage

The Sacred Tooth's sojourn in Myanma engaged massive donation drives marked by the politics of giving in national and transnational contexts. Each day, the *New Light of Myanmar* (NLM) conspicuously depicted donation rituals, reported exact amounts donated by individuals and collectives, and featured both donors and SLORC functionaries who officiated as ritual recipients of such donations. The newspapers published daily lists of donors and amounts they contributed in excess of 5,000 kyats.[4] Also published were tallies of funds received each day and the accumulated totals to date. Altogether, the donations collected during the procession of the Sacred Tooth exceeded 162 million kyat and 13,700 pieces of jewelry. On June 5, the day prior to the relic's return to China, the NLM reported:

Today's donations included over 5.81 million kyats by pilgrims, 244 US dollars, 520 (Thai) bhat, ten Bangladesh taka, 65 Indian rupees, 4 Jamaican dollars, 1,100 Brazilian cruzeiros, 276 Chinese yans and three jiaos, 1,000 Indonesian rupias, four Singapore dollars, five Israeli shekels, five Nigeria nairas and 20 kobos, ten Philippines pesos, 250 Taiwan dollars, 650 Cambodian riel, two Venezuela bolivar, 1,000 won and three Malayasian dollars.

Such detailed accounts of monies were intended to attest not only to accurate bookkeeping. At a symbolic level, they were intended to legitimate the State Law and Order Restoration Council's ritual sponsorship and hence its religious patronage over national and international communities of Buddhists paying homage to the Tooth Relic. While the largest portions of funds were raised by collectives and the general public, a considerable portion was received from major private donors.

The list of donors provided a rough profile of the economic and political elite. Prominent members of the government and of the business community made significant donations on several occasions. Some business families donated as much as 100,000 kyats. A second group of major donors included representatives of professional and ethnic religious associations whose collective donations exceeded the required minimum.[5]

4. In 1994, though the official exchange rate gave a much higher value to the kyat, 200 kyat were roughly equivalent in purchasing power to one American dollar.

5. Officially, a minimum of 5,000 kyat was required for inclusion of one's name among the published lists of donors. In actuality, however, donations made by families or other private citizens typically amounted to at least twice that amount. Donations collected

The contributions of a third group also featured in the press comprised those who volunteered their services to facilitate crowd management and provide first aid, fans, and soft drinks to exhausted pilgrims waiting for many hours in long lines to pay homage to the relic. A fourth group consisted of foreign dignitaries from religious, economic, or political backgrounds whose large public donations were especially lauded in the press. A number of foreign political dignitaries who visited Myanma during this period, such as the prime minister of the Socialist Republic of Vietnam, the Indonesian foreign minister, the Yunnanese governor, and a military advisor from India made donations to a variety of religious causes.

The state provided donors with certificates of honor and arranged for select groups of donors to perform daily rituals to share merit and to acknowledge their ritual participation. These ceremonies were performed at the sites of the relic's temporary residence at Kaba Aye in Yangon and at the State Pariyatti Monastic University in Mandalay. While such membership entitles one to privileges, it also entails continuing obligations to the patronage of a political elite. Public portrayals of generosity in support of a renewed Burmese national ethos suggest implicit competition among donors for political recognition and can be seen as a demonstration of one's allegiance to prevailing power structures. Despite the large-scale public outpouring of generosity, the perception prevailed that contributions furnished access to political power and involved more or less formalized membership in a ritual community under the auspices of SLORC.

Traditional and Modern Contexts of Interpretation

The recent ritual procession of the Sacred Tooth in Burma can be interpreted against the background of the textual and historical themes in the Theravada tradition. In traditional Theravada polities, the popular veneration of Buddhist sacred objects like relics and images was shaped by mythic constructs that often are modeled after texts like the Mahaparinibbana Sutta which tells the story of the Buddha's cremation and distribution of his relics to the kings of surrounding kingdoms. A theme reflecting the righteousness of Buddhist rulers is also found

---

through organizations tended to be less predictable, but often exceeded most individual donations.

in the Cakkavatti Sihanada Suttanta where the Buddha tells the story of a world conquering *cakkavatti* (wheel-turning) king whose reign is established through the submission of lesser rulers who voluntarily become his vassals. Since this king possesses and rules by the *Cakka*, which is the Wheel of the Dhamma (Truth or Law), the well-being and prosperity of his realm is assured. Theravada myths and mythological histories include numerous stories of many kings who honor particularly potent relics (such as the famous Tooth Relic in Sri Lanka), give special veneration to particularly powerful images (such as the Emerald Buddha in Thailand), and construct highly impressive monuments (for example, the 84,000 stupas or funeral mounds constructed—according to the legends—by King Asoka, the great patron of Buddhism in ancient India). Living memory also recalls an earlier, government-sponsored visit of the Chinese Sacred Tooth to Burma and Sri Lanka at the time when Theravadins were celebrating the 2,500th anniversary of the founding of Buddhism.

The veneration of the Buddha's physical remains (*dhatu*) is integral to the practice of cosmological Theravada Buddhism in traditional Buddhist kingdoms. A significant aspect of popular Theravada practice, relic veneration, the construction of stupas, or, more generally, state patronage of the Buddha's *rupakaya* create a field of merit and source of political legitimation separate and distinct from merit made through giving to the *sangha*. These practices also establish a socially and ritually differentiated hegemony within which power relations are negotiated and consolidated. First, relics and similar sacred objects stand for the entire body of the Buddha and, by extension, the totality of his dispensation. They map a cosmic center and establish structural orders between a microcosm, its periphery, and an encompassing macrocosm, thus linking, for example, the Southeast Asian periphery to the universal Buddhist order of things (*dhamma*). Secondly, a teleological significance is attributed to the presence of relics in a given location by mytho-historic narratives that link the historical present to a pristine time in the life of the Buddha. Sacred realities are thus mapped onto temporal polities, and ritual acts localize the Buddha's presence in cosmological, social, and political domains to generate merit for the eventual transcendence of this world (*samsara*) and attainment of enlightenment (*nibbana*). Thirdly, the ritual veneration of relics engenders a hierarchically ordered, religio-political community. It endows social actors with charisma and historical events with significance beyond the immediate contexts of cultural performance. A just ruler (*dhammaraja*) acts as ritual patron of some of the tradition's most evocative root metaphors. He does so within the ritual and social structures of an economy of merit. Homage and generosity (*dana*) toward the Buddha's spiritual and material remains are seen as indications of religiosity, social status, and political legitimacy.

Yet, 1994 in Myanma no longer denotes a time in which traditional, cosmological Buddhism is deployed in the context of a pre-modern religious and political ethos. The ritual structures created by the procession of the Chinese Sacred Tooth throughout the nation encompass multiple interpretations framed by competing contexts, including the contemporary and frequently contested notions of Burmese history, culture, and national community. The SLORC military clique seeks to strengthen its hegemony through patronage of the Chinese Tooth Relic, through the creation of historically linked and socially overlapping fields of merit throughout the contemporary nation-state of Myanma, a process that necessarily involves the mobilization of diverse communities and resources. The state's appeal to the symbols of cosmological Buddhism in a modern setting aims to create a particular ethos and vision of the Burmese nation, its history, culture, and territory—an ethos and vision that are depicted as, at the same time, "essentially" Burmese and "essentially" Buddhist. The state seeks to project to its citizens and to outside observers an ethos and vision of Buddhism in which the state, the *sangha*, and the laity speak in a single voice, emphasizing righteousness, scripturalism, and morality (*sila*).

While the rituals described here may be modeled after traditional paradigms rooted in cosmological Buddhism, in modern contexts competing visions of authority contest traditional orders and provide alternate avenues for interpretation. Some, though by no means all, of the competing Burmese interpretations share salient presumptions about the veneration of the Buddha's relics and its social import. The range of ritual interpretations encountered only underscores the cultural and symbolic significance of relics as root metaphors of the Theravada Buddhist tradition.

Voices that speak within Myanma's national boundaries for alternative visions of Buddhism, the nation, and moral authority have become seriously muted. As the state controls social discourse about public merit-making, alternate voices must be gleaned from silence, in absence from ritual participation, and in the countertexts of expatriate communities beyond Myanma's national boundaries. Burma has a long-standing tradition of voicing political dissent in religious terms. In recent years, this has sometimes taken the form of disparaging remarks about the legitimacy and splendor of the grand Mahawizaya Pagoda built by the preceding Ne Win government next to Shwedagon Pagoda, a national symbol of Burma. Others may ruminate about the stupa's night-lit silhouette serving as a backdrop for entertaining foreign businessmen in posh restaurants that have opened in this part of Yangon. Voices of dissent also emerge from religious donations that circumvent the state's collection network. Especially among dissident elites, political resentment is expressed in perfunctory donations to the state's religious causes, while more generous offerings are made to sources of merit that reflect a personal choice and are deemed more worthy of support. Widespread mobilization of donations to state-sponsored religious causes has at times reinforced popular resentment as some consider it to be merely another form of taxation. The government-dominated media responds to such everyday forms of resistance mostly with silence.

Outside the nation's territory, some expatriate voices expressed doubts about the use of the donations that are collected. Some—including Buddhists who are historically aware—question the authenticity of the relic and its supposed connections to Burma and the Burmese tradition. While Burmese have traditionally venerated various Buddhist relics, issues such as these are being raised with increasing frequency in the present social and political contexts.

In conclusion, it is worth emphasizing that the many forms of venerating the Buddha's relics are primarily individual acts of meditative devotion or ritual service with little relevance to the type of social interpretation discussed above. Historically, however, Theravada Buddhist culture established or perpetuated hegemonic structures through the construction and patronage of Buddhist relics and reliquaries. The perspectives that emerge from the modern Burmese Buddhist relic veneration in large-scale state rituals show how sacred objects can legitimate a specific vision of authority over diverse communities, and how such rituals can become a focal point for the articulation of national culture, history, and community.

Some general observations emerge. The first concerns the role of relics as root metaphors that evoke conceptions of power universal to the Buddhist tradition. As root metaphors, relics exhibit universal relevance across the tradition that can be "translated" into specific local contexts and cultures sharing the same religious heritage. Universal conceptions become particularized in social, political, and historic contexts.

A second commonality in the interpretation of relics as root metaphors rests in the transformation of ritual service to the Buddha's remains into particular patterns of political patronage. In state rituals, they support the creation of fields of merit, status, and power and are therefore readily appropriated by political ideologies and in the mobilization of ritual clients. They often become, as they have in contemporary Myanma, important currency in the economy of power.

Figure 4. A scene from the Vessantara Jataka in which Prince Vessantara, Maddi, and their two children walk to their forest hermitage. A mural from Wat Luang monastery in Laos. Photograph by Donald K. Swearer.

CHAPTER 4

Village Rituals and Ceremonies (Thailand)

In virtually all cultures in which Buddhism is well established among the populace as a whole, Buddhist temples hold regular calendric festivals. Especially in the village context, these rituals and ceremonies often cover a range of social interests and concerns. They generate merit for the devout. They produce merit for the dead and departed and assist them on their way to better states of rebirth. They sustain communication and exchanges among different villages, towns, and temples. They establish and maintain what are considered to be proper gender, monastic, and lay relations and roles. They instruct the larger community with and through the life, virtues, and moral principles of the Buddha and Buddha-related figures. They celebrate good harvests and agricultural cycles and attempt to ensure the prosperity of those to come. They please village guardian deities and function as modes of requesting continued supernatural protection and blessing. Finally, they provide a context for social amusement, creativity, and fun. Thus, temple rituals and ceremonies, especially annual ones, function as definitive moments in communal identification, social cohesion, and collective expression. To put this point another way, annual temple rituals and ceremonies help to develop and sustain a community's understanding of the world at large and to orient its ongoing religious and social life based on that understanding. The following excerpt illustrates one

The essay in this chapter was taken from S. J. Tambiah, *Buddhism and the Spirit Cults in North-east Thailand* (Cambridge: Cambridge University Press, 1970), 160–68. Copyright © Cambridge University Press, 1970. Reprinted with the permission of the Cambridge University Press.

such annual temple ceremony as it takes place in and around a monastic complex in northeast Thailand.

BUN PHRAAWES

S. J. Tambiah

Bun Phraawes is the grandest merit-making ceremony in the village of Phraan Muan. The name of the festival derives from the story of *Phraa Wes* (Prince *Vessantara*), which relates the story of the Buddha in his last birth before the one in which he attained Buddhahood. For all Buddhists this is preeminent for its moral implications of selfless giving and its deeply moving drama that leads from tragedy to final vindication and triumph. In Thailand it is often referred to as the *Mahachad* (great *Jataka*) and is recited in merit-making rites in the form of 1,000 verses divided into thirteen chapters.[1] Villagers count *Bun Phraawes* as merit from listening to a sermon. Listening to the recitation of this long text is believed to confer great merit and the fulfillment of the devotee's wishes.[2]

But *Bun Phraawes* is not merely an annual religious ritual. It is the village's major festival, appropriately occurring after harvest, and combines merit-making with secular interests. In terms of the agricultural cycle it reflects two themes—thanksgiving and looking forward to the next cycle. Occurring as it does in the middle of the dry season, it looks forward to the onset of rains. The particular interest this festival has for our study of village Buddhism is that it embraces a number of themes and interests which are given theological integration under the auspices of Buddhism.

Structurally, the *Bun Phraawes* rites divide into three sequences. First comes the invitation to Uppakrut to attend the festival; he is a Buddhist guardian deity who is associated with protecting the village and ensuring the rains. In this sense the first phase is man's communion with natural

1. Editors' note: *Jatakas* are stories recounting an episode or series of episodes in one of the Buddha's many previous lives. They play an important role in Buddhism, particularly, though not exclusively, in the Theravada Buddhism of Sri Lanka and Southeast Asia.

2. Editors' note: The story recounts the many gifts of Prince Vessantara including, ultimately, the gift of his wife and two children to a despicable Brahmin priest. In the end the god Indra intervenes, and Vessantara is reunited with his wife and children and becomes king. For a full translation of the Pali version of this story, see Margaret Cone and Richard F. Gombrich, *The Perfect Generosity of Prince Vessantara: A Buddhist Epic* (Oxford: Clarendon Press, 1977).

forces. The next phase, the inviting and propitiation of the divine angels (*thewada*), is man's communion with the upper spirit world. Uppakrut mediates with nature, the *thewada* with the divine. The ideologically central part, enacted in the third phase, is merit-making by recitation of and listening to the great story (and other subsidiary sermons). Every night of the festival the village fair is held in the precincts of the Buddhist temple or *wat*.

I shall give a brief ethnographic description of these sequences and analyse their implications.

Preparations

Preparations go on during the two days preceding the first major ritual sequence. Stages are built for *maulam* (folk opera) and *ramwong* (popular Thai dancing); a pavilion to store paddy contributions is constructed; four posts are planted to enclose the reception hall, with large flags attached to them at the top and baskets fixed at the bottom; the reception hall is decorated with painted cloths and special decorations connected with this festival. Special ritual articles connected with Uppakrut, *thewada*, and *Phraawes* have to be made locally or purchased.

A striking pattern of the preparations is the differential male-female roles. Old women roll cigarettes, make betel-nut packets, candles, etc. This is a role that in fact old women perform in every religious or social ceremony in the village. The men—both old and young—decorate and construct pavilions (or in other contexts coffins or other ritual furniture), the old doing the lighter and the young the heavier work. Young girls and young married women are the cooks. It is they primarily who, supervised by older women, bring food for the monks on ceremonial occasions.

In the afternoon of the second day the Buddha image is brought down from the monks' quarters and installed in the pavilion. Monks sit in the pavilion with begging bowls, waiting for villagers to bring them gifts of paddy. Paddy contributions are the main gift made by villagers at this festival.

The Invitation to Phraa Uppakrut

In the late afternoon is staged the first main ritual of the series—the invitation to Phraa Uppakrut, who lives in a perennial pond or swamp.

Villagers said that before preaching the story of *Phraawes* it was the custom to invite Phraa Uppakrut to the temple.

The set of ritual articles important in this rite is called the *kryang* (things) of *Phraa Uppakrut*. They are: a monk's bowl, a set of monk's yellow robes, an umbrella, a pair of monk's sandals, two small images of the Buddha, *karuphan* (made of various kinds of flowers), puffed rice, two banana-leaf trays containing locally made cigarettes, and a kettle. All these articles were placed on a cushion which rested in the centre of a wooden sedan chair. The procession actually started from the temple compound and was led by three monks, who were followed by elderly leaders carrying the sedan chair. Then followed a large body of villagers—men, women, and children. Guns were carried, and music was provided by a bamboo flute and drums. Conspicuous were the flags with pictures of Nang Thoranee (goddess of the earth), a mermaid, a crocodile, etc., which represent Buddha's victorious battle with Mara.[3] The procession, after passing through the hamlet, headed for a pond in the paddy fields. The ponds selected must have water all the year round.

After the usual preliminaries in any Buddhist ceremony—lighting of candles, offering of candles and flowers to the Buddha, and requesting of the five precepts—Uppakrut was invited. An elder placed the two small Buddha images on the cover of the monk's bowl. Another held a dish of flowers and a candle in his hand (as an offering to Phraa Uppakrut), while the former chanted the invitation to Uppakrut to come and be guardian of the ceremony. As he chanted, he threw some puffed rice onto the sedan chair, again as an offering to Uppakrut. Next the guns were fired several times, the drums were loudly beaten, and all the people shouted "*chaiyo*." (It was said that the guns were fired to frighten off *Praya Mara* and "*chaiyo*" was shouted in order to proclaim victory.) After this the monks chanted "*chaiyanto*," the victory blessing—this was to bless all those who had joined the procession. The kettle was then taken by an elder to the pond and filled with water, and placed on the sedan. The Buddha images were put in the bowl, and the sedan chair lifted. The procession returned by a different route, entered the temple by a different gate, and circumambulated the reception hall three times in the usual clockwise direction. The sedan chair was carried into the re-

3. Editors' note: One of the most important stories in the biography of the Buddha concerns his victory over Mara, a powerful deity who is the personification of desire. The victory prepared the way for the Buddha's attainment of Enlightenment, and during the battle itself, the Buddha called the goddess of the earth to be a witness to the virtues he had perfected in the course of his previous lives.

ception hall, and the articles (*kryang*) were put on a shelf in the corner. All the flags were placed near the pulpit. The kettle of water was put on a high shelf. (Informants said that when the entire merit ceremony was over, the water would be ceremonially thrown away: "*Uppakrut lives in the water; that is why the water is brought.*")

Later in the evening, the monks chanted blessings and sprinkled holy water on the congregation, which consisted only of old men and women.

The events of the next two days form one continuous series, but I shall in the following subsections separate out two major ritual sequences: the *thewada* ceremony and the recitation of the *Mahachad* that tells the story of Phraa Wes.

In the afternoon of the day following the invitation to Uppakrut, a sermon concerning Pramalai (Malaya Sutta) was preached by the monks. Since listening to such sacred texts is considered a highly merit-making act, a large congregation consisting of men, women, and children of all ages was present. The gist of the sermon is as follows: Pramalai was a monk who went to hell to preach to all sinners. His visit and his preaching helped to alleviate their sins. Then he ascended to the heavens— with sixteen levels—to preach to those who had made merit. He then came to the world of human beings and told them what he had seen in heaven and hell. This sermon in a sense appropriately reflects the three major sequences of the *Bun Phraawes* festivities—the inviting of Phraa Uppakrut who lives in the swamp, and of the *thewada* who are heavenly beings, followed by the great sermon addressed to human and supernatural devotees.

The Homage to *Thewada*

On the morning of the third day, at 2:30 A.M., when the village fair was in full swing, a ceremony was staged in which respects were paid to the *thewada* (divine angels). It was village dogma that before the *Phraawes* story could be recited (or as a matter of fact any merit ceremony begun), *thewada* must be invited to come and be witnesses to the act. What is of significance here is that in no other ritual are the *thewada* propitiated in a special rite and made the sole recipients of offerings. It was said that if the *thewada* were invited and worshipped they in turn would make the villagers "live well and in health," that rain would fall as usual and much rainfall might be expected.

A procession consisting primarily of old men and women (except the drummers, who were young men) formed at the reception hall with candles and flowers in their hands, and bowls containing balls of glutinous rice (which in theory should number 1,000 to represent the number of verses of the *Phraawes* story). It is in fact called the "procession of 1,000 lumps of rice." No monks took part in the procession. It went round the reception hall three times in a clockwise direction, and whenever it passed one of the four posts with a flag at the top and a basket at the bottom, rice balls, candles and flowers were dropped into the baskets. These posts were called *han* (*ran*) *bucha,* and were said to be *khong* (things) of the *thewada.* The offerings, informants said, were intended for both *thewada* and *Phraawes,* but they were unable to say why the processions and offerings had to be carried out in this particular fashion.

The *han bucha* can perhaps be related to Buddhist symbolism unknown to the villagers. They appear to resemble the "trees that gratify the desires of men." These trees have no likeness to any tree at all, but are hollow wicker baskets on the ends of long poles. In popular Buddhism they are said to represent the four trees that will blossom at the four corners of the city in which the next Buddha, Maitreya, will be born. They will then produce all kinds of delicious fruits in fabulous quantities. The money trees that appear in merit-making rites may also be seen as associated with this symbolism.

The Recitation of *Mahachad*

When the circumambulation was over the participants in the procession entered the reception hall, placed the bowls of glutinous rice near the pulpit, and took their seats. The ritual articles associated with merit-making for *Bun Phraawes* as such are: betel-nut packets, locally made cigarettes, small flags, candles, joss-sticks; each of these items must be 1,000 in number. Other items are: four pans filled with water containing fish and turtle, and these represent four ponds in the forest in which Phraawes lived in banishment; a bee hive (in memory of a monkey's offering to Buddha); bunches of coconuts and bananas.

The main sequences in the recitation of the story were as follows: after presenting flowers and candles to the Buddhist trinity (the Buddha, Dhamma, and Sangha), and the request for the five precepts (which refer to the recitation by monks of the precepts against killing, lying, theft, sexual licence, and the use of intoxicants), two elders in turn invited the *thewada* to come and listen to the great story. "*Chaiyo*" (victory) was shouted three times.

The next sequence was the sermon called *Teed Sangkaad*, delivered by a monk. Its delivery has to be requested by a village leader of the congregation. This invitation, called *aratana Sangkaad*, is a recounting of episodes in the Buddha's final life as Gotama—his renunciation of the kingly life and his wife and son, his departure on his best horse, Maa Keo, one of the seven treasures of the Emperor (Chakravartin), the death of this horse through sorrow, the Buddha's cutting off of his hair and its reception in a golden vessel by God Indra, who took it to his heaven and deposited it at the Phra Choolamani monument.[4]

The theme of the monk's sermon which followed was the well-known story of the defeat of Mara, especially the tricks resorted to by Mara in order to defile Buddha's state of enlightenment. Mara sent his three daughters to excite Buddha's sexual passions. He rejected them, and the girls "finally became old women." Informants said that this sermon was an essential prelude to the *Mahachad* recitation. Monks took turns in reciting the long text of the *Mahachad*, and the recitation, which started early in the morning, did not conclude until 8 P.M. First a Pali verse was recited; then the audience threw puffed rice at the Buddha image; then the monks told the story in Thai.[5] People came and went and the attention to the sermon was not intense.

At the conclusion of the recitation, villagers brought money trees and presented them to the monks and the temple. People came in procession in groups. Finally a monk made lustral water (*nam gatha phan* = water of 1,000 verses) and sprinkled it on all those present. Villagers took home some of the sacred water to sprinkle on their buffaloes in order to drive away illness. Thus were concluded the *Bun Phraawes* ritual and festivities.

There is a belief associated with the *Mahachad* recitation that it must be completed in a day; if not, unfortunate accidents and misfortune will occur. This is why, we were told, the *thewada* ceremony had to be staged in the early hours of the morning, so that the recitation could be started very early and concluded in the evening.

The themes of the monks' preaching of the *Dhamma* were renunciation of the kingly life and family, selfless giving in the *Mahachad*, rejection of sexuality and passion in the encounter with Mara's daughters, and the after-death phenomena of heaven and hell. It could be said that

---

4. Editors' note: The Phra Choolamani monument is a stupa located in the heaven presided over by the god Indra.

5. Editors' note: As mentioned in the general introduction to this collection, Pali is the sacred language in which the scriptures of the Theravada tradition are preserved.

the last phase of the *Bun Phraawes*, the sermonizing and recitation of texts, recounts the great episodes of the Buddha's life: renunciation of secular glory and comfort, the ardours of the search for truth, and final achievement of detachment and salvation. At the same time the paradox is that these words of renunciation and selflessness (as well as the other ritual sequences) are viewed by the participants as endowing them with merit, and ensuring a "good and healthy life," and plentiful rain. Mara, the enemy of Buddha and man, is held at bay, and the lustral water of the thousand verses confers health on man and buffalo. Thus a problem is posed as to the mechanics of the Buddhist ritual—how the use of sacred words which deal with the virtues of renunciation transfers to the participants the seemingly opposite benefits of life affirmation.

The Activities of the Fair

I have thus far concentrated on the Buddhist rituals. I must now describe the fair briefly in order to give a rounded picture, for *Bun Phraawes* combines with merit-making robust fun and sheer entertainment. The annual temple fair is the chief recreational event in village life and characteristically Buddhism shows its robustness for combining it with conspicuous merit-making.

The fair ran for three days and two nights, the nights being the time of peak activity. Shops—mostly selling food and drink—were set up in the temple compound. The chief attractions were the *ramwong* (popular Thai dancing), conducted by a professional orchestra and dance hostesses from a nearby village; *maulam* (folk opera), also performed by a visiting professional troupe; and movies.

The monks, true to their rules of priesthood, avoided the *maulam* and *ramwong*, but they did not avoid interest in the movies. They were, however, mainly involved in ritual merit-making activities in the pavilion with the Buddha statue. There, two main activities were carried out: laymen put money in the monks' bowls and in turn were sprinkled with holy water; and laymen bought pieces of gold leaf and daubed them on the Buddha statue. (Additionally, laymen brought flowers in order to present them to the Buddha.)

Persons of all ages and both sexes attended the fair. Most old persons, male and female, first engaged in merit-making by contributing money, then looked at the movies for a while, and then gravitated towards the folk opera. Adults watched the movies and *ramwong* and also found the *maulam* of absorbing interest; the young men were primarily interested in the movies and *ramwong*, while young girls of the village found the movies and *maulam* their chief attraction. Children were the most consistent audience at the movies. No local village girl took part in the dancing. The fair was an occasion for flirting between the sexes. Some ritual sequences of *Bun Phraawes*, which ran parallel with the fair, were largely ignored by the young people.

A few words about the scale of participation. *Bun Phraawes* in all the villages around Baan Phraan Muan is staged with a fair. It therefore attracts devotees and pleasure-seekers from a number of adjoining villages. People from at least seven or eight *tambon* (communes) were present at the Phraan Muan proceedings: they made merit, contributed money, and had fun. Particular hamlets or groups of villagers from elsewhere often acted as a merit-making group, each contributing a gift of paddy or a money tree. Twenty-six monks from other temples took part in the *Bun Phraawes* proceedings. It is usual to send out invitations to other temples, and for the latter to send representatives. The following distribution shows the range of inter-temple co-operation—15 monks came from 15 temples in the same *tambon* in which Baan Phraan Muan is located; 6 monks came from 6 temples in the adjoining *tambon* of Mumon; the remaining 5 monks came either from the same district (Amphur Muang) or from the adjoining districts of Pen and Pue. The vendors of food and drinks also came from a widespread area. Of a total of 40–45 vendors, only 5 were from the local village; 4 came from the town of Udorn and the rest from at least 8 adjoining *tambon*.

These facts, I think, establish the nature of festive Buddhism as a supralocal religion. It is true that it is local people who primarily patronize a village temple; but merit-making is a society-wide ethic and such prominent merit-making occasions as a temple fair attract many others who see participation in them as a chance of acquiring greater merit than usual. Just as outsiders attend grand merit-making rites at Baan Phraan Muan, so do residents of the latter participate in the *wat* festivals of other villages. By contrast, the cult of the village guardian spirit is of an essentially local character, being bound up with a settlement and its land and people. All the villages around Phraan Muan propitiate the same village guardians; the cult is widespread but no outside villager needs to propitiate the guardian of another village. But traditionally the villages in the region combined to propitiate a common swamp spirit in a Buddhist festival that expressed a regional identity and interest.

PART II

Monastic Practices

Figure 5. A novice ordination ceremony in Sri Lanka. Photograph by John Ross Carter.

CHAPTER 5

The Ordination of Monks and Novices (Korea)

Many Buddhist texts and traditions—some the earliest-known expressions of Buddhist culture—depict the ideal Buddhist community as intrinsically constituted by an order of monks (*bhiksus*), an order of nuns (*bhiksunis*), and a laity composed of laymen (*upasakas*) and laywomen (*upasikas*). In the next five chapters, we will focus on the Buddhist monastic orders and those who participate in them. We begin with an excerpt that concerns the order of monks—specifically with the ritual processes through which novices and full-fledged members are ordained

The ordinations of novices and monks are crucially important events in the life of the Buddhist community, since they both confirm and restrict certain degrees of religious legitimacy and authority. They function as crucial and highly self-reflective moments that establish monastic commitment, perpetuation, propagation, organization, and hierarchy They also maintain distinctions among different Buddhist sects, schools, and traditions. Thus, like much ritual activity, they involve considerable preparation, formality, and structure. So, too, these ordinations are often associated with a great deal of public performance and display

In various Buddhist traditions, novice ordinations play quite different roles. In Myanmar, for example, novice ordinations followed by a short stay in the monastery have become regular features of life for boys and young men and have developed into elaborate life-cycle ceremonies last-

The essay in this chapter was taken from Robert E. Buswell, *The Zen Monastic Experience: Buddhist Practice in Contemporary Korea* (Princeton: Princeton University Press, 1992), 81–90. Copyright © 1992 by Princeton University Press. Reprinted by permission of Princeton University Press.

ing several days. These ordinations hold particular importance and status because people consider them to be extremely meritorious for the initiate and also for the immediate and extended family.

Similar differences can be observed in the ordinations of monks. In most cases these ordinations involve vows of celibacy and are considered to imply a lifetime commitment. However, there are important exceptions. In Japan, for example, most Buddhist sects have come to assert the appropriateness of clerical marriage. In Thailand, where many monk ordinations serve as a rite of passage from male adolescence into adulthood, traditionally it has been common for men to move in and out of the monastic order as they pass through various stages in the life cycle.

The excerpt that follows describes novice and monastic ordinations as they are performed among Son (Zen) monastics in Korea. More specifically, it explores novice and monastic ordinations among members of the Chogye Order, the bearer of a rather conservative tradition.

ORDINATION IN THE CHOGYE ORDER

Robert E. Buswell

After their six-month postulancies are over and they have mastered all the chants and books of monastic regulations, the postulants are finally ready to ordain as novice monks (Skt. *sramanera*). During my years in Korea, I observed that many large monasteries still held their own ordination platforms. At Songgwang-sa (a monastery), a complete ordination platform was held only once a year, during the third lunar month (usually in April), during the spring vacation period. The entire ceremony lasted three days. On the first day, the sramanera ordination was held in the early morning before breakfast, followed in the late morning and afternoon by the full ordination for monks. (The final two days were devoted to bodhisattva ordinations given to members of the laity.)

Novice Ordination

The novice, or sramanera, ordination is held around four in the morning after the service in the main buddha hall. If the weather is warm, the ceremony will be held in the larger Solbop-chon (Speaking the Dharma Basilica), the main lecture hall; if heating is necessary, the ceremony will be transferred to the great room in the kitchen compound. Songgwang-sa held two novice ordinations each year, one in conjunction with the large ordination platform in the spring, the other in the early winter, to accommodate the next matriculating group of postulants.

All postulants of the monastery who have completed a full six months of training at the monastery are invited, though not required, to participate. Disciples of the abbots or senior monks of the monastery's branch temples will also join the ceremony. The Son master (a master of a particular form of meditation and teaching) may have nuns in other parts of the country who are his disciples; they too may send their own disciples to the main temple for the novice ordination, since the *Vinaya* requires that nuns be ordained by both the monk (*bhiksu*) and nun (*bhiksuni*) samghas. The Son master may conduct the novice ordination himself, but during the spring ordination platform the specialist in ordination procedure may instead be in charge.

Each of the postulants will be assigned a "beneficent master" (*unsa*), a senior monk who serves as the formal sponsor of the postulant's candidacy for ordination, rather as does the "vocation father" in Catholic monasticism. No bhiksu with less than ten years of seniority is allowed to serve as an unsa. The prospective monk's relationship with the unsa is one that will last for life and will be crucial for a successful vocation. The new monk's identity will be defined by his home monastery and the reputation of his unsa, so it is essential that the unsa be carefully chosen.

Competition is especially keen among the postulants to have the Son master as their unsa. The Son master is quite choosy in accepting new disciples and accedes to only a limited number of requests from postulants. Monastic "families," like their secular counterparts, maintain the earlier Chinese emphasis on the primacy of the senior line within the lineage. This superior status of the Son master's own line accounts for why the postulants are so intent on becoming his direct disciples. Unsuccessful candidates he assigns instead to the abbot and other senior monks in the monastery family. The unsa chooses a dharma name for the postulant, the unsa's dharma family usually being indicated by the use of the same Sino-Korean logograph in the names of all his disciples or generations of disciples. Many postulants are heartbroken when they learn they will not become the disciple of the Son master, and I knew of several cases where rejected candidates left the monastery without taking ordination to start their postulancy over again elsewhere.

Before the novice ordination begins, each postulant has been given a set of formal robes by his unsa. If the postulants have done their preparation at the main monastery, robes will have been made by the monastery's own in-house seamstress, considered a bodhisattva.

The novice ordination is quite simple. Unlike other ordinations, the novice ordination does not require the participation of official witnesses in order to validate it. Laypeople are allowed to attend if they desire, but this is uncommon; usually only senior monks from the main monastery and branch temples will be present, along with all the represented unsas. Never once did I see the family of the ordinand attend the ceremony.

For the ceremony, a dais has been placed in the middle of the room, where the master presides. A small table has been placed in front of the dais, on which are placed two candlesticks and the regular sacristal instruments—the water holder and censer. Wearing the *changsams* (a full-length, formal robe with butterfly sleeves worn over a monk's regular clothing), the ordinands file into the room one by one, prostrate three times before the master, and stay kneeling on their heels in what we in the West know as Japanese fashion, one of the few times Koreans adopt that style of sitting. As the candidates remain seated in line, the master goes into a lengthy explanation of the meaning of the ten precepts that novices must follow, and the importance of their new vocation. This lecture can often last an hour or more, during the whole of which the ordinands force themselves not to shift positions. I have seen many cases where the candidates could not rise afterwards, their legs having gone completely numb. The master repeats for them the ten precepts: (1) not to kill; (2) not to steal; (3) not to engage in sex; (4) not to lie; (5) not to drink alcohol; (6) not to sit or sleep on high or wide beds; (7) not to wear garlands, ornaments, or perfumes; (8) not to dance or sing to oneself or intentionally attend such performances; (9) not to handle gold or silver; and (10) not to eat in the afternoon or raise domestic animals. At the end of his recitation, he asks the ordinands, "Can you keep each and every one of these precepts without transgressing them?" The repetition of this simple formula three times constitutes the act of ordination. The candidates then vow to keep the precepts for as long as they remain monks. The Son master's attendant then places a miniature *kasa* (a square cloth that, when worn, hangs around the neck and covers the belly) over each ordinand's head, and at that moment they have become novices.

At the conclusion of the sramanera ordination, a waxed wick, called the *sambae,* is placed on the inside forearm, lit with a match, and left to burn down to the skin. This ritual is called "burning of the arm." While the burns are usually not severe, the novices are in obvious pain as the wick burns down, pain they try to bear stoically. Later, as the scab begins to heal, the novices sometimes pick at it so the resulting scar will grow larger and larger, another mark of monkish machismo.

Ilt'a *sunim*, the *Vinaya* master at Haein-sa (a monastery), who is one of the most popular catechists because of his genius for storytelling, explained to me that burning the arm is done to symbolize the new novice's nonattachment to the body and disentanglement from worldly affairs. According to Ilt'a, the sutras mention three types of physical burns to which monks subject themselves: burning the arm, burning the fingers, and burning the body. The custom is therefore validated in the basic texts of Buddhism, he claimed. The Koreans do not go so far as the Chinese Buddhists, who light a grid of multiple wicks on the top of the ordinands' heads at the time of their ordination. Ilt'a denounced this Chinese practice as having no scriptural basis. He speculated that the idea of burning the top of the head came from Chinese medicine, in which applying heat to acupuncture points on the head was considered to be a powerful curative agent. But he did note that some elderly monks who came originally from north Korea had such burn marks on their heads.

The novice ordination usually ends just before breakfast at six. In the few minutes before the meal is served, the audience of monks will congratulate the ordinands, often teasing them about being unable to stand after sitting through the master's interminable talk. After the monks have finished breakfast, they stay seated in the refectory and the new novices are led into the hall to be introduced formally to the samgha. The novices file into the hall and prostrate themselves three times before the buddha image. Turning toward the back of the room, they then bow three times to the Son master and the rest of the samgha. As the novices remain kneeling, the proctor introduces them individually to the assembly, informing the monks of the dharma names of the new novices, the names of their unsas, and their home monasteries. This same information will be repeated for the rest of their careers each time they are introduced at a new monastery. The Son master might then make a few further comments about how important and exciting it is to have new monks in the monastery. When the master indicates his remarks are finished, the novices prostrate themselves three more times and file out.

There is no formal certificate presented to the novices during the ordination. Later, however, each new novice will be given a monk's identification card and number. The card has a small picture of the monk and his identification number, dharma name, home monastery, and unsa teacher. The identification numbers are issued by the national Samgha headquarters in Seoul, with the supreme patriarch given the number *1*, and the rest of the national hierarchy following in order. Each monastery has its own series of numbers, again with either the Son master or abbot being given the number *1*, and the rest of the numbers given out in succession as people ordain. These numbers are not registered with the secular government, I was told, but are only on file with the Chogye Order. Wherever the monk travels, he will always carry this card with him. The back of the card is divided into spaces and the monk is supposed to have recorded in those spaces the temples where he spends his periods of retreat, and in which section of the monastery he resided (for example, meditation hall, seminary, etc.). When the monk later travels to other monasteries, this information will help the guest prefect assess the quality of the monk's training and decide whether he should be admitted to the temple as a resident.

Koreans recognize a substantial difference in the degree of commitment made by the novice and the monk. The monastery would not view so negatively a novice who decides to return to lay life, whereas it would be a major embarrassment to the monastery, and especially the unsa, if one of its bhiksus should disrobe. Despite this difference in commitment, both classes nevertheless receive equal treatment in the monastery and are allowed to participate together in all temple functions. Virtually the only difference in treatment is in seating assignments, monks sitting according to seniority within each of the two groups.

Bhiksu Ordination

The bhiksu ordination is procedurally more complex than the novice ordination. In the 1970s there were only five monasteries in the country permitted to hold ordination platforms conferring the complete precepts (*kujok-kye*) of the bhiksu and bhiksuni. These occurred at various times throughout the spring and the novice had his choice of which ceremony to attend. "Family" connections and monastery ties came into play, as they always do, in making the decision. In 1981, the Chogye Order instituted new limitations on ordinations, restricting sramanera and bhiksu ordinations to T'ongdo-sa, the Buddha-jewel monastery, which was the traditional center of the *Vinaya* school (Yul-chong) in Korea. Other monasteries thereafter were allowed only to confer the bodhisattva precepts, the precepts taken by both lay and ordained Buddhists in Korea.

Three senior monks are officially in charge of a bhiksu ordination: the preceptor, usually the Son master of the monastery, who serves as the spiritual mentor to the ordinands; the confessor, who oversees the conduct of the ceremony and ensures that it is performed correctly; and the ordination catechist, who delivers extensive sermons on the 250 bhiksu precepts and the 348 bhiksuni precepts. For a valid ceremony, a number of witnesses, drawn from the ranks of the most senior monks in the monastery, were also required to attend the ordination as certifiers. These witnesses may number anywhere from six to nine monks, though most of the ordinations I observed used seven. None of these witnesses has any specific role to play; they are simply to be present throughout the entire ceremony. The three presiding monks and the various witnesses all sit in front of the hall on a long platform raised about four feet above the ground—hence the name "ordination platform." While the Koreans are not as strict as the Theravada orders of Southeast Asia in observing to the letter the ordination procedure detailed in the *Vinaya*, they do maintain considerable propriety during the ceremony.

The bhiksu ordinations I witnessed at Songgwang-sa were held in conjunction with the bodhisattva-precept ceremony, vastly expanding the size of the audience because of the large number of laypeople in attendance. On the first day of the ceremony, after the novice ordination is finished and breakfast eaten, all the monks and nuns who have come to receive the complete precepts sign the roster of participants. The ordinands are required to bring their changsams and bowls, though if they have forgotten their bowls the monastery supplies them with a temporary set. The monastery provides each ordinand with a large brown *kasa* (a dyed cloak which is draped around the changsam), which can be worn only by the fully ordained bhiksu and bhiksuni. I never knew of there being any restriction on the numbers of monks and nuns allowed to participate in the ordination; since such ceremonies occurred infrequently in Korea, however, it was not unusual for Songgwang-sa to have upwards of a hundred ordinands in attendance.

At eight in the morning, after breakfast and morning work, the ordinands gather in the lecture hall for a dress rehearsal. Although I had already received full ordination in Thailand, which the Koreans accepted without reservation, after two years in Korea I chose of my own accord to reordain as a bhiksu to mark to myself my commitment to the Korean church. At my reordination as a bhiksu, the ordination catechist, Ilt'a *sunim*, explained in detail the steps in the ceremony and the four most important precepts. These are the *parajikas* (expulsion offenses), transgression of which are grounds for permanent expulsion from the order: engaging in sexual intercourse, murder, grand theft, and false claims of spiritual achievement.

We ordinands were also told where to get information on the seemingly myriad lesser precepts of the fully ordained monk, though the parajikas were the only precepts about which the ordination catechist showed real concern. In his discussion with us, Ilt'a spiced his lecture with commonsense advice, including his own teacher's counsel to him when he first became a monk. His teacher told him that of course he hoped he would have a successful vocation. But if the compulsion to transgress the precepts became strong, he warned, it would be better to disrobe and return to lay life than to break one of the parajika precepts and be expelled from the order, which would shame both himself and his dharma family. He also discussed the basic etiquette and decorum of the monk's life in greater detail than was done for the novices. His purpose was to impress upon the candidates how fortunate they were to have become monks in the first place and what an opportunity they now had to further their vocations by assuming the complete precepts of the bhiksu. He finally sought to instill in the ordinands a sensitivity for the greatness of the religious tradition we were now joining as full members. Ilt'a was one of the first contemporary Korean monks to travel widely throughout Asia, and he described for the ordinands the Buddhist traditions he had experienced in other countries. He described Korean monastic life as offering a happy medium between the austerities of the Theravada monasteries of Southeast Asia and the laxity he had observed in Japanese monastic practice. He also stressed how fortunate we were to be ordained into a tradition where Son practice still flourished.

There is no immediate pressure placed on novices to become bhiksus or bhiksunis. Typically, a postulant remains a novice for at least three years before taking bhiksu ordination, to ensure his contentment with the celibacy demanded in Korean monastic life; he should also be at least twenty years old. There is, however, tacit understanding within the order that once a novice decides to take full ordination, thereby acknowledging his total commitment to the tradition, he should subsequently maintain his vocation for life; but there are no formal vows stating this commitment. In traditional Korea, monks might remain novices for most of their careers, feeling themselves unworthy of assuming the responsibility to the tradition that comes with full ordination.

In recent years, there have been attempts to revive the original Indian

Buddhist custom that any monk over the age of twenty was eligible to take the bhiksu ordination, even if he had not been a novice for at least three years. When this reform was first proposed at an ordination platform held at Songgwang-sa in 1976, there was much disagreement among the presiding senior monks over its wisdom. Many felt that such relaxation of the eligibility requirements would encourage monks still relatively new to the order to make virtually a permanent commitment, placing undue pressure on them. Others ascribed this reform to political motivations from some of the larger monasteries, which have the greatest number of ordinands, to exert more control over ecclesiastical affairs by having more bhiksus from their temples in the order. No consensus has yet emerged within the Chogye Order on this issue.

No one in Korea expects the new monks to observe all of the 250 bhiksu precepts or the 348 bhiksuni precepts found in the original Indian monastic codes followed by East Asian Buddhists. Many of the precepts are considered to be anachronistic in Korea, such as the restrictions against digging the soil or entering the harem of a king who is a member of the *ksatriya* (noble) class/caste. Others are so contrary to long-observed custom in East Asia that they are ignored, such as not eating in the afternoon. But the catechist encourages all the ordinands to keep all the precepts at least for that day so that they will have a sense of how monks in the Buddhist homeland of India would have lived.

The dress rehearsal for the ordination continues until about ten in the morning. After the noon dinner, the formal ceremony begins. Only monks ordaining and those supervising the ceremony are allowed to attend, a throwback to the Indian custom that the *sima*, or boundary lines of the ceremony, should not be transgressed by outsiders for fear of polluting the ordination. The ceremony is officially administered by the catechist and witnessed by the other senior monks on the platform. In fact, however, the director of the meditation hall, or another senior meditation monk, has primary responsibility for ensuring that the ceremony runs smoothly and punctually.

The actual ordination begins with the ordination catechist's giving a short explanation of the responsibilities that come with being a fully ordained monk. Monks respond in unison to all questions. When asked, for example, their names and the names of their teachers, they all answer in unison with the different information. In this regard, Korean ordinations are rather unlike those held in Theravada countries, where each person must answer individually to ensure that he has not been coerced into ordaining. In Theravada countries only three monks can ordain at once, but there is no such limit in Korea: virtually any number is allowed.

During the ceremony, the monks have their bowls and kasas on the floor in front of them. Toward the end of the ordination, after the ordination catechist has asked whether they have their bowls and robes ready, the ordinands will begin walking in a sinuous, snaking line, tracing a figure eight around the hall, while chanting the *Great Compassion Mantra* three times. During the walk, the ordinands place their folded kasas on top of their heads and hold their bowls in front of them. After the third repetition of the mantra, they return to their places, put the bowls back on the floor, and drape the kasas around their changsams. At that point the ordination catechist has them repeat some of the more important of the *Vinaya* rules (the parajikas and perhaps a couple of the suspension offenses), and finally proclaims them bhiksus and bhiksunis. In the meantime, the office monks have used the roster of participants to prepare official ordination certificates for everyone. The ordination certificate is a large document giving the date of ordination and names of the monks who officiated over the ceremony.

One of the more controversial moves made by some *Vinaya* masters in Korea was to arrange a special ordination of Korean monks by Theravada bhikkhus from Thailand. These *Vinaya* masters were concerned about the potential aspersions that could be cast against the purity of the Korean Buddhist ordination lineage because marriage had been officially permitted during the Japanese colonial period. Organized by Ch'aun *sunim,* the foremost *Vinaya* master in Korea, and Ilt'a *sunim,* one of the most popular ordination catechists, the ordination was held at T'ongdo-sa on 22 February 1972. The abbots of Wat Benjamobopitr, Wat Sukkot, and the Thai temple in Bodhgaya presided over the ceremony, with five other Thai monks witnessing it. This ordination was conducted within the Thai Mahanikaya ordination lineage, the largest of the two main Thai Theravada sects. In a daylong ceremony, twenty-three Korean monks received reordination in Theravada fashion, accepting the saffron robes and large iron alms bowl that the Thai monks had brought along with them. Twenty-three other Korean monks received reordination with traditional Korean robes and bowls.

Controversy ensued immediately. Many opinion leaders within the Chogye Order viewed the ordination as a complete fiasco, because it implied that Korean Buddhism was corrupted and that the only orthodox ordination lineage remained in Thailand. Koreans also were aware that the Thai Mahanikaya tradition was in fact introduced to Thailand from

Sri Lanka, which had in turn received it from Burma, so that Thailand could hardly be considered a bastion of purity in its own right. The affair grew into a full-fledged scandal when the Thais made claims, published in Korean newspapers, that they had come to Korea not to help the Korean Buddhists reestablish their *Vinaya* tradition but instead to convert them to the orthodox Thai tradition. Many of the monks who had participated in the ceremony subsequently renounced their reordinations in prominent public displays. To my knowledge, this was the last foreign ordination performed on Korean soil.

Figure 6. Cambodian nuns clad in white attend a new robes ceremony for fully ordained Theravada monks. Photograph by Christian Jochim.

CHAPTER 6

Female Renunciants (Myanma[r]/Burma)

The presence, legitimacy, and proper role of female renunciants have long been important issues within the Buddhist tradition. The earliest-known accounts concerning the order of nuns hold that the Buddha himself first rejected the requests of his aunt to institute female ordination. They also hold that the Buddha ultimately allowed women to be ordained as full nuns, but only after a request came from one of his leading disciples. The accounts further indicate that the Buddha declared that the formation of an order of nuns would accelerate by five hundred years the decline and disappearance of the religion he was founding. Presumably to prevent an even faster decline, he initiated additional rules for the conduct of nuns. These included rules that established a clear hierarchy of status in which the male order of *bhiksus* was superior to the female order of *bhiksunis*.

This having been said, it is important to recognize that in the early Buddhist tradition the *bhiksuni* order enjoyed a high level of prestige and played a significant role in Buddhist life. In the Mahayana and Esoteric traditions of Tibet and East Asia, the *bhiksuni* order has been maintained, though the prestige it has enjoyed and the role that it has played have varied from time to time and from place to place. In contrast, in the Theravada traditions of Sri Lanka and mainland Southeast Asia, the continuity of the *bhikkhuni* (Pali for the Sanskrit *bhiksuni*) order has been lost. This loss of continuity has been crucial since it has,

The essay in this chapter was taken from Hiroko Kawanami, "The Religious Standing of Burmese Buddhist Nuns (*thila-shin*): The Ten Precepts and Religious Respect Words," *The Journal of the International Association of Buddhist Studies* 13 (1990): 17–28.

by strict Theravada standards, made the full ordination of *bhikkhunis* impossible. As a result, the female renunciants of Theravadin traditions no longer retain a status even roughly equivalent to that of ordained Theravada nuns. In recent years there have been efforts to reestablish the *bhikkhuni* communities in various Theravada contexts. Up to this point these efforts have had only limited success.

The excerpt that follows focuses on the situation of female renunciants in Myanmar. It highlights many different difficulties, ambiguities, and possibilities that confront women who, though adopting a life of renunciation, are prohibited from attaining the status of fully ordained nuns.

THERAVADIN RELIGIOUS WOMEN

Hiroko Kawanami

The "official version" of Buddhist texts in the Theravada tradition may serve as the starting point for understanding the religious status of contemporary Buddhist nuns. While doing my fieldwork, I found that stories of *bhikkhunis* and "religious women" in the Buddhist texts were frequently referred to by monks and laity in an attempt to explain the present position of *thila-shin* in Burma. The formation of the *Bhikkhuni* Sangha and the textual account of *bhikkhunis* who once existed were important components of the story. Tradition also tells us that the lineage of *bhikkhuni* ordination has become extinct and there exists no *bhikkhuni* who can confer ordination on contemporary Buddhist nuns. Therefore, present-day *thila-shin* are not *bhikkhunis*. The pseudo-ordination ceremony that initiates laywomen into the Order is considered a ritual that provides them with a religious status no more than that of pious laywomen who abide by additional sabbatical vows. Ironically, the assumption that their predecessors once held a legitimate religious status seems to stress all the more the "illegitimate" religious status of present-day Buddhist nuns. These explanations are repeatedly referred to by monks and scholars to remind the general public of where a contemporary Buddhist nun "should stand," in order to perpetuate the ideology that "she is not a *bhikkhuni* and that she can never become one."

According to traditional Buddhist classification, the Buddhist assembly comprised four kinds of people: *bhikkhu* (almsmen), *bhikkhuni* (almswomen), *upasaka* (devout laymen) and *upasika* (devout laywomen). Both male *upasaka* and female *upasika* were pious layfolk who followed the Buddhist morality of five precepts (eight on sabbatical days). These people were above all householders and material benefactors of the Sangha, called *dayaka* (donor) or *dayika* (female donor), and responsible for the upkeep of both the *bhikkhu* and *bhikkhuni* communities. The number of precepts taken is usually a major index of the religious status of an individual, and from this viewpoint, a *thila-shin* is categorized as an *upasika* (laywoman) who takes eight precepts. However, strictly speaking, a *thila-shin* does not fit into the category of *upasika*, because she is not a productive householder but an almswoman who is dependent on the laity.

Historically and socio-culturally, it seems that women have always been discouraged from spiritual renunciation. In the Hindu tradition, from which Buddhism arose, married status was the only acceptable way for women to pursue their religious goal. The institutionalized body of male renouncers was and still is dependent on lay householders for material support as well as for recruitment of celibate monks. Women were expected to look after the family and children, and be responsible for the perpetuation of the Buddhist faith to the future generation. Stories concerning pious laywomen were far more numerous and elaborated in the texts than those relating to Buddhist nuns. This implies that the role of female lay householders was far more acknowledged and encouraged than that of female renouncers in the Buddhist tradition.

Present-day Buddhist nuns in Burma are called *thila-shin*. The Burmese term *thila* derives from the Pali word *sila*, which designates that virtuous behavior, ethical conduct, and moral practice which Buddhist texts list as the initial point of departure towards higher spirituality. The precepts Buddhists observe are also called *thila*. The Burmese word *shin* means the "holder" or "one who possesses." Therefore, *thila-shin* means a person who observes the Buddhist code of morality, one who is virtuous and moral in every way this word would apply.

The legal position of a *thila-shin* in Burmese Buddhist law makes it clear that she is still a member of the secular world; she is not deprived of social rights to inherit estate and property, whereas monks and novices are governed by monastic rules that oblige them to renounce all secular rights. Nevertheless, in most cases a woman, should she become a *thila-shin*, voluntarily hands over her property to her family or donates her wealth to the nunnery, considering it incompatible with the pursuit of a religious life; alternatively, she may use her inheritance to build her own accommodation inside the nunnery premises; after her death, it becomes communal property of the institution.

With regard to civil status, a *thila-shin* is put in the same category as a monk. The Constitution of Burma (No. 180, 1974) stipulates that "any religious persons" or "any member of the religious Orders," whether Buddhist, Christian, Muslim, etc., whether male or female, may not vote in elections. "Religious persons" are denied certain civil rights so that they do not engage in political activities. This reflects fear on the part of political authorities in Burma that "religious persons" may exert their power in secular forms. The assumption is that "religious persons" should be confined to the religious realm, and in this respect, both monks and nuns are considered to belong to the *lokuttara* (the realm of Buddhist attainment that transcends the boundaries of ordinary social existence) rather than to the *lokiya* (the world of ordinary social existence).

In order to understand the present standing of the *thila-shin* in Burma, we have to understand the distinction between *lokiya,* worldly and mundane, and *lokuttara,* transcendental and spiritual. In Burma, this distinction is frequently referred to and understood as that between the secular and the religious. Members of the Buddhist community who have committed themselves to the "higher ideal" are referred to as those who belong to the *lokuttara,* contrasted to those who belong to the *lokiya.* The *lokuttara* person is unproductive, and thus completely dependent on the productive members of the *lokiya* for material support. The Buddhist community provides a field of religious merit for secular people. Accordingly, "giving" is encouraged as the most meritorious and ethically valued activity for those in the *lokiya,* while "receiving" is the norm of life for those in the *lokuttara.* The difference in ways of life is well recognized and the boundary between the two worlds is firmly maintained. They are dependent on one another, and this complementarity provides the basis for Burmese Buddhism.

Thila-shin stand in between the *lokiya* and the *lokuttara.* Their position may be perceived as both *lokiya* and *lokuttara,* or part of either, depending on the situation and context, and according to the standing of the speaker in relationship to a *thila-shin.* Almost all my Burmese lay informants asserted that *thila-shin* did not belong to the *lokiya.* Having said that, some consider *thila-shin* as indispensable members of the *lokuttara,* vital to the maintenance of the Buddhist community, while some disregard them as a mere burden on the productive population. Monks, who officially adhere to the doctrine that contemporary nuns are "laywomen," tend to discount their importance in everyday life. The *thila-shin* themselves strongly identify with the Buddhist community as far as their lifestyle and affiliation are concerned, yet their religious activities tend to centre around merit-making, entailing the act of "giving" that is the focus of members of the *lokiya*.

A *thila-shin* seeks to clarify her standing by distinguishing her status from that of the permanent or semi-permanent *yaw-gi* (*yogin* in Pali) woman. Most Burmese laity, young and old, male and female, married and single, spend a certain time in meditation centres as *yaw-gi*. They are usually clad in brown, follow eight precepts, and meditate in religious premises. Most permanent or semi-permanent *yaw-gi* are old women relieved of their domestic chores and responsibilities. When asked why they had not become *thila-shin,* many of them said that they were too old to pursue a professional life. Furthermore, in contrast to a *thila-shin,* whose commitment to a religious cause is demonstrated by her shorn head, the retained hair of the *yaw-gi* was frequently derided as evidence of the lack of spiritual worth that made it difficult for them to detach themselves from the *lokiya* world.

Even though *yaw-gi* observe the same number of precepts and lead a stoic lifestyle in religious premises, they are regarded as basically outside the *lokuttara*. Still, *thila-shin* envy *yaw-gi* because they have more time for meditation and personal religious pursuits since, unlike nuns, *yaw-gi* are not expected to provide menial services for the monks or the Buddhist community. Also, *yaw-gi* cannot, nor do they wish to, live on "receiving" alms like the *thila-shin*. Therefore, in order to lead a religious life as *yaw-gi,* they have to be materially self-sufficient and fairly well-off, which suggests that they have not given up their role as "donors" who are responsible for "giving" to the Buddhist community.

At one level, the *thila-shin* claim that they have renounced the lay world to take up a life of stoic discipline and hardship. They say they have symbolically become "daughters of the Buddha" and entered the Order of sisterhood for the pursuit of spiritual advancement. The keeping of Buddhist morality obliges them to abstain from sex, alcohol, eating after midday and from such worldly pleasures as singing and dancing and cosmetics and garlands, which may hinder their effort to purify the body and soul. *Thila-shin* say that their life is cool and clean compared to the hot and filthy life of the secular world. This gives them a reason to feel spiritually superior to the laity, both men and women.

As mentioned before, the daily life of *thila-shin* is centered around merit-making activities that involve menial services to the religious community of the monks. Perseverance and hardship are endured as "giving" and sacrifices are believed to lead to the acquisition of merit. Many *thila-shin* said that they were enabled to acquire more merit than those living in the secular world, since they could devote themselves wholeheartedly to a lifestyle with a religious cause, another reason for their spiritual superiority to the general laity.

However, there is a contradiction between the spiritual worthiness felt by *thila-shin* themselves and the mundane degradation to which they are subject. In order to cope with the embedded tension, they distinguish their relationship with the secular world on two levels: that of spiritual supremacy and that of economic dependence.

On an economic level, *thila-shin* seem to be reminded of their worldliness. They feel down-graded, inferior, and "bad," being obliged to be economically dependent on their lay benefactors despite their "illegitimate" religious status. *Thila-shin* are aware that theoretically they are not full members of the Buddhist Order. Therefore, they feel that they are not fully entitled "to receive" like the monks and novices whose legitimate religious status, backed by the Sangha, gives them full rights to receive from the laity. The alms received by monks and *thila-shin* appear to be fundamentally different. *Thila-shin* are given raw rice and money, which indicates that they can cook and look after themselves, in contrast to the monks, who are given only cooked food. The degree of autonomy maintained by the *thila-shin* shows that they retain a closer link to the secular than monks, who are completely dependent on the laity.

In most big monasteries, there usually are lay helpers to offer the monks menial services, such as cooking and washing, so it is not necessary for the *thila-shin* to perform these duties. Nonetheless, *thila-shin* are eager to take part in merit-making activities by offering food to the monks. They like to "be in need of the monks" and this becomes almost a religious objective for some of them. However, it must be added that not all *thila-shin* spend their time cooking for and serving the monks; those who are students and teachers of Buddhist scriptures and philosophy devote most of their time to the work of education. Therefore, there is a division of labour among the nuns, and the basic economic unit within a Burmese nunnery is usually comprised of a partnership between a nun who teaches and a nun who is in charge of the household. It is wrong to assume that most nuns are servants for the monks, and to my surprise, I met many educated *thila-shin* who were not even able to boil water!

In a Buddhist culture, "giving" (*dana*) is encouraged, but receiving gifts may become problematic. Although it is theoretically unnecessary for *thila-shin* to reciprocate a material gift with a material countergift, they feel comfortable in "giving," but "receiving" makes them feel "indebted." While monks and novices enjoy the privilege of receiving to the full on the supposition that they are providing the laity with a chance to acquire religious merit, the role of recipient for *thila-shin* constantly reminds them of their ambiguous religious standing, such that they are not fully exempted from the social rules of reciprocity.

When they receive, *thila-shin* recite and give out religious blessings in return. They may chant for the donor the "powerful" Buddhist protection-formulas called *paritta*. These are believed to ward off evil spirits and confer upon the recipient prosperity, safety, luck, and happiness. *Thila-shin* also show their utmost hospitality and kindness, and offer whatever humble food they have whenever a lay guest visits their nunnery. But these acts are not sufficient to convince them that they have paid back their debts in terms of the religious merit acquired by their lay benefactors. The feeling of having to receive all the time becomes a psychological burden, and seems to make them feel inferior. At times, they expressed this as a wish not to descend to the status of a mere beggar who receives alms with no religious significance.

Officially, "Buddhist nuns" observe eight precepts. Novices observe ten precepts and monks abide by the 227 rules of the Vinaya. Five precepts are considered as fundamental to Buddhist morality, so devout lay Buddhists abide by at least five. On *uposatha* days (determined by the waxing and waning of the moon), days during the *Vassa* (a three-month period—a kind of Buddhist "Lent"—that coincides with the rainy season in eastern India, Sri Lanka, and mainland Southeast Asia), and on other special days, such as the day of the week when they were born, Burmese people make special efforts to observe an additional three precepts and interrupt their ordinary lay life by taking religious disciplines. "Celibacy" and "no solid food after midday" are important and difficult additional abstinences on these occasions.

There are *thila-shin* who attempt to abide by ten precepts, the same number taken by novices. These precepts may be the same in content, but different in context and significance. This derives from the precept-takers' difference in status. A novice is "on the way to becoming a fully ordained member of the Sangha," whereas further religious status for a *thila-shin* is closed. This difference becomes clearer when we examine the manner in which the basic Buddhist precepts are taken.

Novices and *thila-shin* recite and take the first six precepts in the same manner. For novices, the seventh and the eighth precepts are separated and recited as two precepts: (7) abstinence from dancing, singing, music, and shows, and (8) abstention from garlands, perfumes, cosmetics, and adornment. *Thila-shin* and laity take these precepts as two precepts merged into one, which makes one long precept, counted as the seventh. The ninth precept—abstention from sleeping on luxurious beds—is ninth for novices only; the same precept slides into the place of the eighth for *thila-shin* and laity. Therefore, it is recited as the ninth for the novice and the eighth for *thila-shin* and laity. Technically speaking, this means that there is no ninth precept for *thila-shin* and laity, and the artificial gap created between the eighth and the tenth precept marks the boundary between their religious status and that of a novice. If a *thila-shin* wished to abide by the ten precepts, the present custom is to fill in the gap of the ninth position by reciting the phrase which sends loving kindness (*metta*) to all sentient beings, especially to the spirits. This allows her to carry on to the taking of the tenth precept. However, this so-called "ninth precept" is not a precept of abstinence, but rather a code of behaviour set up for instrumental reasons.

It seems that the gap stands as a reminder that the religious status of *thila-shin* is that of *upasika,* and the manner in which the precepts are taken seems to confine them to the same level as the laity, or *lokiya.* In the meanwhile, a novice confronts no gap which hinders him from following further precepts and he is led to a higher religious status in the *lokuttara.*

The tenth precept prohibits the taker from handling gold and silver, which means, in effect, money. This precept has a considerable religious significance for contemporary Buddhist nuns, while it is taken for granted by monks and novices. Most *thila-shin* in Burma receive and handle money, and are rarely in a position to abstain from it. They live under the constant pressure of low income, since their daily life has to be maintained on humble donations of 1 to 5 kyats, while monks receive 50 to 100 kyats for attending a religious function. Threatened by the insecurity of their financial base, *thila-shin* cannot abstain from fussing over money, haggling at markets and living as thriftily as possible—this seems to result in a general image of nuns as greedy.

On the other hand, *thila-shin* are often indispensable to the administration of monasteries on behalf of the monks, who are not allowed to handle money. Still, they do not consider this role of treasurer as an important base of power from which to demand further influence. The negative value attributed to their capacity "to be able" to handle money makes them feel worldly and degraded, and it is regarded more or less as a shackle that keeps them away from spiritual advancement. Abstinence from handling money comes to be regarded as a special privilege for *thila-shin.* Not having to deal with it is aspired to as a "cool" state of detachment from "hot" matters, an unobtainable state of bliss. As one *thila-shin* expressed it, if only she were relieved from worries about money and maintenance, she would be able to concentrate fully on Buddhist studies and meditation. Such a state was considered to give her the physical and spiritual freedom to concentrate wholeheartedly on her basic spiritual pursuit.

Only a few *thila-shin* in Burma are able to follow all ten precepts. To become a ten-precept *thila-shin*, a woman has to have either a wealthy family background or a highly successful academic career, or both, so as to be able to attract numerous donors and benefactors who can give her a solid financial standing. It may sound paradoxical, but to be in a position of detachment, she must have sufficient resources and backing to be able to afford it. She must also have a reliable layperson or a nun serve as a *kat-pi-ya* to attend to her needs. A *kat-pi-ya* will act as secretary and treasurer and attend to the daily needs of the ten-precept *thila-shin*. If money is donated to the *thila-shin*, her *kat-pi-ya* will receive and deal with it on her behalf. The actual difficulty lies in the fact that *thila-shin* are rarely in a position to be looked after like monks, since they usually cannot attract sufficient respect or attention from the laity to require being attended on a full-time basis. On the contrary, *thila-shin* themselves often act as *kat-pi-ya* to monks, looking after their financial interests and, as we have seen, acting as manager and treasurer for the running of monasteries.

Thila-shin who have attained the ten-precept status are regarded as those who have attained a higher stage of detachment, endowed with spiritual peace. They do not necessarily have to commit themselves to a lifestyle of collecting alms and receiving donations, which reverses the power relationship between the *thila-shin* and her lay donors. In general, ten-precept *thila-shin* still maintain close relationships with their lay donors, but give a general impression that they are not desperately in need. Having a secure backing gives them a feeling of assurance so that they do not feel servile or inferior in any way to their lay benefactors. The inner tension felt between their spiritual worth and economic dependency gradually resolves as the former gains strength. Ten-precept *thila-shin* are well respected, regarded as higher on the spiritual ladder than ordinary eight-precept *thila-shin,* and perceived to have a special quality called *gon*.[1] Moreover, their status of "not having to receive" gives them more importance, hence reasons for the laity to give; thus,

---

1. *Gon* (*guna* in Pali) was translated by my informants as "good quality" or "virtue, worth, prestige, honour"; it connotes for Burmese Buddhists a special quality inherited from previous incarnations.

they become the centre of worship among Buddhist nuns. However, the formal religious status of ten-precept *thila-shin* is still considered to be that of *upasika,* since they have not been through an "official" ordination ceremony. The only implication may be that they have succeeded in renouncing their role of service to the monks and novices, and achieved a certain state of religious autonomy within the Buddhist community.

As a current movement in Sri Lanka shows, nuns clad in yellow who are ten-precept observers aspire to a higher religious status than ordinary eight-precept nuns.[2] They are attempting to secure a proper religious status between that of lay *upasika* and *bhikkhuni.* The aim of this movement is to raise their religious status into a different category through strict morality, meditation, and recitation of the *dhamma,* so that they can approximate the ideal of "sainthood" (*arahantship*). Similarly, in Burma, *thila-shin* are eager to enhance their spirituality in spite of many obstacles. The taking of ten precepts is a valid religious statement which signifies that a *thila-shin* has overcome the "uncomfortable" position of being materially dependent on the laity. Some *thila-shin* take the ten precepts in the evening, even though it has no practical effect, since they go to markets and attend religious functions in the mornings. Some *thila-shin* keep the ten precepts on *uposatha* days, on the day of week on which they were born, or during the *Vassa.* A nun may save up her whole donation income for the rest of the year to be able to abide by the ten precepts during the three months of *Vassa.*

The abstinence enjoined on the ten-precept abider is often combined with one or two austere Buddhist practices called *dhutanga,* which also enhance one's spiritual stature. Among the most common of the thirteen kinds of *dhutanga* are the taking of one meal a day and the mixing up of all the food and taking it directly from the bowl, with no second helpings. To these basic *dhutanga, thila-shin* may add vegetarianism, eating only beans, no sleep, and so on. The observation of these trials is by no means forced upon them, but a matter strictly of individual choice and decision. If a *thila-shin* is healthy and committed enough to take upon herself this kind of hardship, her efforts and sacrifice are met with respect by the laity. The *thila-shin* herself also believes that she is on the path to a higher spiritual level.

Officially, *thila-shin* are not obliged to abide by as many rules and

2. Editors' note: The reference is to the *dasa sil maniyo* (ten-precept mother) movement that is discussed by Tessa J. Bartholomeusz in *Women under the Bo Tree* (New York: Cambridge University Press, 1994).

regulations as monks. However, in practice, their daily life is governed by far more rules and minor details than that of monks and novices. These include both verbally transmitted rules[3] and written regulations.[4] Moreover, it is often the case that *thila-shin* explicitly display their seriousness towards their religious profession and give the impression that their commitment is stronger than that of the monks. *Thila-shin* seem to know that their religious position depends on their outward image—on how they are perceived in society—so they try all means to keep up their religious stance in good manners, clean clothes and pious behaviour, etc. It can be argued that the insecurity of their religious position drives them to make far more efforts in observing rules and regulations. The only way of keeping their religious position intact is by constantly working on it and displaying their "super-devoutness," so that their pious image becomes widely acknowledged by the laity. It is this recognition and the general approval of society that give *thila-shin* a secure place in the *lokuttara*.

3. Verbally transmitted rules are primarily about the everyday behaviour of *thila-shin*. Sneezing, laughing, talking loudly, big gestures, yawning, abusive words, big strides in walking, noisiness, laziness and lack of respect towards elders, etc., are all frowned upon as improper behaviour.

4. Every *thila-shin* in Sagaing Buddhist community (a community in Upper Burma) is required to memorize the "Regulations for Thila-shin" written in 1914 by the influential abbot of Maha Ganda-yon monastery. The rules stipulate details from the acceptance of newcomers, and daily routine, duties, and obligations, up to minor details of everyday behaviour, such as going out for alms, and behaviour towards monks, senior nuns, and towards laymen. Respect, obedience, mindfulness, moderation, and good manners are emphasized. It is interesting to note that proper conduct towards a monk is stipulated in every possible situation, which shows the full apprehension of the danger of monks and nuns living side-by-side in a small community. Punishments following the violation of these rules are also specified in detail.

Figure 7. Inside a Shingon temple in Koyosan, Japan, the headquarters for Shingon Buddhism. Photograph by Don Farber.

CHAPTER 7

Meditation (Japan)

Historically, meditation has played an important role in Buddhist thought and practice. The centrality of meditation to Buddhist understandings of spiritual attainment derives from the paradigmatic actions of the Buddha himself. Indeed, the Buddha's perfection through meditational practice made possible his supreme enlightenment.

Over the years Buddhists have developed a large number of meditational disciplines and practices. These include techniques—employed by monks and laypeople alike—to calm the mind to better deal with the exigencies and problems of everyday life. They also include more advanced techniques that are used primarily though not exclusively by monks.[1]

Many of the more advanced meditational techniques are, in their general features, shared by many Buddhist traditions, including Hinayana/Theravada, Mahayana, and Esoteric. Such techniques include various degrees of asceticism; accepting the guidance of an already accomplished master; the use of various objects, including the physical functions of the body, for contemplation and concentration; the concentrated, often rhythmatic recitation and/or repetition of sacred words, formulaic phrases, or texts; and the use of specific bodily postures and activities. To these techniques may be added others that are also very common, but

The essay in this chapter was taken from Taiko Yamasaki, *Shingon: Japanese Esoteric Buddhism* (Boston: Shambhala, 1988), 182–90. Reprinted by arrangement with Shambhala Publications, Inc., 300 Massachusetts Ave., Boston, MA 02115.

1. Here and in similar contexts the word *monks* will refer to both monks and nuns. These are contexts in which the group in question is made up primarily, though not exclusively, of male practitioners.

limited more to Mahayana and especially Esoteric traditions: the sustained use of bells, chimes, and other musical devices; the visualization of cosmic Buddhas, bodhisattvas, and other deities; and the manipulation of mental and material symbols representing cosmic totalities. To these we can add a meditational technique found expressly in certain Esoteric traditions: sexual activity.

The advanced meditational techniques typically have three primary purposes. They are aimed at the acquisition of supranormal states of consciousness. They are also aimed at the attainment of various powers—for example, the ability to remember one's past lives—accessible through, during, and from those states of consciousness. Last, these advanced meditational techniques are ultimately aimed at the attainment of the highest religious goal, which is, in all Buddhist traditions, a product of the highest form of mental and bodily cultivation.

Generally speaking, the highest religious goal for the advanced meditational practitioners of the Hinayana/Theravada traditions is the attainment of nirvana. Nirvana is a goal that breaks the practitioner free from phenomenal becoming—a becoming that is especially produced by desire and a steadfast attachment to a permanent "self" and is ultimately characterized by the absence of self, by impermanence, and by suffering. Ideally, the advanced Hinayana/Theravada meditational techniques allow one to purify the mind and body of all desire and the attachment to self. These techniques are designed to facilitate and produce the complete mental and bodily calm that puts an end to the "burning" psychosomatic forces that produce phenomenal reality. It is therefore not surprising that a common Theravada image of complete attainment to nirvana is that of a flame being extinguished.

Like their Hinayana/Theravada counterparts, the more advanced meditational practitioners in most if not all Mahayana and Esoteric traditions view the production of the phenomenal world in light of the volitional forces of desire and attachment to self. However, there are significant doctrinal differences between the two types of meditational practitioners and thus differences in their perceptions of the highest religious goal.

Doctrinally, for instance, although many Mahayana and Esoteric practitioners also believe that suffering and impermanence warrant serious religious concern and attention, these practitioners also view existential suffering and impermanence to be the product of a deluded mind that ultimately inhibits one's ability to act in the world for "the sake of all." In this religious view, various types of meditation can function as significant methods for increasing one's capacity to engage—in an extremely proactive manner—in the phenomenal world out of existential concern for the "suffering" of others.

Many Mahayana and Esoteric practitioners have used very diversified, complex, and multisensory meditational techniques focusing on the attainment of a Buddhist goal that is rather different from the Hinayana/Theravada one. These modes of practice aim to achieve a kind of enlightenment through which the practitioner attains the unifying and liberating recognition that all reality, including all cosmic reality and all individual reality, is constituted by an emptiness or voidness that simultaneously pervades every time and place. Mahayana and Esoteric practitioners often specifically identify this emptiness or voidness with the Buddha and Buddhahood itself.

The excerpt that follows describes an advanced form of Esoteric practice that has been developed in Japan by adherents of the Shingon sect.

A MORNING STAR MEDITATION

Taiko Yamasaki

The Morning Star meditation (*gumonji-ho*) is a practice in which the mantra (a sacred word, sound, or phrase) of the bodhisattva Kokuzo is recited one million eighty thousand times ("one million" in Shingon terms) over a set period of time. The Morning Star ritual manual instructs the practitioner to become one body with the universal Dharma Realm. (The Dharma Realm is the realm of Truth as understood within the Shingon tradition.) Following the Morning Star ritual instructions, the practitioner uses one mudra (a symbolically significant positioning of the hands) and one mantra in a concentrated meditation focused on direct experience of the universe through union with the deity of the morning star.

The name *gumonji-ho* means literally "technique for seeking hearing-retaining," meaning that this practice is supposed to result in the ability to remember everything seen and heard. The Morning Star meditation was, in fact, practiced in Japan as early as the Nara period (710–784 C.E.) to develop the memory and aid in memorizing sutras. Its esoteric purpose, however, is to deepen the samadhi (meditative concentration) state in order to experience the self as universal void of potentiality. It is here called the Morning Star meditation because it involves visualization of the deity Kokuzo in the form of Venus, the morning star. A central Mikkyo meditation both in the past and today, it is one of the important esoteric practices of Shingon. (Mikkyo is a type of teaching and practice that is believed to culminate in the transforming activity and presence of Wisdom experienced in the complexity of day-to-day life.)

The source text of this practice is the *Kokuzo Bosatsu Noman Shogan Saisho-shin Darani Gumonji-ho* (Kokuzo Bodhisattva's Power-Filled Wish-Fulfilling Supreme-Mind Dharani Technique for Seeking Hearing and Retaining). This text was translated from the original Sanskrit by Shubhakarasimha in China in 717, and brought to Japan the following year. The Morning Star meditation was therefore known and practiced in Japan some time before Kukai (774–835) brought the Shingon lineage from China. It is considered to be among the early elements of "pure" Mikkyo to arrive in Japan.

Various ritual manuals of the Morning Star meditation were written in Japan based on Shubhakarasimha's Chinese translation. Although the ritual was formalized in Japan, it clearly originated in India, where, for example, at the beginning of the ritual the practitioner would seal milk, symbolizing the nectar of enlightenment, into a container. When opened at the end, the manner in which the contents had fermented was believed to indicate how successful the practice had been. In Japan, however, milk was uncommon, and during much of the year is as likely to freeze as to ferment, necessitating a change in this part of the ritual.

Shubhakarasimha's translation of the source text still exists, and its most important steps have been adhered to in the Japanese ritual manuals. Although the title of this text is long, the contents are brief, emphasizing recitation of the mantra "one million" times. Kukai used this text to perform the Morning Star meditation, and Shingon considers this to be the practice by which he first experienced the nature of the esoteric teachings. An important practice not only in Kukai's own life but in the history of Shingon, the Morning Star meditation traditionally has had a strong appeal in Japan. Kakuban (a significant and controversial Shingon innovator and reformist who lived from 1095 to 1143), for example, performed it eight times—a prodigious feat.

The Morning Star meditation is not a required practice for Shingon priests, nor does it have any relationship to the system of seniority within the priesthood. Because of its rigors, however, there are relatively few priests today who have completed the Morning Star meditation. It seems to have been much more widely performed, though probably in less rigid forms, during the eighth century, when laymen were also initiated into its practice.

It is not known who transmitted the practice to Kukai. Legend has it that a priest named Gonzo, among the first masters of the Morning Star meditation in Japan, was Kukai's teacher. In any case, after encountering his nameless master, the young Kukai sought out isolated places on the Pacific coast and amid deep gorges on the mountainous island of Shikoku in which to practice the Morning Star meditation. Kukai wrote in the *Sango Shiiki* (Indication of the Basis of the Three Teachings):

Here a priest gave me the Morning Star meditation of Kokuzo. In the text was written, "If one follows this technique and recites this mantra one million times, the ability to memorize the words of all the teachings will be gained."

Believing the words of the great master to be true, I hoped to kindle a blaze out of this flying spark. I climbed to the peaks of Tairyu Mountain in the country of Awa, and immersed myself in recitation at Cape Muroto in Tosa. In the echoing valleys the image of the Morning Star appeared.

Celestial Bodies and Meditation on the Universe

Mikkyo actively employs celestial bodies for meditation on the Dharma Body (a name for the ultimate reality as understood within the Shingon tradition). In the Morning Star meditation the focus of ritual is the mantra, while the subject of esoteric union is the universe symbolized by Venus. Shingon considers the Morning Star meditation to refer back to the historical Buddha's experience of seeing the bright morning star at the moment of his enlightenment under the bodhi tree.

Mikkyo also has a number of star rituals derived from Chinese Taoist astrology, performed to avert misfortune and to prolong life.[2] Unlike the Morning Star meditation, these star rituals are for material benefit, but remain, nevertheless, representative esoteric practices.

Within the Morning Star meditation hall hangs a painting of the deity Kokuzo Bodhisattva, whose qualities are also symbolized by the morning star. The actual planet (Venus) is also used in the meditation, and is viewed through a special window. Although Venus is not always visible, the subject of the practice is not simply the planetary body but the dynamic cosmos which, in the esoteric understanding, is embodied in the painting as well. The practitioner employs the planet, the painting of the deity, and the visualized image of the planet-deity as a means to experience suprapersonal truth.

In the painting used in the Morning Star meditation, Kokuzo is depicted in color on wood within a moon disk about one foot in diameter.

---

2. Editors' note: Taoism is a Chinese religion that influenced Buddhism in East Asia.

His body is gold, radiating beams of light. Seated on a lotus throne, he wears the crown of the five Buddhas. His left hand holds the stem of a pale red lotus on which rests a blue wish-fulfilling gem emanating yellow flames. His right hand is extended, palm up, fingers bent down, in the wish-bestowing (*yogan*) mudra.

Kokuzo is a deity of wisdom, virtue, and good fortune, whose activity is to fulfill all wishes. His direction is south. The esoteric tradition considers this the direction from which all treasures come, and south is also associated with the Buddha Hosho, whose name means "giving birth to treasure." Kokuzo's name literally means "repository of the void," void here indicating not merely nothingness, but the mysterious potentiality that gives rise to all phenomena. The samadhi (concentration) state of the Morning Star meditation focuses on the wish-fulfilling gem, a symbol of void-potentiality. The wish-fulfilling gem embodies Kokuzo's enlightenment energy, the universe itself which evolves eternally in perfect freedom, oblivious to humans' attempts to delimit it in their own understanding.

In the Morning Star meditation the practitioner concentrates exclusively on the single practice of union with the deity, the planet Venus. Focusing his being in this way on the distant morning star (symbolizing the universe), he seeks to unite with the source of the mind.

The Practice of the Morning Star

The Morning Star meditation hall traditionally is built in an isolated, natural setting where the sky and stars are visible. (In ancient times it was also performed in the open.) Only a few temples exist in Japan today where this meditation may be practiced: Tairyu-ji in the Awa region on Shikoku, Kongo-ji in Kochi, Mount Misen on the island of Miyajima in the Inland Sea, and the Shinbessho on Mount Koya.

The practice hall for the Morning Star meditation is built so that its east, west, and south sides are open and uncrowded, facing natural landscapes in the distance. The east side in particular must not be closed by trees or other buildings. The hall is small, usually four and one-half tatami mats (about nine square feet) to six mats in area. High in the east wall is a small window through which the practitioner, who sits facing this wall, can see the stars. Hanging on this same east wall, the painting of Kokuzo is kept covered with a white cloth except during the time of meditation. The room is lit only by a small oil lamp which is kept burning throughout the ritual.

The source text for the Morning Star meditation contains a brief reference to a "wooden mandala," a four-legged wooden platform about forty centimeters square, which is still used today. Like the larger platform altars, it functions as a place to summon the deity from its essential realm.[3]

Symbolizing the deity's enlightenment, the altar is immediately below the painting, and offerings are placed on a stand before it. To ensure its tranquility and ease of concentration, the altar is not touched during the practice; neither is the water in the flower vase changed, though fresh water is added. The "flowers" are made from the leaves of the *kaya* tree (*Torreya nucifera*), and *kaya* oil is burned in the lamp. In fact, every ritual performed with the six offering implements employs some part of this tree.

In the past, the Morning Star meditation took one hundred days, but now ordinarily takes fifty days. The date for beginning the meditation is chosen by counting back from the day on which it ends, which must be marked by a solar or lunar eclipse. The closing ritual takes place at the exact time of the eclipse.

The number of recitations to be done each day is calculated precisely according to the length of the practice. If fifty days, for example, the practitioner must recite the mantra of the Kokuzo Bodhisattva "twenty thousand" times (actually 21,600) daily. Each day has equal sittings of the same length and intensity, so that a continuous rhythm can be maintained throughout the practice. Special rituals mark the opening and closing days, but the ritual performed during all the intervening days remains exactly the same.

Since the mantra recitations must be counted, the practitioner uses a rosary and a device rather like a cribbage board with pegs, each of which stands for a certain number of recitations counted with the rosary. The rosary is made of *kaya* wood (or sometimes oak), and has only 54 beads instead of the usual 108. Although the ritual manual specifies a crystal rosary, crystal was found too heavy to be practical and was replaced with the wooden beads.

The Morning Star meditation is physically and mentally demanding. Practiced by a solitary meditator in the mountains over a long period of time, it may not be interrupted by illness or discouragement. It is not rare for practitioners to learn they are unable to bear its rigors. Its practice is not, therefore, taught indiscriminately, and its secrecy is strictly

3, Editors' note: *Mandala*, in this context, refers to a visual representation of the cosmos as understood within the Shingon tradition.

maintained. Since much of the Morning Star meditation is revealed only by direct oral transmission, only certain aspects are described here.

In outline, the ritual format is that of the usual single-deity practice, but differs in that only one mudra and one mantra are used throughout. The right hand forms the mudra of the wish-fulfilling gem, while the left hand forms the Vajra Fist at the hip.[4] The mantra is that of Kokuzo. Since the practice comes under the category of a benefit-increasing ritual, the practitioner, following ancient distinctions maintained in few other rituals today, faces east and wears a yellow robe.

During the time of the practice, all activity, such as eating, bathing, sleeping, and so on is ritualized. Strict rules govern diet. Intake of salt, for example, thought to increase nervousness, is reduced before and during the practice. The morning meal consists of a simple rice gruel, and nothing may be eaten after noon, though the practitioner may drink water.

The general daily procedure during the Morning Star meditation is as follows:

Before entering the hall in the morning, the practitioner ritually worships the morning star, then performs a ritual of drawing two buckets of *aka* water from a well, one for the practitioner and one for the deity. Techniques of purification are used in which he scoops up water in his left hand, transfers it to the right, sips it, then washes his hands and face. The practitioner recites the mantra while visualizing himself purified within and without.

The mantra is NO BO AKYASHAKYARABAYA ON ARI KYAMARI BORI SOWAKA (In the name of Kokuzo Om Flower-Garland Lotus-Crown may it be accomplished).

Having prepared the offerings, the practitioner, wearing over his nose and mouth a white mask that is removed when the practice proper begins, enters the meditation hall. He performs obeisance to the deity, sits in the half-lotus position, and with a special stick raises the cloth covering the painting.

BEING-PROTECTING TECHNIQUE

The practitioner performs the mantra and mudra focusing at five points of the body. He then visualizes Kokuzo and all the Buddhas absorbing

---

4. Editors' note: The *vajra*, often associated with a thunderbolt, is used in many forms of Esoteric Buddhism as a symbol of ultimate wisdom or truth.

him into themselves, causing all his delusions to vanish and his body-mind to become pure.

WATER SPRINKLING

Forming the mudra, the practitioner recites the mantra to empower the water, then sprinkles it on the offerings, the altar, and the floor.

After the ritual of powdered incense, the practitioner empowers the offerings and the altar. Recitation of prayers invoking the protection of the deities is followed by the rituals of purification of the three activities, all-pervading homage, awakening the enlightened mind, and so forth.

The practitioner establishes the sacred space for practice, and within it visualizes the "sublime meditation hall." With eyes closed, he contemplates Kokuzo's essential oneness with the painted image, after which he summons the deity to the altar.

Taking up the container of *aka* water, the practitioner manipulates it while visualizing the feet of the deity being washed. The deity, visualized seated on a flower, is welcomed by ringing the bell and making the five offerings. The universal offering and homage to all Buddhas follow. The practitioner then performs mutual empowerment with Kokuzo, reciting the mantra while forming the mudra at various parts of the body and contemplating his essential identity with the deity.

The core section of the Morning Star meditation then begins, in which the practitioner forms the mudra and recites the mantra while counting with the special rosary. In Kokuzo's breast he visualizes a moon disk in which the syllables of the mantra appear. Emitting a golden radiance, the mantra flows from the deity to enter the practitioner through the crown of his head, leaving through his mouth and reentering Kokuzo through the feet. Forming the same mudra throughout, the practitioner visualizes his recitation in this manner until the prescribed number is reached.

This complete, the practitioner performs "entry into the Dharma Realm," in which, with the same mudra held at the breast, he visualizes the moon disk and the syllables of the mantra gradually expanding to fill the universe, then gradually contracting back to their original size. After repeating mutual empowerment with Kokuzo, the practitioner performs the "diffused recitation" to Dainichi Nyorai (a personification of the entire universe and all manifestations of Buddha-nature, identified as Mahavairocana) and four other deities, repeating this action several hundred times.

Next the ending offerings are performed, followed by recitation of praises, the verses of all-pervading offering and of the mutual empowerment of the three universal powers, the five great vows, and homage to the Buddhas. The practitioner offers the merit gained by this practice to the benefit of all beings, after which he dissolves the protections surrounding the sacred space and dispatches the deity. After completing the being-protecting techniques, the practitioner leaves the meditation hall.

An Experience with the Morning Star Meditation

Taiko Yamasaki describes his experience with this practice as follows:

I performed the Morning Star meditation at Mount Misen temple in Miyajima in 1955, from 10 October to 13 November, the date of a lunar eclipse. My master in this practice was Kanayama Bokusho.

I rose at two o'clock every morning, bathed, and then performed the ceremony to Venus and the ritual of drawing *aka* water, after which I entered the practice hall for two meditation periods totaling ten hours. During the practice I was isolated from the everyday world. The temple was surrounded by the great trees of a primeval forest, and stars in a clear sky were visible to me on awaking in the morning and before sleep at night.

At the beginning, I had pain in my legs and back from the long hours of sitting, making it difficult to concentrate on meditation. Gradually, however, my body and mind came into harmony, creating within me a feeling of lightness and tranquility. During meditation, my body came to feel almost transparent, while my mind and what I saw around me were clear, like crystal. Far from being a hallucination, this came from increased clarity of consciousness—as though I had come to a place where heaven and earth join.

When I came out of meditation and left the practice hall, the sense of the vastness of the universe would remain, as though I were seeing the world for the first time. The trees were no longer separate from myself, but seemed a part of me, as though we were a single being. Although my emotions were involved, this was not an experience of ordinary, sentimental intimacy, but rather an experience of consciousness, a realization that one is made of the very same substance as everything else and that nothing in nature is unrelated to the self.

At night, after finishing the day's sitting, I would go up to the mountaintop and meditate in the open, feeling the stars in the late autumn sky surrounding me on all sides, as though I were hanging in space. This sense of unity with all things remained in my mind even after the practice ended and I returned to the world. A profound feeling of gratitude and a new appreciation for life came to affect everything I did.

Because the Morning Star meditation consists of a single ritual that must be performed at an even, unbroken pace throughout, it requires great determination. Initiation into the practice is not granted unless the candidate fulfills requirements of ability, training, and experience in meditation. To meditate concentratedly for so many hours day after day is physically strenuous, demanding good health and emotional balance. This meditation is a serious practice not to be undertaken lightly, and I have heard of many stories of people who experienced considerable difficulty with it.

For instance, it is difficult at first to adjust to solitary practice after life in the everyday world. Unexpected things happen in the mind. Delusions and attachments come welling up, and subconscious fixations can grow out of all proportion because one's concentration is so deep. I had hallucinatory experiences of such intensity that it is difficult for me to imagine a physically weaker or older person withstanding them.

Hallucinations can become intense during the practice because one is going directly to the deep level of the mind. They should not be cut off, however, but recognized for what they are without either enjoying them or fearing them. Shubhakarasimha wrote that he was offered the secret of invisibility while doing this practice. I experienced something similar when a mysterious "priest" appeared and offered to teach me a secret mudra. The image was so vivid that I had difficulty realizing that it was not real. I understand now how unfortunate it could have been had I had the slightest inclination to accept, since it would have disturbed the entire practice.

During the course of the practice the hallucinations gradually diminished, my concentration deepened, and eventually I came to experience continuous samadhi. All my senses became clearer and sharper, including my smell and hearing, to the point that I felt I could hear the sound of incense burning—an experience recorded in Mikkyo texts.

The Morning Star meditation strengthens the inner spiritual faculties, and may produce unusual experiences, but the point of the practice, of course, is to experience truth.

Figure 8. Ani Yeshe Drolma (b. 1908). Photograph by Hanna Havnevik, Dharamsala.

CHAPTER 8

The Monastic Quest:
A Biographical Example (Tibet)

Throughout Buddhist history, serious monastic practitioners have devoted themselves both to learning and scholarship and to the disciplines of meditation. Although some have placed particular emphasis on one or the other, most have pursued their spiritual quest by combining these two different approaches according to their own distinctive needs, capabilities, and traditions.

For many of the most committed monks and nuns, the spiritual quest has extended over a lifetime and has been embedded in a variety of communal contexts. Among these communal contexts, two have special importance. For monks and nuns, pilgrimages to sacred places associated with Buddhas, bodhisattvas, and/or other Buddhist deities and saints have constituted important occasions for receiving inspiration, expressing devotion, and cultivating understanding and personal introspection. More extended visitations to various temples, monasteries, and hermitages have also played a crucial role. These visitations have provided the occasion and context for receiving instruction from many learned scholars, for becoming acquainted with a significant number of important religious texts, and for being introduced to a variety of different meditative rituals and techniques.

The following biographical account, presented by Hanna Havnevik, of a Tibetan nun illustrates the varied, cumulative, and often peripatetic nature of the Buddhist monastic quest, as well as the communal contexts

The essay in this chapter was taken from Hanna Havnevik, *Tibetan Buddhist Nuns: History, Cultural Norms and Social Reality* (Oslo: Norwegian University Press, 1989), 239–51.

within which it takes place. Tibet has historically been an environment pervaded by esoteric trends and traditions—an environment particularly conducive to seeking out individual teachers who are thought to possess special supranormal powers and who can offer distinctive types of "initiations" or "ordinations." However, despite these idiosyncrasies, the nun's biographical trajectory shares a number of general features with the biographical trajectories of many deeply committed monks and nuns living in many different Buddhist cultures.

One of these features is her sustained exposure to Buddhist teachings, practices, and role models as a child and young adult. Another shared feature is her persistent pursuit of religious knowledge and experience, even in the face of serious social and cultural disruption.

THE BIOGRAPHY OF A NUN

Hanna Havnevik

The nun Yeshe Drolma is known by Tibetans in Dharamsala to be a very good meditation practitioner.[1] In fact she is called *gomchen* which means great meditator. Tashi Tsering arranged for me two meetings with her, which each time lasted for several hours. Yeshe Drolma had agreed to tell me the story of her life and this is how she herself wanted to tell about her life and her religious practice. I am greatly indebted to Tashi Tsering for the translation of this interview.

The time I spent with the nun Yeshe Drolma made a great impression on me. We visited her in the end of December 1983, and there was a very good atmosphere in her small room (about two by three meters). In her room there was a bed, a kerosene stove, and a beautiful altar, with all the necessary ritual objects and pictures of bodhisattvas, *dakinis* (a class of female goddesses), and lamas (respected religious leaders in the Tibetan Buddhist context) that have been important to her. Yeshe Drolma constantly offered us Tibetan tea, biscuits and sweets. She all the time kept saying that her story was not worth recording, that she was only one religious practitioner among several others. She kept stating that she has not been doing any great things in her life.

"I was born in 1908, in the Tibetan Earth Ape Year, at Sangshung

---

1. Editors' note: Dharamsala, a city in northern India, has become a major center for Tibetan refugees who have fled from the Chinese invasion of their homeland.

Shodrug north of Lhasa.[2] The nomad tribe my family belonged to was called Surug. Surug is the name of one of the six nomad tribes of Sangshung. My father's name was Tender and my mother was named Karmo. We were nine children in our family and I was the youngest.

"Our family was well-to-do and we were very religious people. Constantly there were three monks employed to recite *sutras* and *tantras* in our home. One of these monks was called Nelchorma and during his employment he read Milarepa's biography, the hundred thousand songs of Milarepa, and the text *Thardo* one hundred times each year.[3] He also recited the twenty-one Tara prayer seventeen hundred thousand times.[4] Since he was always reciting, he never had time to talk. When I was young, very few women in the northern region of Tibet learnt reading and writing. I was lucky to have Nelchorma as my first teacher, and thus it was he who opened for me the door to spiritual life.

"Many lamas were invited to our home. I only remember the names of the most important ones, which were: Taglung Shabdrung Rinpoche, Matrul Rinpoche, and Tsetrul Rinpoche.[5] I was too young at the time to understand their religious teachings, but I received initiations from them all. Matrul Rinpoche gave me the name Yeshe Lhatso.

"My parents took me to Lhasa twice, when I was nine and when I was thirteen years old. After returning from Lhasa the second time, I did a pilgrimage, circumambulating Namtsho, a lake north of Lhasa. Back at home I did an offering-prayer. I recited *mani mantras* one hundred thousand times and I started doing morning prostrations, one hundred at a time.[6] This I have done every morning since.

"When I was about thirteen years old, I started going to the meadows and pray to the Buddhas in the four directions. I asked that I may live a spiritual life and not the life of a laywoman. I feared this as I saw that my elder sisters were being sent off in marriage to different tribes. Suitors had already asked me to marry, but I refused. They did not ask me because I was particularly pretty, but because I came from a wealthy family, and my father was well known in the area. My brothers and sis-

2. Editors' note: Lhasa is the capital of Tibet.

3. Editors' note: Milarepa is a famous Tibetan saint who lived during the eleventh and twelfth centuries.

4. Editors' note: Tara is a female deity who plays an important role in the Tibetan Buddhist pantheon.

5. Editors' note: *Rinpoche* may be translated as "precious" or "very precious" and is a term of respect especially reserved for those who are considered to be reincarnate lamas.

6. Editors' note: *Mani mantras* are "seed mantras" associated with particular deities in the Tibetan Buddhist pantheon.

ters were having successful marriages, and thus they thought me to be a desirable partner. My family asked the suitors to wait until I was twenty years old, as they thought that I would have changed my mind by then.

"When I was fifteen years old, I did one hundred and thirteen circumambulations of Tshepag Lhakang in Lhasa. Two years later, I did one thousand seven hundred prostrations while circumambulating three stupas called Taglung Kumbum in Taglung Monastery north of Lhasa.

"When I was seventeen years old, my mother died (1924). My father now decided to do a retreat for three years. When the three years were up, he started another retreat called sealed-door retreat. Each day he did four sessions of meditation and prayer. He stayed in the retreat for twelve years, and died in the cave during a fourth meditation session. He was reciting *Vajra Guru Mantra* of Padmasambhava (a very important Buddhist saint ca. the 8th century who is believed to have contributed to the conversion of Tibet by quelling local demons), and before he died a small new tooth grew in his mouth.[7]

"There was another outstanding religious person in my family who inspired me much. This was my younger uncle. He was sent to his in-law's house, and his wife's family made him work very hard. They did not give him any free time for religious practices. During work he used to recite *mani mantras*. He had a pocket hanging around his neck, and when he had finished one hundred *mantras,* he put a pebble in the pocket. Then, in the evening, in candlelight or in the shade of the moon, he counted the pebbles and changed them into beads. Thus he was able to count the *mantras* he recited, and in this way he counted one hundred million *mani mantras*. As time passed he was given more rights in the household, and he could do his prayer and visualization sessions without being interrupted. Altogether he recited six hundred million *mani mantras*.

"One of my elder sisters had been a nun from when she was eight years old. Her name was Peldzom Drolma. She, together with a friend, meditated in Tongshong Phugpa, a cave near Phumdo. They were followers of the Kagyu tradition and their teacher was Gangshar Rinpoche. In 1925, partly to avoid being married, I joined my sister Peldzom Drolma, a nun called Sangmo Chodon, and her mother on a long pilgrimage to Mt. Kailash.[8]

"On the way we visited many holy places, such as Tashilunpo Mon-

---

7. According to Tibetan belief, when a religious practitioner recites certain mantras one hundred thousand times, he or she grows a new tooth, called *dungso*.

8. Editors' note: Mt. Kailash is a sacred mountain located in western Tibet.

astery, Sakya Monastery, Dingri Monastery, and Shelkar Monastery. In Mustang we visited pilgrimage sites such as Sala Mabar, Dola Mebar, and Chumig Gyatsa. On our trip we also went to Purang and saw the images Khorchag Jowo and Namkha Khyungdzong. Here I met the famous Lama Degyel Rinpoche. Now I undertook my first haircutting ceremony, and Degyel Rinpoche looked in the scriptures he was reading and gave me the name Drolma Yangchen. I received religious teachings from Lama Degyel, but I do not remember which.

"Our pilgrimage lasted for one year and three or four months. During all this time we did not waste one day, we were always receiving religious teachings from lamas or visiting holy places. I do not remember the names of all the sacred sites, but we visited them all in the western region of Tibet. I came back to my tribe in 1926, then nineteen years old. The spiritual master of my father, Potrul Rinpoche Karma Yinpa Dargye from Dzigar Monastery in Kham, told me that he had done the same pilgrimage, and that it was equal to seven preliminary practices.

"In order to obtain religious teachings from Potrul Rinpoche, I did the preliminary practice called *Chagchen Ngondro*. This religious practice consists of one hundred thousand prostrations, one hundred thousand prayers of refuge, reciting one hundred letters or *mantras* one hundred thousand times, then one hundred thousand *mandal,* and finally Guru prayers one hundred thousand times.

"In the following years I continued doing my religious practice as before. In 1928 I went to Lhasa and twice circumambulated the Lingkor, and I did one circumambulation with prostrations around the Bamye, the Radre, and Drigung Thil. Three times I went on pilgrimage to Bumri Barkor. When I was twenty-three years old (1930), I was ordained a novice by Potrul Rinpoche, and given the name Tshultrim Palmo.

"My father's guru, Potrul Rinpoche, had been to many pilgrimage places all over Tibet and received religious instructions from different teachers. He was destined to have a monastery somewhere, and he had looked all over Tibet for a proper place. While staying with our tribe, he found the place he had been searching for. He reported this to the Thirteenth Dalai Lama, who shared his aspirations and allowed him to found a monastery.[9] The monastery's name, Thosam Changchub Ling, was given by the Thirteenth Dalai Lama. The monastery was situated in the south of Surug, and it was of the Drugpa Kagyu School.

9. Editors' note: The Thirteenth Dalai Lama was the head of the Buddhist theocratic state that ruled Tibet at the time. His successor, the Fourteenth Dalai Lama, is presently the leader of the Tibetan community in exile.

"At that time (1935–1936) Kunsang and I decided to build a hermitage. Kunsang came from a poor family and was a distant relative of mine. Our families supported us during our building project, and our brothers helped us with the work. The hermitage was to be a sub-branch of Thosam Changchub Ling and it was situated ca. twenty minutes walk north of the monastery. The hermitage was generally known by the name of Dragkhu. At first we had only three rooms, but the hermitage expanded as we were joined by eighteen to twenty more nuns. In the daytime we went to the main monastery for religious teachings and came back to our hermitage after dark.

"From 1935 to 1958 Kunsang and I stayed most of the time at Dragkhu. Sometimes during these twenty-two years of hermit life, my family sent a horse for me so that I could come and visit them. This usually happened during the summer. Otherwise, I spent my time at Dragkhu. Some of the winters I followed my nephew Changchen Khentrul Rinpoche to Drigung Monastery. At Drigung I stayed for some time to receive religious teachings and to visit pilgrimage sites.

"In Drigung there is a place called Tshaphug and here I obtained religious teachings on Tara from Lama Dorje Lhokar. In Terdrom I received the initiation of Vajrakila, and Nyentshe. I recited certain seed-syllables one hundred thousand times. I also recited one hundred thousand seed-syllable *mantras* to Vajrakila. In Dringung Thil, I did ten periods of fasting, each period lasting for twenty days. Then I received initiation from a nun called Nene Choden Sangmo, a very accomplished religious practitioner, who left her footprint on solid rock. She was born near Drigung at a place called Drupang. Her root-guru was Drigung Dripon Ngawang Rinpoche. At another time, I met Shugseb Lochen Rinpoche, who was another highly accomplished religious practitioner.

"Later, I received precepts (*lung*), initiation (*dbang*), and instructions (*khrid*) from the text *Rinchen Terdzo* from Lama Dzigar Kongtrul. In order to obtain the above-mentioned instructions, I had to do certain practices like the *Jetsun Ngondro*. Furthermore, I promised to meditate in an absolutely dark room. This meditation is called *Yangti Nagpo*, and I did this for one month. The instruction was given by Lama Ngawang Rigdzin in his hermitage called Langdong Osel Ling. It was a sealed-door retreat, and there was a small window through which the teacher every day gave instructions on how to proceed with the meditation.

"Fifteen or twenty days after this retreat, on the fifteenth of the fourth Tibetan month 1950, my friend, the nun Kunsang, Lama Ngawang, and

I went on a pilgrimage to Bata. Our teacher said that if we did one circumambulation of Bata in one day, it would be equal to one circumambulation of the holy Mt. Tsari in southern Tibet. Bata had been blessed by Machig Labdron and Yeshe Tshogyal. My father's spiritual teacher Karma Yinpa Dargye had left his footprint on a rock there.

"We were told by our lama to bring all the articles for offering. Early in the morning, we set out on the journey. Ngawang Rinpoche told us that the day was auspicious, and we therefore requested him to do some miraculous deeds. We thought he might want to do a miracle since he had asked us to bring all the objects for offering. Lama Ngawang did not answer our request, he was simply smiling.

"After some time we reached a big plain, where in the distance we could see the hills of Bata. From the hills a big hail and thunderstorm was coming towards us. Since we had not brought any shelter or raincoats, we asked our lama to stop the storm. He told us to recite this prayer:

> While crossing the forests and isolated country of Bayul
> No matter the way was beclouded and impeded
> It is doubtless that Ogyen, the earth-lords
> And his retinue of guardians lead us
> On the way in the right direction
> I offer my salutation to Ogyen Padmasambhava

"Lama Ngawang himself went a short distance ahead of us, put a shawl on his head and started praying. Then we noticed that the hailstorm changed direction and went away from us. We thanked our teacher and told him that he had really done a miraculous deed. He was simply smiling, not acknowledging whether he had stopped the storm or not.

"We went on with the journey and we crossed a pass called Shela at the place Tsaza. Before reaching the valley on the other side, we came to a place called Menlung Dzongnag Sumdo. There was a temporary nomad camp here, made by one of the wealthiest families in the area. The name of the family was Kokhen Tshang. The Rinpoche knew these nomads since he had grown up in the same area as them. The nomads welcomed us and brought us yoghurt and fuel. The Rinpoche was invited to their tents, and we went to a beautiful spot near a stream nearby. We started making lunch, my friend prepared the tea, and I started making offering cakes. Kunsang made an offering of the first tea, and then she poured us each a cup.

"We were getting worried because Lama Ngawang had not come back, and we looked to the sky to check the time. There, in the sky we saw numerous rainbows moving around, like clouds before a storm. The sky was full of these rainbows, moving very fast in a criss-crossing way. Slowly the rainbows turned into the shape of a red-coloured triangle. I asked my friend what all this was, and Kunsang looked up. We were both amazed and forgot completely about our tea.

"Then, on the red triangle the form of Guru Padmasambhava took shape. The image covered the upper part of the valley. Anyone could have seen this huge form of Padmasambhava, but it was difficult to make out the details of his face. We were feeling very blissful and happy and we could hardly think clearly. Kunsang suddenly remembered the short sevenfold recitation, *Tshigdun Soldeb*, which we both prayed.

"Again the five-coloured rainbows started moving, and the form dissolved. Then the clouds slowly became green and formed into a lotus on which the form of Tara sat. Her left leg was crossed and her right hand was pointing downwards. Her left hand was holding a lily and her right leg was stretched. The image was much smaller than that of Guru Padmasambhava, but it was more clear. The image was made up of clouds and rainbows in space, but it was very near to us. Tara was laughing, rejoicing. We were both dazed and we recited the prayers and seed-syllables of Tara. Slowly the rainbows and the clouds started moving again and Tara's face turned red. She was slowly fading away, but she was still smiling at us. Thereafter, the sky turned very chaotic, the rainbows again criss-crossing. Then everything was lit up, the nomad tents and their sheep were illuminated.

"Rinpoche, together with a servant from the nomad camp, came slowly towards us. We were overwhelmed by happiness and wanted to tell our teacher about the miracle, but because of the servant we decided to wait. Lama Ngawang told us to start the offerings. We went to the fire but discovered that it had died out. Our tea was cold and the butter hard. Thus the miracle must have lasted for some time, but we did not know how long. The servant lit the fire with his matchlock and we started the ceremony. Afterwards, we offered many items to the servant and he was quite happy.

"Finally we told Rinpoche about our experiences and exclaimed that we had never been so happy before. It was a happiness beyond words. The lama asked if we both had seen the images. We told him one by one what we had witnessed, and he revealed that the display had been created by him. Rinpoche told us that we were both virtuous since non-virtuous people do not see such things. He told us not to cling to what we had experienced. He himself had not seen the display.

"We returned to the hermitage very late and when we arrived Lama Ngawang's mother and nephew were asleep. The mother woke up, and said she had been looking for us in the direction of Bata just before sunset. I asked her if she had seen any rainbows in that direction, but she had not. We thought this was strange, because to us it looked like the whole sky was full of them. Some time before our small pilgrimage, Rinpoche had ordered a new Green Tara *thanka* to be painted for him.[10] We had thought this *thanka* very impressive, but after our vision of Tara, the *thanka* looked pale, as if it had faded.

"The reason why we saw this display in the sky must have been because of my friends and not because of myself. Since then, I have never seen anything like this, so the appearance could not have been created on my behalf. When I was young I used to have many good spiritual dreams, but now I do not have them anymore. Maybe this is because I do not practice religion as much as I ought to.

"While staying in our hermitage, I received religious instructions from Domang Tulku Kunsang Thegchog Dorje, from Detrul Pema le Rabtsel, and from Potrul Rinpoche. I received *Zhi khro'i bKa' dBang* three times and instructions on the Manual of Hermits. Kunsang and I did an abridged *ngondro* written by Dza Peltrul Rinpoche. This religious teaching was given by our teacher, Lama Detrul Pema. Further, we recited one hundred seed-syllables of Tara, and practiced the teachings that we had been given before by lamas. From Domang Tulku Kunsang Thegchog Dorje, I received teachings of the *Terser* cycle. From Lama Detrul Pema le Rabtsel, Lama Dzigor Kongtrul, and Lama Ngawang Rigdzin I received instructions on how to train the mind, from Lama Potrul Rinpoche, I received *Drubpa Kagye kyi Wang,* and from Lama Drigung Rukhen Trul Rinpoche I received the initiation of Chenresig five times. During our twenty-two years in the hermitage, we annually did eighteen days of fasting, and we never failed in this.

"One of our teachers, Potrul Rinpoche, died in 1944. His incarnation was found and installed in Thosam Changchub Ling.[11] In 1959, when he was thirteen years old, he was arrested by the Chinese and he spent eight

---

10. Editors' note: *Thankas* are scroll paintings used in many forms of Tibetan devotion and meditation.

11. Editors' note: In the Tibetan Buddhist tradition, many important religious leaders are considered to be incarnations of a sacred figure in the Buddhist pantheon. This sacred figure will be reincarnated in successive persons who must be identified and installed in the same leadership role. The most famous example is the case of the Dalai Lamas, who are taken to be the successive incarnations of the bodhisattva Avalokitesvara.

years in prison. He is now living as a layman in Lhasa, but he is still a Rinpoche. His name, Karma Shedrub Chokyi Nyima, was given to him by Gyalwa Karmapa (1924–1981), but these days he uses his lay name, Sonam Dondrub.

"We were eight nuns from the hermitage who started our escape from the Chinese in 1958. We took the northern route to India, and on the way we visited various famous sacred places. Among them was Sangsang Lhadrag Karpo where there is a cave of Yeshe Tshogyal. Here we performed rituals. Before reaching Nepal we went to four pilgrimage-sites of Milarepa: Dragkar Taso, Uma Dzong, Kyangphen Namkha Dzong, and Ragma Changchub Dzong. It took us two years to reach Nepal and there we visited Bodhnath, Swayambhu, the Asura Cave, Yanglesho, and the place where Buddha offered his body to the tigress.[12]

"Of the eight nuns from Dragkhu Hermitage, who escaped to India, only the youngest one and myself are alive today. This other nun disrobed and is presently living in Nepal. She recently went back to Tibet. Our hermitage has been totally destroyed, and only the throne is there today. Also, Thosam Changchub Ling Monastery has been destroyed. Only the flowers are still there.

"In 1961 (the Bull year) I reached Dharamsala, but stayed here only one and a half months. The Tibetan Government sent me and one hundred refugee families to Manali. That year I went with my relatives on pilgrimage to Varanasi, Bodh Gaya, Rajgiri, and to the ruins of Nalanda. From Manali I also travelled to Lahoul, Spiti, to holy places called Re Phagpa, Phagmo Drilbu Ri, and Gandola. I also visited Kardang and Tayu Monasteries, and Biling Retreat-centre. In Lahoul and Spiti there is a famous statue of Milarepa owned by the wealthy Khangsar family. I went to see this very auspicious statue, of which it is said that its hair grows.

"From Manali I moved to Dalhousie. Here a nunnery was established in Ashoka Cottage. The abbot of the nunnery at that time was Karma Thinley, or as he is also called, Lama Wangchen Norbu. When staying here my memory was failing. Karma Thinley told me to recite the seed-syllable of Manjusri and Arapaca seven hundred thousand times. After that I recovered.

"Later on the nunnery, which now was inhabited by forty nuns, was moved to Gita Cottage. I was now fifty-eight years old and I started a

---

12. Editors' note: This episode occurred, according to a well-known Jataka story, many lives before the Buddha's birth as Gautama.

two hundred days fasting (equals one hundred sessions of fasting). After one hundred and forty days I fell ill and was hospitalized. Now I received help from the British nun Freda Bedi or Kechog Palmo. After the stay in the hospital, I started another two hundred days fasting and in addition I did a sixteen days fasting to make up for the two hundred days that I broke when I was hospitalized. During my stay in Dalhousie, I received many initiations, empowerments, religious teachings, and precepts from Karma Thinley and from Karlu Rinpoche.

"The nunnery was moved to Tilokpur in 1968 and I stayed here for one month. Thereafter I moved back to Dharamsala and settled in Forsyth Ganj. I did one hundred days fasting and following that a two hundred days fasting in the Nyungne Lhakhang. When the fasting ended a thanksgiving was given in the house of the benefactor Ama Drolma. Ama Drolma then offered me a room in the same house, and this is where I now live.

"From 1970 to 1973 I did a three-year retreat in my room. During this retreat I also finished reciting the *Vajra Guru Mantra* one hundred thousand times. This was started in 1950 when Kunsang and I had the vision of Padmasambhava. We were then told by our teacher to recite this *mantra* every day until we eventually reached one hundred thousand. During the retreat I received the initiations of *Sangha Dupa, Demchog Jigche,* and *Nelchorma* from H. H. the Dalai Lama, his late senior and junior tutors, Ling Rinpoche, and Triyang Rinpoche. Every morning together with three monks I did *Nyenpa* in the Nyungne Lhakhang. We finished one hundred thousand *Nyenpa* of Vajrayogini. This religious practice we did during the daytime, and in the evening I went back to my room. After we had finished, a *Chinsek* ritual was held.

"Then for three months, the mother of the Tibetan doctor, Lobsang Drolma, and I did the *Nyenpa* of Vajrayogini four hundred thousand times. Afterwards, I did a *Chinsek* ritual. Then I helped an old Tibetan lady, Yangchenla, to do a Vajrayogini *Nyenpa* in the Nyungne Lhakhang. We did one hundred thousand. Yangchenla is now living in Switzerland.

"In the Tsuklakhang in MacLeod Ganj, I received a transmission (*lung*) of the whole Kangyur from the abbot of Sera Monastery, and it lasted for nine months.[13] Later, I received a transmission of the whole Kangyur from Pangnang Rinpoche. I received a transmission of the col-

---

13. Editors' note: The Kangyur is a large collection of Tibetan Buddhist scriptures. It contains vinaya materials, sutras, tantras, and *avadanas* (life stories and records of meritorious deeds).

lected works of Tsongkhapa and his two disciples Gyal Tshabje and Madrubje.[14] Also, I received transmission of some volumes of Tengyur.[15]

"Since I settled in my house in MacLeod Ganj, I have participated every year in a one to four days fasting in the ninth Tibetan month and a two days fasting in the tenth Tibetan month. Every winter I go into retreat of *Opagme kyi Tshedrub* for two months. This year I have not been able to do so because my legs are in such a bad shape."

14. Editors' note: Tsongkhapa was an important monk, scholar, and reformer who lived during the fourteenth and fifteenth centuries. He is considered the founder of the Geluk Pa order, which became the dominant order in Tibetan Buddhism.

15. Editors' note: The Tengyur is a large collection of sacred writings composed of Tibetan translations of works by Indian authors. Its contents are diverse, ranging from commentaries on canonical materials to works on grammar and astrology.

Figure 9. The cremation of a senior monk, Mae Sariang district, Mae Hong Son province, northern Thailand (edifice with the corpse of the senior monk situated at the site of the cremation). Photo by Charles Keyes.

CHAPTER 9

Monastic Funerals (Thailand)

The story of the Buddha's passing away, his cremation, and the distribution of his relics is vividly presented in the Mahaparinibbana Sutta—a very important text within the early Buddhist canon. According to this very famous account, the Buddha's passing away, and the funerary process that followed, had at least two crucial components. On the one hand, the events that transpired signaled the Buddha's attainment of final release from the ongoing process of death and rebirth (that is, his attainment of nirvana). At the same time, the funerary process provided an opportunity for the community to express its respect and to continue to profit from the charisma that his very special spiritual achievements had generated.

Clearly Buddhists have considered the spiritual achievements of the Buddha, and therefore the funerary process that marked his death, to be radically distinctive if not unique. However, many of the practices that have been employed to mark the deaths of members of the Buddhist community—especially the deaths of highly respected senior monks—have displayed practices very similar to those surrounding the Buddha's passing away. Such funerary practices have incorporated sophisticated ways of recognizing and honoring a life of spiritual attainment and of symbolizing and assisting the rebirth of the deceased in an appropriately positive place and position. They have also provided a process through which the community and its individual members can draw on the spiri-

The essay in this chapter is an abridged form of Charles F. Keyes, "Tug-of-War for Merit: Cremation of a Senior Monk," *Journal of the Siam Society* 63 (1975): 44–62. Courtesy of the Siam Society and Charles Keyes.

tual capital—the "field of merit"—generated by the deceased through his life of faithful monastic commitment.

In the excerpt that follows, Charles Keyes describes one such funerary process. The senior monk in question, unlike Yeshe Drolma (the nun whose autobiography was recounted in the previous essay), had lived his monastic life in a single monastery, where he had pursued his vocation as abbot and as the spiritual leader within the local community.

THE CREMATION OF A SENIOR MONK

Charles F. Keyes

In February 1973 I observed the cremation of an abbot of a village temple near the town of Mae Sariang in northwestern Thailand. During the three days prior to the cremation, which took place on the 9th day of the waxing moon in the 9th lunar month (northern Thai reckoning)—that is, on Sunday the 11th of February, the temporary "palace" or *prasada* on which the corpse of the abbot had been placed was pulled to and fro by several hundreds of people. Local people call the funeral of a monk which includes such a ceremonial tug-of-war *poi lo,* lit. "ceremony of the cart or sleigh." While the people who participated in the ceremony were predominantly northern Thai or Yuan and while the deceased was also northern Thai, the custom of the tug-of-war is said to be of Shan origin.[1] In fact, the *poi lo* ceremony which I observed is closely related to the usual northern Thai funeral for a monk which is known as *lak prasat* or "pulling of the *prasada.*" Both the *poi-lo* and the *lak prasat* ceremonies share much with the Burmese rites for a monk known as *pongyi byan pwe* which Shway Yoe glosses as "the return of the great glory." In this paper, I will attempt an explanation of some of the symbolism evident in the *poi lo* ceremony which I observed in Mae Sariang.

Cao Adhikara Candradibya Indavanso Thera or as he was known to local people, Tucao Canthip,[2] was born in the village of Nam Dip near the town of Mae Sariang in 1916. After having served as a novice in the local temple, he was ordained at the age of 21 into the monkhood. He remained in the monkhood throughout his life and continued to live in the temple in his home village. While he did not attain any significant scholastic honors awarded by the Thai Sangha, he was locally respected

---

1. Editors' note: The Shan are a Tai people closely related to the Thai and the Yuan, who live in northern Thailand. The majority of Shan live in the hills of northern Myanmar.
2. *Tucao* is the northern Thai title for the abbot of a temple.

as a knowledgeable practitioner of Yuan or northern Thai Buddhism. For many years before his death, he had been the abbot of the local wat and held the title of *cao adhikara* which indicates that he was an abbot who was also a *thera* or monk who has been in the yellow robes for more than ten years. Tucao Canthip passed away, or as it is said, "reached the cessation of his nature" on the 23d of November 1972 following a severe attack of dysentery.

After his death, Tucao Canthip's body was ritually bathed, dressed in yellow robes, and placed in a casket which was kept in the temple in which he had lived. In northern Thailand, as in northeastern Thailand and Burma, funerals for ordinary people are held as soon as possible—often within 24 hours—following death. In contrast, the bodies of senior monks (as well as high-ranking lay people) are kept for some months before the cremation is held.[3] The District Abbot of Mae Sariang explained that this delay permitted the organizers of the cremation to collect from among the congregation, the clergy, and "Buddhist faithful generally" the funds necessary for holding an expensive funeral. Sanguan Chotisukkharat, the northern Thai folklorist, has elaborated on this point in a short note on *poi lo:*

Whenever a Bhikkhu who has been an abbot, has been an important monk of many lenten periods, or has been ordained from youth until his death and has never tasted the pleasure of the world died, it is arranged that his corpse be bathed and placed in a coffin. The corpse is kept several months. This long duration of keeping the corpse permits the faithful to find the money for holding the cremation because it is a major ceremony which requires the expenditure of much money. When enough money has been raised, invitations are sent to Buddhists everywhere and the schedule of merit-making events is made known.

In addition to the need for a period of time in which to raise the necessary funds for funeral expenses, I would add another reason, derived in part from my anthropological perspective, for such a delay between the time of death and the time of cremation. During this period between death and cremation, the deceased is in a state of limbo, having not yet totally departed this world or fully entered the world beyond. This period is characterized by what Victor Turner has called "liminality," that is, it is a period, ritually marked and invested with complex symbolism, which follows separation from the normal structural roles played by individuals and which occur before a reintegration or aggregation back

3. The body of the famous northern Thai monk, Khruba Siwichai, was kept eight years (from 1938 until 1946) before being cremated.

into the normal structural world. This process of separation, liminality, and aggregation has long been recognized in studies of rites of passage. However, it has only been with the work of Turner that attention has been focused on liminality. During the liminal period, Turner has shown, the participants are confronted ritually with ambiguity, paradox, and other challenges to the normative basis of social life. Ultimately a new resolution, communicated symbolically in the form of sacred knowledge, is effected, the participants are thus transformed and can be aggregated back into the world.

The death of a monk ushers in a liminal period which differs from that following the death of an ordinary layman. The corpse of an ordinary person is "dangerous" in that the spirit which adheres to the body until cremation may become a malevolent ghost. The continued presence of the corpse of a highly respected monk poses no such threat. By virtue of the merit which such a man has accumulated through rejection of the "pleasures of the world," his spirit is immune from such a fate after death.

Far from being dangerous, the corpse of a monk is auspicious since it becomes a unique "field of merit" for the lay followers and for Sangha brethren. The coffin containing the corpse of Tucao Canthip was kept in the *vihara* or image hall of Wat Nam Dip and was placed to the left of the main Buddha image. Not only did the corpse receive offerings of funeral wreaths and of incense, candles, and cut flowers in special rites, but similar offerings were also placed before it on the occasion of every ritual held in the *vihara* during the period it remained there. Each offering laid before the coffin was believed to produce merit.

Serving as a channel of merit was not the only religious function served by the corpse. More importantly, the corpse served as a constant reminder of a fundamental message of Buddhism—the impermanence of self and the transitoriness of life. Meditation upon corpses is strongly enjoined in the texts of Buddhism and is ritually recognized in Mae Sariang (as elsewhere in northern Thailand) in the ceremony of *khao kam*—lit., "to enter karma." In Mae Sariang this ceremony is held for seven days each January during which all the monks and novices of the district go into meditation retreat in the Mae Sariang cemetery. The decaying body also finds representation in pictures which are hung in the buildings of a wat. The corpse of a former monk, whose cremation can be long delayed, is perhaps the best of all symbols in bringing into consciousness reflection about the decay and disintegration of man's physical form.

Following the death of a monk, a committee is formed to organize the funerary rites, schedule the events for the cremation, and collect the money to pay for the costs of the ceremony. For the funeral of Tucao Canthip, the organizing committee was cochaired by the District Abbot, representing the clergy, and the Headman of Ban Nam Dip, representing the laity. The other members of the committee consisted of other members of the Sangha in Mae Sariang and members of the lay stewardship committee of Wat Nam Dip. For ordinary lay people, such an organizing committee includes no representation as such from the Sangha. The death of a member of the Order, however, is not the concern only of his clerical brothers as the equal division between lay and Sangha in the organizing committee for the funeral of Tucao Canthip indicates. Tucao Canthip had been both a member of the Sangha community, which in the small district of Mae Sariang included the clergy of the whole district, and spiritual mentor for the congregation of Wat Nam Dip.[4]

There appears to be no set length of time which is deemed appropriate or auspicious for keeping the corpse before the cremation. However, certain considerations, which are symbolically significant, influence the choice of time for a cremation. The District Abbot of Mae Sariang said that it was preferable for cremations to be held in the dry season and that they should not be held during lent. All of the cremations of monks in northern Thailand on which I have been able to obtain information occurred between December and March. Shway Yoe also notes for Burma "that a pongyi byan never takes place during lent." Lent (called *vassa* in Pali and *phansa* in Thai) is the period of rain, of planting, of fertility, of new life as well as the period for retreat for the Sangha.

The committee organizing the funeral for Tucao Canthip chose February as the time for the cremation because by that month villagers in Nam Dip would have finished harvesting rice and would not have yet begun planting dry-season crops (which in Nam Dip consist mainly of groundnuts). The field in which the cremation was to be held was filled

4. For very important monks, the role of both the local clergy and congregation in organizing the funeral may be considerably reduced. For the funeral of Khruba Siwichai, the feeling that he was spiritual mentor to all of northern Thailand, monk and layman alike, and not only for the local congregation of Wat Ban Pang in Li District, Lamphun province, prevailed. The cremation actually took place at Wat Camthewi near Lamphun City and not at his home temple. The committee which organized the cremation of Phra Upaligunupamacarya, the late abbot of Wat Phra Sing, Chiang Mai, who died in 1973, was headed by the regional ecclesiastical chief, the provincial abbot, the acting abbot of Wat Phra Sing, the governor of Chiang Mai Province, and the senior lay steward of Wat Phra Sing. Moreover, as this was a cremation at which the king himself brought the fire, much of the planning was removed from the hands of the local community and undertaken by the palace. Indeed, the date of the cremation (which took place on 15 January 1974) was changed several times to accommodate His Majesty's schedule.

only with the stubble of harvested rice. A Sunday was chosen for the actual day of the burning since it was not a workday for schoolchildren, teachers, and officials. The day chosen for the burning was also purposely not a Buddhist sabbath day (*wan phra*), that is, a day on which the clergy would have normal ritual duties to perform. In short, the time chosen for the cremation linked the unfertile season in which the fields had only dead rice stalks with the death of a man. The liminality of the day of burning was underscored by the scheduling of the cremation for a time when both laity and clergy would not have normal functions to carry out.

The site chosen for the cremation was not the "cemetery" where cremations of most lay people are carried out, but was a field belonging to a relative of the late monk. This field lay to the west of Wat Nam Dip and was on ground which was lower than that on which the wat is located. In the field, several temporary edifices were erected just prior to the beginning of the scheduled events. There were two pavilions. One which faced west was used by the participating monks and the second, at right angles to the first and facing south, was used by a small portion of the laity who attended. Opposite this second pavilion was a stage used for performances of *like* or Siamese folk opera. Next to it was a movie screen, hung on bamboo poles. In front of the first pavilion was the "course" on which the tug-of-war would be held. Prior to the beginning of the funeral, the *prasada* without the coffin was placed on this course 15 or 20 meters away from the main pavilion. Later, during the three days of the ceremony, the *prasada* with the coffin would sit in the same place except when the tug-of-war was taking place. Some hundred or so meters away from the pavilions, etc., were four bamboo poles, rising about 20 meters into the air, to which a yellow cloth which had been part of the late monk's robes was attached. This construction, called *pha phidan* or *pha phedan*, "cloth canopy," marked the place where the burning would occur.

At this point, we should examine the *prasada* in some detail. The one used in Mae Sariang consisted of an outer structure erected on poles about five meters high with a "roof" supported not only by these poles but also by other poles set at diagonals to provide strength. The roof itself consisted of a central tower with five tiers, surrounded by four smaller towers of three tiers each. Each of these towers was crowned by a pole decorated with "flags." Inside this outer structure was another, again elaborately decorated, which contained the casket. The bottom of the *prasada* was decorated on both sides with long Naga figures.[5]

---

5. Editors' note: Nagas are semidivine beings associated with snakes who play an important role in Buddhist mythology. For more associations, see below.

The whole edifice rested upon a sleigh to which heavy ropes had been attached.

In Mae Sariang, the *prasada* just described served both as the vehicle on which the body was transported to the place of cremation and as the funeral pyre itself. This was rather unusual as in most cremations of monks (and high status laymen) in both Thailand and Burma, hearse and pyre are separate structures. In northern Thailand, the cart used at a funeral of a monk was traditionally in the shape of a *hastilinga* bird, a mythical creature which has the head, trunk, and tusks of an elephant and the body of a bird. One still sees carts in this shape in some funerals for monks, although the custom has begun to disappear, according to a former District Abbot of Phrao in Chiang Mai province, because the work required to make the animal is too time consuming and too costly. Few northern Thai whom I have asked know the significance of the *hastilinga* bird and no one had heard of the ritual killing of the animal which used to occur in northeastern Thailand. Nonetheless, the animal, in its strange combination of elements, must appear to those who see it as disturbing and even dangerous since the creature is not of one class of beings or another. Symbols which cause confusion of normal categories of classification play important roles in liminal periods of rites of passage during which paradox, ambiguity, and bafflement arising from actual experience are confronted and resolved.

In Mae Sariang, the only animal symbol present was the Naga which was represented on the bottom part of the *prasada*. The Naga has generally been interpreted as a fertility symbol, but it does not have this meaning alone. It also carries a cosmographic meaning, representing the seas which surround Mount Meru.[6] The *prasada*, in turn, represents Meru, a name by which the funerary pyre is also known. The fertility meaning of the Naga does remain, conveying in this context masculine sexuality which has been suppressed when a man enters the Sangha. The juxtaposition of monk and Naga, here manifest in the body of the monk which lies in the coffin above the Naga, recalls other pairings such as the use of the term Naga as the name of the candidate for monkhood and the depictions in sculpture and painting of the Buddha's conquest of the Naga.

The cremation pyre, whether distinct from the hearse as is normally the case, or combined with it as was the case in the funeral of

---

6. Editors' note: In Buddhist cosmology, Meru is the cosmic mountain that constitutes the center and linchpin of the lower realms of the cosmos, including certain heavenly realms as well as the earthly realm in which human beings live.

Tucao Canthip, is recognized by local people as a model of the cosmos. The tiered roofs represent the levels of existence or heavens located on Mount Meru. Through the fire of the cremation, the deceased monk's earthly model of heaven becomes transformed into actual heaven, that is the abode for the soul of this virtuous man. That monks and high-ranking laymen are burnt in such elaborate *prasada* while ordinary people are not symbolizes the belief that those with great merit (evidenced in the wearing of yellow robes or in possessing power and wealth) will enjoy a heavenly reincarnation.

The *pha phidan* or the yellow cloth canopy mounted on bamboo poles at the site of the burning appears to be a uniquely northern Thai custom. It is found only at the cremation of monks or novices and never at the cremation of lay persons, no matter how high-ranking. Sanguan has written that:

these four poles are planted to form a square. A monk's cloth belonging to the deceased will be stretched as a canopy. . . . [At the burning,] the canopy will be watched to see if it catches fire or not. If the flames burn a hole [in the cloth] this shows that the soul of the virtuous senior monk has departed well . . .

Puangkham Tuikhiao, a former District Abbot of Phrao in Chiang Mai province and in 1973 a research associate in the Faculty of the Social Sciences at Chiang Mai University, says that if the cloth burns, it shows that the monk was "pure" and thus entitled to a high rebirth. If it does not burn, then it indicates that the monk still has "impurities" and must return in a state less than that of heaven. He will still enjoy a better rebirth than ordinary men.

The events scheduled for the cremation of Tucao Canthip began with an "entertaining" form of sermon, a performance of *like*, and a movie in the evening on Thursday, the 8th of February and ended with the collecting of the remains in the early morning of Monday, the 12th of February. The events scheduled, according both to the printed schedule and to the words of informants, provided the lay people who attended with the opportunity to make merit through presentation of food and alms to the participating Sangha, through listening to sermons, and through the unique opportunity of the tug-of-war over the body of the deceased monk. In addition, those who came could observe the burning and enjoy various entertainments. The clergy, in their turn, made merit by performing their ritual roles in the events. Finally, a small group of monks and laymen gathered a few remains to be kept for later internment in a stupa (a traditional Buddhist burial structure).

The entertainments drew the largest crowds of all events save for the tug-of-war and the burning. In addition to the nightly performance of *like* and showing of movies, the entertainments also included some of the sermons. On Saturday evening, a well-known monk from Mae Rim near Chiang Mai delivered a two-hour version of the Jujaka story from the Vessantara Jataka.[7] For the whole two hours, he had the audience in stitches as he made ribald remarks about the love of the old Brahmin, Jujaka, for a young pretty girl, as he described, with imitations of conversations, how this young girl grew into an avaricious bitch and how Jujaka, constantly plagued by flatulence (noted with appropriate sound effects), strived to do his wife's bidding. Such entertainments, which to some Westerners would seem to transgress the boundaries of respect at a funeral, are not as anomalous as they might first seem. "Wakes," which include the playing of games, courting, gambling, and drinking, are found throughout Thailand, Laos, and Burma as part of the activities which take place following a death. Such activities underscore the liminality of the period because they involve watching fantasies (*like* and movies), interacting in social relationships which do not, in the end, alter any normative structure of everyday life (games), or entrance into states which are temporary (drunkenness, courtship).

The funeral afforded those laymen who chose to do so with several conventional ways to acquire merit. One way was to contribute to the costs of the funeral. In the announcement of the events scheduled for the cremation of Tucao Canthip, the presentation of the mid-day meal for the participating clergy on each of the three main days and the presentation of alms to the Sangha were specifically listed. The amount involved was not small since 56 monks (a number equal to the age of the late abbot) and four novices had been invited from various villages and towns in Mae Hong Son province. Thus, the announcement requested that "if anyone should wish to be a donor of alms . . . please contact or make your reservations with the committee." Donors were asked to contribute 100 baht each. The greatest expense involved, that of the construction of the various edifices, was met through the merit-making donations of the villagers from Ban Nam Dip. These donations also paid for the costs of the *bangsakun* robes which are an essential alms-offering to clergy at cremations. In addition to gaining merit through gifts to the clergy, lay people could also gain merit through listening to the sermons

---

7. Editors' note: Vessantara was the birth of the Buddha before he was born as Gautama. During that birth, Vessantara perfected the virtue of generosity by, among other things, giving his children to the Brahmin Jujaka.

delivered. With the exception of the sermon concerning Jujaka, mentioned above, the sermons (which were read from Yuan texts) attracted only older people. Although these conventional ways of making merit were far from unimportant, it seems clear that the merit-making activity which attracted the greatest number of people was the tug-of-war.

After the body in its coffin had been moved from the temple to be placed in the *prasada* on Friday, the first tug-of-war took place. On each afternoon of the next two days, a similar event occurred, lasting several hours on each occasion. The *prasada* was oriented in an East-West direction in the middle of the field. The heavy ropes attached to each side of the sleigh were picked up by men and dragged in opposite directions. Then men, women, and children—mainly northern Thai but with some Karen and Shan as well—took hold of the ropes on either side.[8] There was no special social basis for determining who chose to go on one side rather than the other and I observed many who changed sides. A number of men and even a few women had appointed themselves as coaches cum cheerleaders; several even had megaphones. These people encouraged the side they were on to begin pulling. Usually the side that began would have the advantage, but would be stopped finally as more and more people joined the other side. Sometimes the rope broke and the side having the good rope might pull the *prasada* several dozen meters before they were persuaded to stop. Flags marked the course on which the tug-of-war took place, but there were no "goals," no points which if the *prasada* passed, one side could claim a victory.

To my question as to why the people engaged in this apparently inconclusive competition over the corpse of a monk, I received invariably the same answer: those who participate gain great merit. The same point was emphasized in the mimeographed announcement of events which concluded: "we invite all faithful and good people to join in the merit-making at the cremation of Cao Adhikhara Canthip by contributing strength and spirit in the tug-of-war of the *prasada* which is the local custom. [By doing so,] we believe that we gain great merit." Shway Yoe gives a similar explanation for the same ritual action in Burma, although he said that the merit "falls to the share of those who win in the tug-of-war." In Mae Sariang, no distinction was made between those who participated on one side as distinct from the other. Sanguan, the northern Thai folklorist, has elaborated upon the theme that participation in the tug-of-war brings great merit:

8. Editors' note: Karen are a non-Tai ethnic group that forms a significant segment of the population in the Mae Sariang area.

Poi lo . . . is the supreme merit-making [ceremony] because it is believed that anyone who dies in the yellow robes, having dedicated his life to the religion, has much merit. The funerary merit-making for such a monk, it is believed, will yield strong merit. Thus, merit-making should be undertaken without concern for the expense.

The tug-of-war, in contrast to simply pulling the *prasada* directly to the place of burning, serves to prolong the tapping of merit possessed by the late monk.[9] The purpose of the competition is not for one side or the other to obtain more merit, but to draw out as much merit through pulling the *prasada* to and fro. Inherent in this act is the belief, widely held in Theravada Buddhist societies, that one who possesses great merit —e.g., a highly esteemed monk—can share this merit, and the benefits following from such merit, with others who act in appropriate ways.

The transfer of merit through the pulling of the corpse is not the only meaning of the tug-of-war. As noted above, the course for the tug-of-war was oriented in an East-West direction, with the site of the cremation being located to the West. The West is recognized by Mae Sariang people, as by most Southeast Asians, as the way of the dead, while the East is associated with birth and auspiciousness. The movement, then, from East to West, back again, and so on, clearly symbolizes the cycle of birth, death, rebirth, etc.

The resolution of the tug-of-war was in keeping with the above meaning for eventually the contest ended when the *prasada* was pulled to the site of the cremation which laid to the West. In the late afternoon on Sunday, the District Abbot gave a signal to end the tug-of-war and to begin the burning. Everyone then shifted to the western end of the *prasada* and helped in pulling the edifice to the place under the *pha phidan* where the actual cremation would take place. Once there, several men began to pile dried logs around the coffin inside the outer structure of the *prasada*. Next, members of the lay committee placed packages containing clerical robes on the pyre. These were the *bangsakun* robes which are symbolic reminders of Buddha's enjoinder to the monks that they should use discarded shrouds for their robes. After the monks had claimed their cloths, several laymen poured gasoline on the firewood. Next, an elaborate fireworks system was set off; this involved the light-

9. It should be noted that in usual northern Thai funerals for monks, the *prasada* is pulled in procession for a considerable distance before being taken to the place of cremation. In the most important cremation of a monk in modern history, that of Khruba Siwichai in 1946, the body was carried in procession from the village of Ban Pang in Li District, Lamphun, to near Lamphun City, a distance of about 80 kilometers.

ing of rockets which travelled along wires to lantern-shaped containers of gunpowder which when ignited set off yet another rocket. The final rocket plunged into the pyre itself. Yet other rockets were set off along the ground towards the pyre; it was one of these which actually started the burning.

The pyre burned rapidly and people watched the burning for only a few minutes before turning to go home. Before departing, it was apparent to all that the *pha phidan* was not going to catch fire. A few laymen from the local congregation stayed to see that the flames consumed all the *prasada* and the body contained therein.

On the following morning, a few men from the local congregation, the monks and novices from the local temple, and a few of the late abbot's relatives foregathered at the site of the cremation. They collected some of the remains of the abbot's burnt bones. These would later be enshrined in a small *stupa* called a *ku* in northern Thailand, in the grounds of the wat. While in the case of the late abbot of Wat Nam Dip one would not expect this stupa to have any great significance, some such stupas become the focus of cults. This is the case of the four stupas which contain the relics of the famous northern Thai monk, Khruba Siwichai,[10] and, in Mae Sariang, of the stupa containing the remains of the late abbot of Wat Phapha. This latter monk had been renowned for his holiness and supernatural powers during his life and his cremation was still talked about for the auspicious omen which had occurred at it. A circle had appeared in the middle of the *pha phidan* for which no natural explanation could be given. In the case of this monk, as in the case of Khruba Siwichai, people believe that their great merit has not been exhausted at the cremation and can still be tapped.

Death transforms the monk not into a threat to the aspects of life most valued but into a vehicle whereby the good life can be achieved both by himself and by others. For himself, it is believed that the monk will not be reborn into a more holy state, but will be reborn in heaven where earthly pleasures can be enjoyed without the suffering which accompanies such pleasure in this world. Herein lies the meaning of the *prasada,* whose burning together with the body transforms the monk into a denizen of heaven. Moreover, the monk's great merit which ensures him of a good rebirth can be shared with those who assist in pulling

10. These stupas are located at Wat Ban Pang, Khruba Siwichai's home temple in Li District, Lamphun province, at Wat Cam Thewi in Muang District, Lamphun, at Wat Suan Dok in Muang District, Chiang Mai province, and at Wat Doi Ngam in Sankamphaeng District, Chiang Mai.

his body to the place of burning. Such is the meaning, in part, of the tug-of-war.

Although death is conceived of as auspicious in the case of a monk, it cannot be denied, even in the funeral for a monk, as an ultimate concern. Indeed, shorn of more proximate challenges posed to structure by the death of an ordinary person, the death of a monk becomes the occasion, in the funeral rites which follow, for a clear confrontation with this ultimate concern. The dissolution of self and decay of the body are kept before the eyes of the local people during the long period that the body is kept before the cremation. Again, the choice of the time and place for the cremation reemphasizes the negative side of death. And for all the decoration and elaborate construction, there is no question in anybody's mind but that the *prasada* contains a corpse.

This awareness of death is met by symbolic answers to the question of what death means. These answers are supremely Buddhist. Man is born to die and dies to be reborn once again. Such is the fundamental meaning of the tug-of-war. It is also the meaning of the act of burning which effects the transformation between death and rebirth. While in the case of the monk, this rebirth will be a pleasurable one—how pleasurable being known by whether the *pha phidan* burns or not—it will not be the final one. With the exceptions of *arahans* (renunciatory saints), the likes of whom have not been seen in the world for a long time, monks, like ordinary laymen, have not exhausted their karma at death. Thus, they too will be reborn. And here we return again to the symbolism of the tug-of-war which can be seen as competition between death and life in which there is no ultimate champion. That champion is neither death nor life; but for an understanding of this Buddhist conception it is necessary to go beyond the symbols found in death rites.

Those who attended the cremation of Tucao Canthip came away with a sense of well-being, albeit a few had this sense diluted by hangovers. The sense of well-being was in part a consequence of having gained merit through participation in the tug-of-war. It was also, in part, a consequence of an experience of "communitas" during the tug-of-war and in the entertainments during which social differences were irrelevant. In addition, the power of the symbols of the ritual etched on most minds some idea of the meaning of death. If this meaning were to be reflected upon—and admittedly it is only by a very few—it would be found to be not wholly satisfactory. It is for this reason that Buddhist theology is not confined to ritual symbols alone; deeper understandings come though study and meditation.

PART III

Lay Practices

Figure 10. Worshipers at a roadside shrine to Kuan-yin in Hangchow, China. Photograph by Chen-Fang Yu.

CHAPTER 10

Lay Identity and Participation (China)

In the introduction to chapter 5, we noted that many Buddhist texts and traditions state that the ideal Buddhist community is composed of an order of monks (*bhiksus*), an order of nuns (*bhiksunis*), a segment of laymen (*upasakas*), and a segment of laywomen (*upasikas*). As we have already seen from several examples, the renunciant communities have played an important role in Buddhist life. However, as has been suggested in several of the preceding chapters, laymen and laywomen have also been integrally involved. In fact, most Buddhist communities have typically given the lay vocation an essential and respected role. Further, certain exceptional cases in recent Buddhist history in Japan and China notwithstanding, most Buddhist communities have positioned the lay vocation within the context of a symbiotic relation with the monastic vocation. In the next five chapters we will explore certain aspects and dimensions of the lay religious life and how certain aspects of that life relate to the monastic one.

Typically, Buddhist lay communities are guided by various sets of precepts and injunctions, which are designed to inspire and cultivate a number of personal, devotional, and social attitudes. They are meant to inspire a sense of honor, awe, and reverence toward the Buddha, dharma, and samgha. They are also meant to assuage, limit, and control excessive desire, anger, fear, hatred, anxiety, and frustration. Finally, they

The essay in this chapter was taken from Holmes Welch, *The Practice of Chinese Buddhism, 1900–1950* (Cambridge, MA: Harvard University Press, 1967), 357–66. Copyright © 1967 by the Presidents and Fellows of Harvard College. Reprinted by permission of Harvard University Press.

are meant to encourage good and proper social relations and interactions, including those between oneself and one's family and between oneself and the wider society and world.

The following excerpt concerns lay Buddhist precepts and injunctions as they appeared in China several decades before the triumph of communism. It is especially compelling in its portrayal of the establishment of nonmonastic forms of Buddhist identity as well as different types and degrees of lay commitment and practice.

LAY PRAXIS IN A MAHAYANA CONTEXT

Holmes Welch

First of all, we have to decide what a lay Buddhist is. If we were preparing a census questionnaire for use in China, how would we phrase the entry on religion? This is not a hypothetical problem. The director of the 1961 census in Hong Kong was unable to solve it and therefore no entry on religion was included. Suppose we asked: "Do you believe in the Buddha?" In that case most of the rural population of China would answer in the affirmative, because to them *fo* (buddha) and *p'u-sa* (bodhisattva) are terms that can be loosely applied to all divinities, Buddhist, Taoist, and even Christian. If we asked: "Do you go to worship at Buddhist temples?" almost all would answer that they did, although they might add that they worshipped at other temples too. It would not help to inquire whether they called in Buddhist monks to perform rites for the dead, since this was done even in strict Confucian families that would normally have no traffic with the sangha.[1] On the other hand, if we said "Are you a Buddhist (*fo-chiao t'u*)?" we would find that instead of some claiming to be Buddhists who were not, there would be some claiming not to be Buddhists who were. This is partly because the term "Buddhist" has a little stronger connotation in Chinese than it does in English and partly because, as Gamble discovered, "a man will usually claim that [Confucianism] is his religion, even though he believes in others as well."

There are two questions, however, to which the answer would be revealing: "Have you taken refuge in the Three Jewels?" and "Have you taken the Five Vows?" All who answered either of these questions affir-

---

1. Editors' note: The author of this article has adopted *sangha* rather than *samgha* as the term designating the Chinese Buddhist monastic community.

matively would be likely to have a clear idea of Buddhism as a distinct religion and to have decided that they belonged to this religion rather than to any other. They would acknowledge that they were "Buddhists," since they had become the disciples of the Buddhist monk with whom they took the Refuges.

If they had taken the Five Vows, they would also say that they were *yu-p'o-sai* (male) or *yu-p'o-i* (female), terms transliterated from the Sanskrit *upasaka* and *upasika*. Bhiksus and bhiksunis, upasakas and upasikas, are the four groups that make up the Buddhist community. A somewhat broader term is "devotee" (*chu-shih*), literally "a person who resides [at home]." "Devotees" include not only devout laymen who have taken the Refuges or Five Vows, but those who are merely scholars and friends of Buddhism. Indeed it can be loosely applied as a title of courtesy to anyone who has any interest in Buddhism whatever. But it would not be applied to the peasant woman who offers incense to Kuan-yin in hopes of bearing a son.[2] This would be because, although she might be more devout than most devotees, she does not distinguish the Buddhist religion from any other. She has no affiliation with it. Such a woman, like the Confucian official who has a Buddhist service performed for his parents, might best be called an "occasional Buddhist." In the sections that follow, there will be an effort to keep the reader clearly informed as to what category of lay person is under discussion.

First let us consider the formal steps by which affiliation with Buddhism was celebrated. The first step, taking the Refuges, meant that the lay person declared his faith in the Buddha, the dharma, and the sangha. The second step, taking the Five Vows, meant that he promised not to kill, steal, lie, drink alcoholic beverages, or commit any immoral sexual act. The third step, taking the Bodhisattva Vows, meant that he was committed to follow the bodhisattva path in helping and saving all other creatures. These three steps could either be separated over the years, or be taken close together in a brief period.

Taking the Refuges

When the Refuges were administered by a monk to a layman, the effect was to make the layman the monk's disciple, that is, his Refuges disciple (*kuei-i ti-tzu*) and hence formally a Buddhist (*fo-chiao t'u*). Taking the

---

2. Editors' note: Kuan-yin is a feminized version of Avalokitesvara, the great bodhisattva of compassion, that developed in China.

Refuges might be compared to baptism and confirmation together. A monk did not become the Refuges disciple of another monk, or a layman of a layman.

The layman prostrated himself as he recited the Refuges and received a religious name from the monk exactly as he would if he were entering the sangha. The name included a character, which was the same as the one received by his master's tonsure disciples. The latter, therefore, could be considered his "brothers." Unlike tonsure, however, the Refuges could be taken over and over again with different masters or with the same master. Like most master-disciple relationships, it was not exclusive.

These features were universal. Others varied. Usually, for example, the disciple repeated with his own lips the formula: "I take refuge in the Buddha, I take refuge in the dharma, I take refuge in the sangha." Sometimes, however, he stood in silent assent while the master pronounced the formula on his behalf. This was the procedure, for example, when the Venerable Yueh-hsi administered the Refuges to a crowd of four hundred persons gathered in the park of the Seventy-two Martyrs in Canton before the Second World War. Afterwards they filed past and he gave each a slip of paper with their religious names. He did not give out certificates, however. This may have been because he was old-fashioned or because of the size of the crowd. Certificates became increasingly common during the Republican period (1912–1949), perhaps as a countermeasure to the baptismal certificates handed out by the Christian missionaries. Termed *san-kuei cheng-shu, kuei-i cheng*, or *kuei-i tieh*, they stated that "So-and-so of such-and-such a place has this day taken the Refuges under Reverend So-and-so," whose signature was affixed below. Usually the text of the certificate admonished the disciple to do nothing evil, but good to all, and in particular, to forsake other religions. For example, one certificate lists the following prohibitions: "If you take refuge in the Buddha, you may no longer take refuge in other religions, whether they deal with Heaven or demons, for they do not provide escape from the cycle of birth and death. If you take refuge in the dharma, you may no longer accept the scriptures of other religions, for their principles do not reflect the true reality. If you take refuge in the sangha, you may not become the disciple of a master who belongs to another, heterodox religion, because that would be the blind leading the blind." I have never seen a Refuges certificate from the Ch'ing period (1644–1912) and I do not know whether they were marked by the same sort of exclusivism.

Usually the Refuges were administered to a group, but it could just as well be done individually. One of my lay informants went to get them from the Venerable Yin-kuang. He found the great Pure Land monk in sealed confinement, and the ceremony was performed through a wicket. Yin-kuang recited the formulae and my informant repeated them after him. Next came a short explanation, and finally he was handed his Refuges certificate. Another informant, who was unable to go to Yin-kuang to take the Refuges in person, applied by letter. He soon received a certificate, already filled out, together with instructions on what to do with it. He was to place it in front of the Buddha image at home, make three prostrations, recite the formulae, and then make three more prostrations. Having done this, he could consider himself Yin-kuang's disciple. Later he took the Refuges with the abbot Hsu-yun in exactly the same way, except that a monk he knew acted as his sponsor, asking for the favor by letter and presumably assuring Hsu-yun that he was a worthy applicant.

Most masters felt little concern for worthiness. What concerned them was the opportunity to make another convert. One monk told me with pride that he had administered the Refuges to over two hundred persons. In most cases, he admitted, it had been in the form of "expedient Refuges," that is, with a simplified version of the ceremony. I was present when he made such a convert. A young woman had come to the monastery for an outing. She got into conversation with my informant, who soon suggested that she ought to take the Refuges. She seemed reluctant, so he gave her a five-minute sketch of the Buddha's life. To clinch his argument he pointed out that Buddhism was not superstitious and was being studied by foreign scholars like this American who was listening to them. Perhaps out of politeness she appeared to find the last argument irresistible. We were standing at the time some distance from the monastery buildings. He had her recite the formulae "I take refuge . . ." and bow to the south after each sentence. (I asked why the south and was properly reminded that the Buddha nature was everywhere.) Then he gave her a little talk on her future conduct. She was not to worship any popular divinities and she was to try to eat a little less meat and to avoid killing animals at home. Finally he took her name and address so that he could send her the Refuges certificate.

Such a "conversion" should not be laughed off. A seed was planted: perhaps it grew. But it is certainly fair to say that this first step in the lay Buddhist career was not necessarily an important one. While some devotees only took it after a long study of Buddhist doctrine, for other disciples it made their "occasional Buddhism" only a little less occasional.

Their master might write to them from time to time asking for money. They were usually glad to send it, since it made them feel that some of the merit he was accumulating by his pure life would be transferred to them. If he were a great abbot, like Hsu-yun, even the indifferent Buddhist would take great pride in the connection he had established by becoming his disciple. But pride too can start people along the path to enlightenment.

Lay Ordination

If the Three Refuges were an initiation, the Five Vows were an ordination. They were usually administered in a monastery as part of an ordination of monks. The ceremony was elaborate and solemn, and at the end of it a lay "ordination certificate" was conferred.[3] Serious obligations resulted. The devotee who took the vow against killing could not, for instance, hunt or fish. So seriously were the vows looked upon, in fact, that not all five were necessarily taken. When one or two were taken, it was called a "minor ordination (*shao-fen chieh*)." When three or four were taken, it was called a "major ordination (*to-fen chieh*)." When all five were taken, it was called a "plenary ordination (*man-chieh*)." In the printing of some lay ordination certificates, a space was left before the word *fen,* which could be filled in to show which of these three categories the holder belonged to. A businessman, for example, might be reluctant to take the vows against lying and stealing, since this would interfere with the conduct of his business. A person who felt unable to forgo the pleasures of the "flower house" would omit the vow against sexual license. Almost everyone, however, included the first vow: not to take the life of any sentient being. It may be argued with some force that if the Five Vows were a mere form, there would not have been such scrupulousness in taking them.

An increasing number of male devotees took the Five Vows outside monasteries during the Republican period. T'ai-hsu, for example, administered them to four hundred members of the Right Faith Buddhist Society in Hankow in 1929.[4] The ceremony was held at the

---

3. Many certificates had borders composed of three rows of tiny circles. A circle was burned each time the holder recited a text or buddha's name. When the border was completely burned, the certificate could serve as a passport through hell and was often placed in his coffin.

4. Editors' note: T'ai-hsu was the leading figure in the modernist Buddhist reform movement that developed in China during the early decades of the twentieth century.

Society's headquarters. Those being ordained first recited the Three Refuges (many of them for the first time) and then, kneeling, responded to T'ai-hsu's catechism. "Can you accept the prohibition against killing living creatures?" he asked the assembly. All those who were prepared to undertake this answered "I can," and prostrated themselves. Even some of those who were *not* undertaking it prostrated themselves, although there would have been no embarrassment if they had simply remained on their knees (or so my informant said). After the other vows had been administered, everyone received a certificate bearing his religious name as well as his surname, domicile, age, and so on—data taken from a form that they had filled out ahead of time.

More typical instances are provided by an informant who took the Three Refuges and the Five Vows under the Venerable Hsu-yun on two occasions several years apart. The first time was in Chunking during the war. A great crowd had gathered, perhaps four to five thousand persons. They were packed together so close that it was impossible to kneel or even to bow as they accepted the vows, which were relayed to them by monks standing in different parts of the field where they were assembled. According to my informant, another crowd of the same size took the vows on the following day and again on the day thereafter. "Ten to twenty thousand people became disciples of Hsu-yun in those three days," he said. This caused a delay in the delivery of their ordination certificates, which they came back to collect a week later.

Perhaps because he felt that this sort of mass ceremony was too casual, my informant took the Five Vows under Hsu-yun again, this time at the Nan-hua Ssu, Kwangtung, in 1949. The procedure was largely the same as at other large monasteries. The lay ordinees arrived at the beginning of a regular ordination of monks and nuns, and took the Three Refuges and the Five Vows on the same day that the novices took the Ten Vows. Many stayed on while the novices went through the second part of the triple ordination, and then took the Bodhisattva Vows during the third part. The night before they performed the same penance as the monks and nuns and during the actual ordination they left the hall only when the latter recited the articles of the *Fan-wang ching*. Whereas the monks and nuns were burned on the scalp, the lay ordinees were burned on the inner side of the forearm—three scars or more.[5]

---

5. Here at Nan-hua some preferred to burn six marks, some nine. At Pao-hua Shan, according to one informant, the lay ordination always involved nine scars, burned on the head, not on the arm. In his description of this monastery Prip-Moller agrees that they were burned on the head, but states that in the case of women, at any rate, there were

They too received ordination certificates (with a different text) and their names were printed at the end of the ordination yearbook.

There was no fixed charge for all this. Most of the lay ordinees made whatever donation they felt they ought to, considering the fact that they had been living in the monastery for a couple of months. The rich might give the equivalent of one or two hundred silver dollars.

Some devotees who took the Three Refuges did not go on to take the Five Vows. Some who took the Five Vows did not go on to take the Bodhisattva Vows. The relationship between those three principal steps in the lay Buddhist career is controversial. Several lay informants have insisted that the Three Refuges were never taken alone, but always in conjunction with the Five Vows. Other informants had themselves taken the Three Refuges alone. It was common to do so in a local hereditary temple under one of its heirs, and then after a few years had passed, to go to a large monastery and take the Five Vows in a group organized by one's master.

I have found similar disagreement as to whether a majority of lay people who took the Five Vows did or did not go on to take the Bodhisattva Vows. On the whole, it seems that they usually did if they went to a monastery for ordination, although there was no obligation to do so. If, however, they went to a secular place of ordination (like a lay Buddhist association) the Bodhisattva Vows were usually omitted.

In general the monastery ordinations were far more impressive. The layman who kneeled for a few minutes one morning in an auditorium cannot have felt so fully initiated as the layman who had spent two months in a secluded monastery, studying with the monks-to-be, drilling with them in the courtyard, taking part in the same night-long vigils, and burning scars onto various parts of the body (especially the scalp and forearm). Furthermore, they emerged feeling a connection with the ordaining establishment. One devotee described himself as an "heir" of the monastery where he had been ordained. He was speaking loosely, of course, because he had acquired no proprietary rights whatsoever. On the other hand, he had undoubtedly become an "ordination

---

only three, burned in a small square shaved on the middle of the scalp. An informant from Peking had only one scar burned and said that this was common there, perhaps because piety was at a lower pitch than in central China. Scars on the forearm would have the advantage of being visible evidence of the ordeal, whereas those on the head would be covered by hair. On the other hand, none of the four hundred persons who received the lay ordination from T'ai-hsu at the Right Faith Buddhist Society in Hankow had any scars burned at all. T'ai-hsu is said to have considered it "superficial."

disciple" of that monastery as much as any of the monks ordained there at the same time. Ordination disciples could—like Refuges disciples—be approached for support if it was needed.

Observance of the Lay Vows

The Bodhisattva Vows formalized the lay resolve to follow the bodhisattva path and to help all living creatures. Taken word for word, they did not appear to add a great deal to the Five Vows already accepted. Most of my informants, however, maintained that they added the obligation to be a vegetarian. The first of the Five Vows, they said, meant simply to avoid killing animals oneself or eating an animal that had been killed on one's account, while the Bodhisattva Vows forbade contributing in any way to the use of animal products.

Other informants, on the whole better qualified, took a different view. They maintained that the first of the Five Vows carried with it the clear obligation to become a vegetarian. They were quite indignant at the idea that this obligation arose only from the Bodhisattva Vows. There was a similar difference of opinion about sexual abstinence. All informants agreed that the third of the Five Vows (against illicit sexual activity) prohibited visits to a brothel or even intercourse with one's wife in an improper place at an improper time or with the use of instruments ("improper" meaning, for example, in the living room during the afternoon, which, I was told, has been in vogue among those of modern outlook). But some informants said that a devotee who had taken the Five Vows was required to put away his concubines. Others said that he was merely prohibited from taking additional concubines. Still others maintained that these restrictions did not begin until he had taken the Bodhisattva Vows. One upasaka I know, who had not taken the latter, avoided intercourse with his wife when its purpose was to satisfy sexual desire. He only had relations to beget children and, he said, children begotten without sexual desire were always superior. I have heard of devotees (though my informants were not among them) who avoided sex and animal food on holy days like the festivals of Kuan-yin and the 1st and 15th of the lunar month. There was obviously a wide variety of interpretation and practice.

Breaking the vows was distinguished from suspending or "opening" them. In the treatment of some illnesses, for example, the doctor would prescribe eggs or wine. In that case the upasaka could consume prohibited foods with a clear conscience. Nor did his conscience trouble him if he violated the vows he had *not* taken. It was up to each individual how far he wanted to go in abstinence and how much merit he wanted to accumulate. As one devotee remarked: "There is nothing embarrassing in being unprepared to give up sexual immorality. The embarrassing thing would be to take the vow and then not to carry it out."

Some lay people practiced abstinence without any formal ordination. One informant, for example, had been afflicted with eye trouble since she was a child. It was suggested that she promise to become a nun if the affliction were healed. When her grandfather vetoed this proposal, she and her two sisters promised instead a vegetarian meal on the twentieth of every month for the rest of their lives. Her eyes did improve and so every twentieth they ate vegetarian food, dedicating the merit arising therefrom to repay the merit transferred by the bodhisattva to bring about the cure.

Figure 11. The Lord of Death clutches the round of rebirth in a mural at Thiksé Monastery, Ladakh. Photograph by Matthew T. Kapstein.

Cosmology and Law (Tibet)

Buddhism is, in many important respects, a cosmological religion. Buddhists have considered dharma to be the truth about the structure and dynamics of cosmic reality (including all physical and mental realities). They have also considered dharma to be the truth about how one can attain nirvana—that is, how one can achieve "salvation" by breaking free of the ultimately unsatisfying character of all experiences that occur within cosmic reality. Finally, Buddhists have also considered that the dharma constitutes the cosmological principles that underpin the possibility for a relatively satisfactory and harmonious individual and communal existence. Given these points, it is not surprising that in early Buddhism, and in most subsequent Buddhist traditions, the basic cosmological and soteriological conceptions have been closely integrated with guidelines for proper behavior. In the case of the renunciant components of the community, these guidelines have been worked into a rather comprehensive legal system articulated in the Vinaya Pitaka and later vinaya literature. This legal system, which has developed and been adapted to changing locales and historical circumstances, has persisted for approximately 2,500 years, and is still used in monasteries and nunneries around the world.

In the case of the lay community, as we have seen in chapter 10, the guidelines have been worked into moral codes designed to guide the behavior of ordinary Buddhists. In most contexts, however, the Bud-

The essay in this chapter was taken from Rebecca Redwood French, *The Golden Yoke: The Legal Cosmology of Tibet* (Ithaca, NY: Cornell University Press, 1995), 61–67. Copyright © 1995 by Cornell University. Used by permission of Cornell University Press.

dhist community has not developed a distinctively Buddhist legal system to deal with the secular aspects of social life in a more institutional and formal way. One exception developed in Southeast Asia, where a Theravada tradition of secular law began to emerge in Myanmar around the beginning of the second millennium C.E. and was subsequently diffused and adapted in Thailand, Laos, and Cambodia. The other exception was in Tibet, where a tradition of Buddhist secular law had its origins in the seventh century C.E. This tradition continued to mature for well over a millennium, during which Tibet experienced two periods of Buddhist theocratic rule (the thirteenth to fourteenth and the seventeenth to twentieth centuries). In the following excerpt, Rebecca French analyzes various ways in which Mahayana/Vajrayana notions of cosmology informed this Tibetan tradition of Buddhist secular law as it functioned during the decades immediately before the Chinese invasion of 1959.

BUDDHIST SECULAR LAW: DOCTRINES IN CONTEXT

Rebecca Redwood French

> *A man is walking a narrow path in a sun-dappled forest. Before him on the path, amid the leaves and streaks of light, he suddenly sees a very large coiled snake. Shocked and afraid, he noiselessly turns to hide behind a tree and waits, anxiously aware of the great danger. In time, he ventures a look around the tree once more and refocuses his eyes. He focuses again. Then he comes back to the path and stares down at the snake. He sees that it is not a snake but a heavy, coiled rope in front of him. With a wave of relief, he bends down to pick it up and finds that the rope, worn with age, disintegrates in his hands into tiny strands of hemp.*
>
> Tibetan Buddhist Parable

Among the basic Tibetan concepts that affect the law are those of reality and illusion, the role of karma and the nature of rebirth, radical particularity and nonduality. These concepts are interrelated; each builds upon and is structured by the others. For example, the tripartite nature of Buddhist reality is related to the level of "afflictions" of the individual perceiver, and these afflictions are affected by the cyclical path of karma. Similarly, the awareness of the illusory nature of the world leads one to see interrelatedness rather than opposition. The role of these basic ideas in the legal system of Tibet is illustrated in the Case of the Wandering Monk.

The Illusory Nature of Reality

For the Tibetan Buddhist, the parable in the epigraph above demonstrates an essential, core truth of this life: everything we apprehend in the world is mere illusion. Like a delicious meal conjured up by a magician, our present observed reality is entirely an illusory feast; it has no substance. Appearances or "mental obscurations," as Tibetans call them, occur around us because we do not yet have the ability to see their insubstantiality. Because of our ignorance and grasping attitudes, we can see only the illusion.

The parable's images of the snake, the rope, and the hemp represent the three levels of reality available to a sentient being in this world. The first is an illusion that the man took to be real and responded to emotionally and physically. The snake is the level of appearance, the imagined aspect of reality. The second level, represented by the coiled rope, is the functional or relative aspect of reality. Finally, the tiny strands of hemp are the perfected aspect of reality, the essence of the composition of what lay before the man on the path. To see the snake, therefore, is to see an illusion. A person who cannot see the hemp does not see the world as it truly is in its perfected aspect.

In Buddhist belief, we suffer from attributing significance to the dreamlike appearances resulting from the preconceived notions and categories that we carry with us and constantly use to interpret the world. These categories of data, acquired through our senses, keep us ignorant of the true nature of reality. A Buddha, seeing the world as it actually is, sits down at the magician's table but finds no meal before him, walks down the path but finds no snake before him—only tiny strands of hemp.

This notion of illusion is of profound importance in comprehending the Tibetan view of reality, including legal reality. These realities are states of awareness for individual minds. In essence, what we see and experience daily is only one type of "is," the type of "is" our minds are capable of perceiving. Even though Tibetan judges and petitioners often commented that they could deal with a legal problem only in terms of a this-worldly or apparent reality, at the same time there was a general recognition that this-worldly facts were not ultimate or perfected facts. Disputes were engendered by mental afflictions that hinder one from understanding the perfected aspect of the world. Any dispute was, therefore, comprehensible in an entirely different way by one with a more relative or perfected vision, one not afflicted by certain mental contaminations.

It was not an uncommon move in a dispute to make reference to another frame of reality in which the same circumstances could be understood differently. For example, an old man's argument, "You may think I am just a common beggar, but how do you know I am not an enlightened saint?" immediately shifted his beating of a small child from the this-worldly reality frame of child abuse to the perfected vision of an enlightened being helping a child to burn off bad karma from a previous life.[1] Mitigation of punishment too was commonly argued with otherworldly reasoning.

Tibetans accept the presence of several simultaneously operating levels of reality, each giving clues to the next, each crafted of a degree of deceptive illusion except the last, each coexisitng with the other in a nonnirvanic space. If all a person knows of the world, legal or otherwise, is illusion, one must attempt to operate within these limitations as a legal actor with the knowledge that there are other levels of Buddhist reality. As Clifford Geertz puts it: "The movement back and forth between the religious perspective and the common-sense perspective is actually one of the more obvious empirical occurrences on the social scene. [Human beings move] more or less easily, and very frequently, between radically contrasting ways of looking at the world, ways which are not continuous with one another but separated by cultural gaps across which Kierkegaardian leaps must be made in both directions."

In Buddhism, an individual experiences rebirth into this world and begins the volitional production of both good and bad karma which will determine his or her future rebirth and chances for enlightenment. Avoiding wrong action, seeing the world without mental afflictions, and taking part in religious activities produce good karma in this life. At death the individual goes into an intermediate state and then is reborn into one of six realms.[2] Every human has had countless previous lives and will have innumerable future lives unless enlightenment is achieved. This is the cyclical nature of rebirth, a chain-of-lives connecting past, present, and future.

---

1. Editors' note: The full story is recounted by the author in chapter 18 of *The Golden Yoke*.

2. Editors' note: The six are the realms of the gods, demigods, human beings, animals, hungry ghosts, and beings in hell.

Thinking about their own and others' past and future lives comes very naturally to Tibetans; examples of this point of view abound in conversations. One Tibetan will tell you that the incarnation of his grandfather, who was a lama and is now a nineteen-year-old boy, is coming to visit him to ask for advice; an elderly Tibetan will say that he is going home to do his mantras so that he will be reborn in America; a third will talk about the future low rebirth of a man who is a known thief.

Tibetan law, both philosophically and cosmologically, is situated in a present that expands into otherworldly realms of the past and the future. Since every act done by anyone at any time is the result of both previous karma and the present possible exercise of will, a crime could have its cause in a previous life, its commission in this life, and its punishment in a future life in a lower or more difficult rebirth. In the refugee community in India, for example, when one Tibetan child made strange noises and threw a picture of the Dalai Lama on the ground, her behavior was taken as an indicator that she had been a dog in her previous life and would be reborn in a hell realm. A parable told by a Tibetan official illustrates the same idea:

The throneholder of Ganden monastery was from Khams, and he was once asked by a layman, "Holiest one, why are all Westerners so very clever?"
Then the monk said, "Why do you think that they are clever?" And the man replied, "Holiest one, they have so many things!"
So the throneholder of Ganden replied, "Westerners are not clever at all. They are fools because they engage their entire lives in working very hard to make things now for themselves. What they produce is only for this life. What we produce is for the next life, which is much more important."

The impact of these views on the legal system was significant. In any dispute settlement proceeding, a good petitioner or witness was expected to be aware of future lives and their importance. Tibetans told stories of conciliators and judges asking parties about this directly, for such awareness indicated religious and moral depth. Judges were expected to consider the past and future lives of defendants when assigning penalties. Although self-responsibility for acts and choices in this life is an essential aspect of Buddhism, there is also a recognition that karma can dictate present circumstances. Thus, Tibetans would often comment that one did not always know the reasons for particular legal circumstances, because these were rooted in a past life. And if no punishment was forthcoming for a crime in this lifetime, the presumed repercussions of future karma served as a rationalization.

Cycling in and out of lives with not just one but infinite chances for enlightenment reduced the impact of death but increased the possibility of perpetual suffering. A meritorious life now would result in less suffering in the next time around; an unmeritorious life now would result in more suffering, possibly even a rebirth in a vividly depicted hell realm. There are many stories of robbers and other criminals who, coming to the realization that they were destined for a future life of torture, converted and became religious mendicants.

Radical Particularity and Nonduality

The Tibetan world view is radically particularistic. This means that it focuses on the small component parts as ultimately real rather than the larger entity, the pieces of hemp rather than the snake. Persons are made up of infinitesimal units which are themselves in constant flux, much like the tiny strands of hemp. At its most essential, everything is in constant movement, changing its composition continuously, never stable, combining and recombining into the various accumulations that we mistake for permanent objects and individuals. Rebirth is the total recombination of millions of these units and karmic seeds. One consequence of this view is that no "self" exists in any deep sense in Buddhist philosophy, no ego or actor, no constant or permanent individuality. Tibetans believe that it is one of our common illusions to see human beings as having permanence, when they are merely combinations of tiny elements. In law, however, these notions of radical particularity rarely surfaced as a part of the legal commentary except perhaps in recitations of religious verse.

Nonduality, one result of radical pluralism in the Buddhist world view, is difficult for Americans to grasp. Nonduality eliminates binary opposition—a cornerstone of Western thought in both everyday and scholarly reasoning. At this most fundamental level two orders of truth (absolute and relative), two types of worlds (supramundane and mundane), two phenomenal levels (nirvana and samsara) do not make sense within the nondualist bounds of Buddhist philosophy. There is no actual duality of subject and object, no independent existence of anything anywhere at any moment. Any duality is an illusion. Terms that present dualistic oppositions are used for explanatory purposes only.

An enlightened being in the Mahayana context, a Buddha without mental afflictions, is not subject to the duality viewpoint of lower states of consciousness, does not see subject and object, existence and nonexistence. All Buddhas, all Bodhisattvas, and deities with this higher consciousness also realize that they are one and the same. Everything is composed of the same small parts, which are constantly realigning, forming new identities and entities. Thus, real wisdom in Tibetan Buddhist philosophy consists of comprehending the radical particularity of all existence, the nonsubstantiality of things, and the ultimate union and interrelatedness of all persons and things.

Lay Tibetans and most Tibetan nuns and monks understand basic conceptions such as radical particularity and nonduality as a sort of story about the constitution and composition of the world. These ideas perfuse Tibetan thought and discourse; they are reiterated in liturgy, incorporated into proverbs, employed as idioms and jokes, used as rationalizations, explanations, and morals. Although apparently contradictory and difficult for the non-Tibetan to comprehend, they form the background for all Tibetan jurisprudential concepts and legal rituals.

The Case of the Wandering Monk

How did notions of reality and illusion, karma and rebirth, radical particularity and nonduality operate in the legal system of Buddhist Tibet? Listen to the following narrative of a case that came before a local headman from the area of Sakya in the 1940s:

There was a headman of a region named Tseten which had a well-known monastery. One of the monks in that monastery, when his teacher died, began to leave the monastery and wander about the countryside. That monk often left during the day, and at night he came back to the monastery to steal food from the private rooms of the other monks. There were many complaints about this monk, and so a case was brought to the headman of the area by the complainants who had been burglarized.

Finally, the monk was caught and whipped and put in a jail cell in the main town of the area. The headman went to offer him food. Then, this first time, the monk returned the stolen articles and had another man pledge as a guarantor that he would not do it again, and he was freed.

But the monk continued to wander, and he returned many times to prison after this for stealing offenses. One time he escaped and went a long way away to Tsong Thopgyal, another time to the city of Gyantse, another time to Penam. He escaped several times when the jailers or guards slept and was recaptured. The first several times he was not chained in any way, and so he escaped easily. Then they put iron fetters on his legs during the night. These are the same fetters that we use on horses in the summer by putting the front and back leg together. No one knew how he escaped with the fetters on, but he did. The punishments of whipping and prison had no effect at all on him.

So the headman from that area had real pity for this monk because he was like an animal. Again, the headman had to make a decision about the wandering monk who had stolen once more, but the decision was hard for him. So the headman asked an old jailer in the prison to speak to the monk. He told him to ask the monk why he stole and how to keep him from stealing in the future. And so the monk told the jailer why he stole. He said that he was used to enjoying all the foods in all the monasteries and families that he visited, but after a little while they kicked him out. Then he didn't know how to get more food, and so he stole. After this investigation into the reasons why the monk stole, the headman asked others to see if what he said was true. People said what he said was true, and the wandering monk had never killed or stabbed anyone.

When the headman was told these reasons, he made up a new program for the wandering monk. He decided to send him home and told his father to take his son back and give him food and work to do. But his family came to see the headman and said that they didn't want the monk because it would create a bad name for their household. And so the headman had to think again, for this was a very big problem.

Finally, the headman went to see the monk. He told him that if he kept stealing, no one would like him or even want to see him. He said that he was creating very bad karma, and this karma would cause a bad rebirth. Then the headman told the monk that he was to stay in the headman's house from now on. Since he had a big family, there was enough food, and the monk was to have food, clothes, and a salary. The headman said that he hoped the monk would do this and remain good; if he didn't, both the headman and the monk were in serious trouble because many people were very upset.

And so the wandering monk came to live with the headman. He changed greatly then, and all the people were very surprised. Because he was a healthy monk and good at working, he was put in charge of all the cattle, yaks and goats of the family. The monk stayed with the family and never stole again. In time, the wandering monk became so trusted in the area that during the irrigation supply time when water was distributed, he was asked to be the one to decide which farmer should receive the water first.

At the core of this legal case are the underlying notions of karma, radical particularity, and illusion. All the Tibetan participants considered the previous life of this monk and reasoned that he was acting like an animal because he perhaps *was* an animal in a previous life. The story even hints that the monk was in some way a different sort of being, since he could get out of leg fetters, escape prison, and remain unaffected by whipping. His current self was not a constant; he was obviously afflicted with several mental obscurations that caused his actions. The headman reasoned that the monk was not motivated to commit crimes; instead, raised in a communal environment, he had a view of the world which did not privatize food.

The headman did not deal with this case from a dualistic perspective of right or wrong, guilt or innocence, correct or incorrect rule application. Instead, with a keen awareness of the monk's nature and future life, he moved beyond determination of guilt to investigate the unique causes and circumstances of the case, reveal the illusory nature of the crime, and fashion a unique solution. Such a result is particularist and does not produce a general rule. In the words of one Tibetan commentator, it was as if the headman could look past the snakelike illusion of the crime to the ropelike, relative reality of the monk's nature.

Figure 12. A *yakedura* in trance (Sri Lanka). Photograph by John Ross Carter.

CHAPTER 12

Cosmology and Healing (Sri Lanka)

Traditional Buddhist cosmologies recognize a virtually infinite number of cosmoses. These cosmoses come into being with many different domains and kinds of sentient life, and they persist for very long periods of time. Ultimately, they come to an end. In this Buddhist perspective, the cosmos in which we presently live is only one such cosmos.

One classic formulation asserts that each cosmos, including ours, consists of three realms. The realm beyond form includes a series of very high levels populated by certain exceptional deities (*brahma*) who are associated with the most refined meditative states. The realm of form includes levels of less exalted but still highly regarded deities (also known as *brahma* deities) who are also associated with meditative states. The realm of desire contains six "paths" or "courses" (the same six referred to in footnote 2 of chapter 11): deities (*deva, devata*), demigods or semi-divine giants (*asura*), human beings, animals, hungry ghosts, and hell-beings. While all beings in the Three Realms are said to undergo "suffering," hungry ghosts and hell-beings are said to suffer especially virulent types of torments because of the bad karma they have generated in their previous lives.

Buddhist depictions of our cosmos—and other cosmoses—vary from

The essay in this chapter was specifically written for this collection. It is based on research funded by a 1993–1994 Fulbright grant. In addition to the J. William Fulbright Foreign Scholarship Board, Jason A. Carbine would like to thank John Holt, P. B. Meegaskumbura, Udaya Meddegama, M. Tennakoon, S. N. Wijasingha, and the Reverends Dhammaloka and Sorata, who all helped in different but essential ways.

context to context. However, these depictions almost always crystallize around a clear hierarchical principle. The various domains and kinds of sentient life extend from the highest and most contemplative states through more or less pleasurable states down to the lowest and most abysmal hells. The different domains and types of sentient life ultimately demarcate different degrees of spiritual cultivation, moral activity, and karmic store.

A great deal of Buddhist art and architecture displays visual images associated with the various realms recognized in Buddhist cosmology and with the various figures (divine, human, and subhuman) that populate these realms. Likewise, many Buddhist rituals—very often overseen and conducted by lay Buddhist specialists rather than by monks—can be appropriately understood as an activation and deployment of cosmological components for the benefit of the Buddhist community and Buddhist individuals.

In the following essay, written specifically for this volume, Jason Carbine describes and analyzes a lay Buddhist healing ritual in which attention is focused not only on the Buddha and dharma (referred to as dhamma in this essay) but also on various kinds of sentient beings that populate the Theravada cosmos as it is understood in the highlands of Sri Lanka.

YAKTOVIL: THE ROLE OF THE BUDDHA AND DHAMMA

Jason A. Carbine

This essay describes and then briefly analyzes one type of healing ritual commonly performed among Sinhala Buddhist communities in contemporary Sri Lanka.[1] This ritual is a *yaktovil,* a lengthy (more than nine hours) and quite complex service that prevents malevolent supernaturals from overpowering a patient or patients by, among other things, bringing the patient(s) into the protective manifold of the Buddha and the dhamma (teachings). The discussion that follows derives from my personal observations of one such *yaktovil* performed in May 1994 in Sri Lanka's Kandyan highland area. The service was conducted by a group of six *yakeduras* local to the highland area. *Yakeduras,* the "ones who

---

1. The Sinhalese constitute the largest ethnic group in the country.

know the art of offering," are the ritual specialists who assume primary control over, and authority in, patient diagnosis and the performance of the *yaktovil*.

There was only one patient for the May 1994 *yaktovil*. She was a young married woman who suffered from two supernaturals in particular: the *bhuta* (a disembodied spirit or ghost) of her deceased brother and Kadawara yaka, a nature divinity (*yaka*) considered to have authority over the *bhuta*. Together, the two supernaturals were thought to be responsible for the patient's symptoms. These symptoms included various forms of psychosocial and physiological distress, ranging from troubled dreams and a self-imposed seclusion to an inability to eat solid foods.

My focus in the descriptive portion of this essay (the initial and longer of the two portions) will be to detail the ways in which the *yakeduras* employed the Buddha and dhamma to protect the patient from supernatural affliction. The concluding portion will draw from that description and offer some reflections on the social and cultural function of popular Buddhist practices—such as *yaktovil*—in the history of Theravada Buddhism in South and Southeast Asia.

Description of the *Yaktovil*

THE RITUAL AREA

The *yaktovil* took place just outside a small village shrine (*devalaya*). The shrine was considered to be the "seat" of the "power" and "authority" of all deities and of the goddess Bhadra ("auspicious") Kali in particular. While Bhadra Kali's presence was not explicit during the *yaktovil* itself, the shrine's status as a place especially associated with her presence derived from the fact that the shrine's presiding "soothsayer," a charismatic middle-aged woman, received her "warrant" for soothsaying from her.[2]

The ritual area was rectangular and demarcated on one of its longer sides by one of the walls of the village shrine itself. Four pyramid-shaped

---

2. In Sinhala Buddhist understanding, Kali is considered to be a low goddess; her standing in the cosmic hierarchy is equal to or less than that of Suniyam (Suniyam will be discussed below). People usually view Kali as a fierce supernatural who is closely affiliated with the problems and dynamics of everyday living. However, she is often considered to have—at certain times and in certain contexts—a more pleasant but still very involved character, here identified as Bhadra Kali.

offering baskets, each made of banana tree–trunk wood, sat on a low bench resting against that shrine wall. Three baskets were placed there in honor of several *yakas,* including Suniyam and Kadawara *yakas.* Each basket was of a different size and shape. Suniyam's basket, for example, was the largest (about five feet tall) and had three levels: a top cone-shaped level, a middle square level divided into four sections, and a bottom square level divided into sixteen sections. The *yakeduras* stressed that the size, shape, number of levels, and number of sections in each level of each basket were important: each was designed for a specific supernatural or supernaturals. For instance, according to one performer conducting the rite, Suniyam's basket was intended for his most beneficent form (top level), four lower forms (the middle level), and sixteen lesser male and female forms (bottom level).

Suniyam's basket contained one important item that the others did not: an "arrow" of Brahma.[3] This arrow was a straight branch with one end fashioned into the shape of an arrowhead, and it was used by the *yakeduras* during the ceremony to help command and control certain supernaturals. A live chicken—to be given to the *yakas* during the ceremony as a "craved-for-offering"—was placed under the four offering baskets. The *yakeduras* also set a small offering table to the ghosts (*pretas* and *bhutas*) to the right side of the four offering baskets.

A "flower altar" was positioned at the front of the ritual area, perpendicular to the shrine. It was an elaborate, rectangular-shaped structure standing about six feet high, four feet wide, and two feet deep. It was also made from banana tree–trunk wood, and it held offerings of fruit, vegetarian foods, white, blue, and yellow flowers, bundles of unripened coconut flowers, "weapons" and other symbolic items emblematic of the higher deities (the guardian deities of Sri Lanka, who were considered to be the gods Natha, Vishnu, Kataragama, and Saman and the goddess Pattini), and a "protection thread," which the *yakeduras* said was wound around a bundle of bodhi-tree leaves. The *yakeduras* considered the flower altar, like the shrine itself, to be a seat of the power and authority of the higher deities as well as of the triple gem (the Buddha, dhamma, and sangha).

A small offering table, the "flower-betel-leaf-offering-table," was placed at the left side of the flower altar. In addition to flowers and betel leaves, the table held a mirror, make-up, and a hair brush. All

---

3. Like Kali, Brahma was originally one of the great deities of Indian mythology who was absorbed into the Sinhala Buddhist pantheon.

of these items were in honor of Sri Kanta, the goddess of health and prosperity.

The side of the ritual area directly opposite the shrine was demarcated by a temporary fence constructed from rope and sticks. Standing just inside the fence were two small offering tables. One of the offering tables was for Bhadra Kali, and the other was for Suniyam Gambara Deviyo, an epithet designating the supernatural Suniyam as "protector of the village." Incense, flowers, and lighted lamps were placed on the two tables about half an hour before the *yaktovil* began.

The back side of the ritual area was open. This was the area from which about thirty spectators, myself included, watched the ceremony.

One final ritual offering item, an offering cup made of leaves, was assembled after the *yaktovil* began.

THE RITUAL

The *yakeduras* explained to me that the performance of the *yaktovil* was to follow the "three watches" of the night. These watches were the "evening watch," which lasted from about nine in the evening to about midnight; the "midnight watch," which lasted from about midnight to about four in the morning; and, the "morning watch," which lasted from about four in the morning to about six or seven. The proper sequencing of ritual events according to the three-part time schedule was crucial: certain supernaturals were understood to be most active during certain hours of the night, and they were said to like receiving their offerings at the proper time. For example, as will be shown below, the "time" of the powerful deity Dadimunda, as well as of the other deities above him in the cosmic hierarchy, was the evening watch; Suniyam yaka preferred the midnight watch, and Kadawara yaka preferred the morning watch.

While the following description will remain sensitive to the dynamics and events of the three watches of the night, these watches will not be used as a frame by which to describe the *yaktovil*. Rather, I will focus on one very significant and central curative tactic used in the ceremony. As the *yakeduras* explained the ceremony to me, it was composed of different but often interacting "methods" (*kramayas*, which can also be translated as "systems" or "doings") for the sake of curing patients. Some of these curative methods include the use of mantras, the proper presentation of food offerings to given supernaturals, and devotion to higher deities.

The particular curative method that concerns me here is the use of the power and authority of the Buddha and dhamma. The *yakeduras* understood the Buddha and dhamma to be morally, ethically, and cosmically powerful and thus to be potentially efficacious in curing and preventing illness. To illustrate this point, it will suffice to draw upon and present a few particular aspects of the ceremony.

Specifically, I will describe the *yaktovil* in three parts. The first part will focus on the use of the Buddha and dhamma to tap and orient the creative potential of the cosmic hierarchy. The second will describe the use of narratives about the Buddha, dhamma, and Buddha-related figures to provide a context for the patient to meditate and to establish a protective mental "boundary" (*sima*) around herself. The third will describe the use of the Buddha and dhamma to create a protective magical boundary (also a type of *sima*) around the patient's body.

Part I. Use of the Buddha and Dhamma: The Cosmic Hierarchy

Generally speaking, the *yakeduras* considered the most powerful deities (Natha, Vishnu, Kataragama, Saman, and Pattini) to be protectors of the dhamma. They did not consider this to be true for the lower supernaturals, such as Kadawara yaka and the *bhuta* afflicting the patient. In fact, the *yakeduras* considered Kadawara and the *bhuta* to be attackers of the patient's mind and body; the two supernaturals attacked the patient because they desired to consume her in various ways (for example, sexually and, more literally, as food). These desires indicated that the two supernaturals did not act, or want to act, in accordance with either the moral model articulated in the figure and life of the Buddha or the moral code (dhamma) that he taught. However, the *yakeduras* argued, with proper guidance from the more powerful supernaturals, and from the power and authority of the Buddha and dhamma, malevolent lower supernaturals could be warded off and/or tamed and transformed to accomplish the patient's cure. For the ritual performers, then, the Buddha and dhamma were to be activated and employed within the context of the entire cosmic hierarchy to repulse the attacks of Kadawara and the *bhuta* causing the patient's physical and mental illness and threatening to bring about her death.

The most explicit linkings of cosmic power with the Buddha and dhamma occurred during the appearances of the four supernaturals in the *yaktovil* area. In order of appearance, these four supernaturals were: (1) Dadimunda, a *deva* (god/deity) understood to be a "commander" of *yakas* who acts under the authority of Vishnu, a supreme guardian deity of the Buddhist dhamma in Sri Lanka; (2) Suniyam, a supernatural situated just below Dadimunda in the cosmic hierarchy and considered to have two primary forms, one *deva* and one *yaka;* (3) the *bhuta* afflicting the patient; and (4) Kadawara yaka, who was understood to be presiding over the *bhuta* on the one hand and acting under the authority of Suniyam on the other.[4] The appearances of the supernaturals were particularly significant in that descending and successive levels of the cosmic hierarchy (*deva, deva/yaka, yaka,* and *bhuta*) received elaboration and were shown to be ultimately subservient to the authority and power of the Buddha and dhamma. In the final analysis, a direction of power obtained, wherein Dadimunda, Suniyam, Kadawara, and the *bhuta,* each representative of different levels of the cosmic hierarchy, became channels through which the cure of the patient was achieved.

Dadimunda appeared in the *yaktovil* area first. At the beginning of the evening watch, *yakeduras* positioned themselves between the flower altar and the patient. They sang a characteristically drawn-out and melodious repetition of "Namo Namo" ("worship worship") and offered homage to the Buddha, dhamma, and sangha. They then called upon the authority, power, and virtues of the Three Gems to "please" most if not all of the supernaturals of the Sinhala Buddhist pantheon so that they would come to the ritual area and help with the cure of the patient.

Upon the invitations that were in honor of him, Dadimunda entered a ritual medium (the soothsayer of the Bhadra Kali shrine) and powerfully danced his way into the ritual area. He approached the flower altar, shook his head back and forth, worshiped the flower altar, and turned to speak with the *yakeduras,* who had moved to the sides of the ritual area.

Dadimunda's attitude was one of protection and overarching be-

4. In the *yaktovil* context discussed here the term *deva* was used to refer to two deities (Dadimunda and Suniyam) who are, in other Sinhala Buddhist contexts, called *devata,* or beings who hold a status between the higher gods and *yakas.* In keeping with the actual ritual usage, I have retained the term *deva* in my description.

Also, the reader will recall the discussion above in regard to Suniyam's offering basket; Suniyam's "four lower forms" and "sixteen lesser male and female forms," according to the *yakedura* who furnished the information about that offering basket, were considered manifestations of his primary *yaka* form. Further, the *yakedura* also specified that Suniyam's most "beneficent form" was his *deva* form.

nevolence. He half jokingly asked the ritual performers why the *bhuta* afflicting the patient had not responded to earlier offerings and efforts to make him leave, and he announced that he would indeed use his own authority to control the *bhuta*. Dadimunda signaled to the *yakeduras* to begin drumming again, and he danced. He then stopped and gave the patient and household members medicinal and protective prescriptions and, having stated his pleasure at the ritual structures, smells, and offerings, departed from the medium. The medium, dazed, slowly walked out of the ritual area.

Dadimunda's appearance verified and emphasized two important points regarding the active presence of divine agency in the *yaktovil*. First, as the *yakeduras* explained to me during and after the ceremony, Dadimunda recognized the authority of the deities above him in the cosmic hierarchy, particularly the authority of Vishnu who was (again, to reemphasize) considered the most important protector of Buddhism in Sri Lanka. Dadimunda, so they said, had received a command from Vishnu to come to the ritual area and to help the *yakeduras*. Second, and more explicitly expressed in his actions, Dadimunda recognized that he should act to uphold certain moral ideals propounded by the Buddha. These ideals included a compassionate desire to assuage the patient's psychosocial and physiological distress.

Suniyam appeared in the ritual area about two hours after Dadimunda, at the beginning of the midnight watch. One of the *yakeduras* instructed the patient to sit and fold her hands to her face. He then waved the arrow of Brahma at the offering baskets and—calling on the power of the Buddha and dhamma—commanded the *yakas* to focus their "gaze" on the offering baskets and the patient. The *yakedura* then picked up the chicken, dangled it in front of the offering basket to Suniyam, and narrated its origin. Suniyam, in his form as a *yaka*, took control of the medium's body, and, sitting in a chair away from the patient, licked his lips and jumped into the middle of the ritual area. He announced himself as Suniyam yaka, grabbed the chicken (but not the arrow of Brahma) from the *yakedura*, trampled over the patient, and danced violently around the area. Suniyam then threw the chicken at the ground in front of the offering baskets, crouched before the patient, licked his lips again, and shook his head in her face. The patient flinched with fright but remained seated. Suniyam, seating himself next to the patient, spoke to the *gurunnanse* (the chief *yakedura*).

Suniyam: I am Suniyam yaka! I accept the offerings! Happily!
[the patient screams]

gurunnanse: This patient is ill. She is sick because of an illness caused by
the *bhuta.* Tell the *bhuta* to go away quickly.

[pause]

   g: Tell the *bhuta* to go quickly.

[pause]

   g: You will be pleased to do this.
   S: Yes.
   g: [waves the arrow of Brahma] Say it!
   S: I am pleased to help this patient!
   g: You promise to do this!

[pause]

   g: You promise!
   S: Yes! I promise!
   g: You will protect this patient!

[pause]

   g: [waves the arrow of Brahma] You will protect this patient!
       Say it!
   S: Yes, I will protect this patient.
   g: And this house!
   S: And this house! [5]

Ultimately assuring his acceptance of the offerings and swearing to command the *bhuta* to leave, Suniyam blessed the patient, careened his way
toward the flower altar, worshiped it, and departed from the medium.
Again, the medium, dazed, walked out of the ritual area.

   The meaning and efficacy of Suniyam yaka's appearance paralleled that
of Dadimunda's. Suniyam recognized the authority of the deities above
him in the cosmic hierarchy. He recognized the importance of curing and
protecting the patient. Most significant, he also recognized the authority and power of the Buddha and dhamma. All these points were made
explicit when, after promising to protect the patient, Suniyam worshiped
the flower altar, which was clearly recognized by all concerned as the seat
of the power and authority of the Buddha and dhamma and of the
higher deities.

   The *bhuta* appeared in the *yaktovil* area about two hours after
Suniyam. *Yakeduras* stood over the patient while she held out part of the
offering basket to the *bhuta;* at this point they narrated a story pertain-
ing to the life of King Bimbisara. (This story involving a king to whom
the Buddha preached will be discussed below.) At the conclusion of the

---

5. This and the other conversations presented below have been abbreviated for purposes of inclusion here.

narration, the *yakeduras* intensified the rhythm of their drum accompaniment, and the *bhuta* took possession of the medium and semi-danced his way into the ritual area. He sat down beside the patient and had a discussion with the *gurunnanse* (who was holding and waving the arrow of Brahma). Their discussion concluded with an emphasis on the power of the Buddhas.

gurunnanse: By the Buddhas, you swear to leave.
    bhuta: By the Buddhas, I swear to leave.
        g: (the Buddhas) Kasyapa, Gautama, and Kakusanda, say their names![6]
[pause]
        g: Say their names!
        b: Kasyapa, Gautama, and Kakusanda.

After repeating the names of the Buddhas, the *bhuta* left the ritual area and, significantly, "departed" from the patient. This meant, according to the *yakeduras,* that he consented to remove his malevolent influence.

Kadawara yaka was the last supernatural to appear in the ritual area. At about 4:00 A.M., the onset of the morning watch, the *yakeduras* prepared and offered his offering cup made of leaves. It contained meat, rice, and fish and was topped with flowers. The *yakeduras* sang poetic songs and intoned mantras, and Kadawara entered the medium. Much like the other supernaturals before him, Kadawara yaka danced his way into the ritual area and crouched beside the patient and spoke with the *gurunnanse.*

Kadawara: I have accepted the offerings! I am happy! I am truly sending away the patient's illness. The younger brother has accepted his offerings. He has happily accepted his offerings.
gurunnanse: By the Buddha, you swear that this is so!
    K: I swear. I am not doing any harm. I swear.
    g: [waving the arrow of Brahma] You must go quickly by the power of the Buddha.
    K: I am going, I am going, I am going! I said I was going by the Buddha's power. Truthfully!

---

6. In Theravada mythology, Kakusanda and Kasyapa are, respectively, the twenty-second and twenty-fourth Buddhas in a standard list of twenty-four Buddhas who precede Gautama (the historical Buddha). Theravada mythology also considers the three of them, along with the Buddha Konagamana (twenty-third of the twenty-four) and the Buddha-to-come, Maitreya, to be the five Buddhas of the present "era."

At this point, there was a pause, and Kadawara yaka asked the *yakeduras*
if they could dance. They answered yes, and a dance and song contest
ensued. Kadawara could not match or keep up with the *yakeduras* in their
rhythms and drumbeat and did not know the words to songs he claimed
to know. Kadawara, now worn out, was addressed by the lowest-caste
ritual performer.[7]

performer: So what is it that you will do?
Kadawara: I will give protection to this place and patient. I will not harm.
I accept your offerings.

After this proclamation, Kadawara departed.

With some resistance Kadawara acknowledged several crucial points.
He acknowledged the authority of the Buddha. He acknowledged that
he was delighted to help the patient. He acknowledged that he had
indeed commanded the *bhuta* to leave the patient. Finally, he acknowledged that he would protect the patient. These acknowledgments were
extremely significant, for it was clear at this point that Kadawara had been
tamed, in the sense of being controlled by human and divine agency. Indeed, he was now subject even to the authority of the lowest-caste ritual
performer. Further, Kadawara had been thoroughly transformed in that
his power had been channeled for creative and protective "this-worldly-
oriented" (*laukika*) ends rather than destructive ones. Thus, the use of
the Buddha and dhamma in the course of the *yaktovil* served to direct
and orient the hierarchy of cosmic powers—from Dadimunda and the
highest deities to the lowest *yaka* and *bhuta*—in a very positive way. It
should come as no surprise that Kadawara's transformation was one of
the final events of the *yaktovil*.

Part II. Use of the Buddha and Dhamma:
Narratives and Meditation

Also important to the patient's cure was a particular type of meditation
known as "recollection" (*anusmrtiya*) of the Buddha. The *yakeduras* intended this meditation to make the patient reflect upon a variety of stories concerned with the power and "morality" (*sila*) of the Buddha and
dhamma. Three such stories were: (1) the Buddha's life; (2) King Vijaya's
arrival in Sri Lanka (a story recounted in the Buddhist mythohistory of

---

7. A caste system continues to exist in Sri Lanka, the only Buddhist country where
this is the case.

the island); and (3) King Bimbisara's efforts to curtail the sordid habits of a malevolent *yaka*.

During the recitation of the story of the Buddha's life, one of the very first events of the evening watch, the *yakeduras* covered the patient with a white cloth associated with the purity and protective power of the Buddha. They then exhorted the patient to listen to, first in prose and then in poetic verse, the story of the Buddha's final birth. The *gurunnanse* jokingly asked the patient, "Who is the Buddha? What did he do? How did he do it?" The audience and even the patient herself laughed. The *gurunnanse* answered his own questions with the important events in the Buddha's life: his birth, his renunciation, his meditation and enlightenment (the conquering of Mara), his acceptance of a gift of milk-rice from the woman Sujata, and his attainment to the "supreme blowing out." This account of the Buddha's life concluded with the proclamation that "By the power of the virtues of the Buddha all illnesses will leave the patient" and with the benediction "Long life! Long life! Long life!"

Sometime after the narration of the Buddha's life, a *yakedura* again exhorted the patient to attentively listen to another story, a narration about the arrival of the first Sinhala king, Vijaya, in Sri Lanka. King Vijaya and his men arrived in Sri Lanka only to find themselves harassed by the *yakini* (female *yaka*) Kuveni and her minions. Vijaya and his men ultimately discovered that she could not harm them because of a protection thread that was given to them by the King of Gods, Sakka, on behalf of the Buddha himself.

Just before the *bhuta* entered the ritual area, the ritual performers recited another story, that of the morally righteous king, Bimbisara. Bimbisara was concerned for his people because they were being harassed and eaten by a *yaka*, and he ultimately protected his people by giving the *yaka* gifts of food. The *yaka*, happy with his gifts, offered to protect the people rather than eat them.

The *yakeduras* narrating the stories of the Buddha's life, of King Vijaya, and of King Bimbisara stated that the patient, on hearing and reflecting upon the stories, became "happy in the mind" or "having good thoughts." They stated this was possible because the narratives were accounts depicting the potential for the alteration or prevention of mental and physical suffering, particularly through the power and morality of the Buddha and his teachings. The narratives, and the meditation upon them, were thus meant to remind and inculcate in the patient the notion that her protection against any malevolent supernatu-

ral stemmed from three things: her understanding of the nature and
efficacy of the Buddha's own meditation, her establishment in the Buddha's dhamma, and the degree to which she herself followed the basic
model of the Buddha and used her establishment in the dhamma to calm
her mind.

Ultimately, the *yakeduras* stressed that the patient could create a mental boundary, thereby preventing Kadawara and the *bhuta* from harming
her. She could do this by recollecting and reflecting on the narratives
about the Buddha and Buddha-related figures. This point is crucial, because it should be understood that the Kandyan *yaktovil* was not simply
framed by a Buddhist psychology. Indeed, the Buddhist meditative ethos
for severing the ties to the cycle of rebirth—an ethos exemplified by
and in the Buddha and his dhamma—was used to assuage the patient's
immediate physical and mental illness. True to the Theravada paradigm
of liberation from suffering, the narratives were meant to provide the
context for the patient to protect herself by the power of her own mind.

Part III. Use of the Buddha and Dhamma: The Protection Thread

In the previous section I pointed out that the story recounting the protection thread's origin functioned as a meditative device for the patient.
The actual protection thread itself, tied around the patient's neck at the
conclusion of the *yaktovil,* may have also served this function. That
is, meditating on what the protection thread embodied (the power and
virtues of the Buddha and dhamma) may have also provided the patient
with a context for the cultivation of mental calmness.

However, the physical employment of the protection thread accomplished something a bit different from the narrative of its origin: It
established a physically efficacious magical boundary around the patient.
To take some license with the imagery, not inappropriate to the physically framing and encompassing function of the protection thread, it
bounded the patient's body within a shield of dhamma.

This shield of dhamma protected the patient from possible mental
and physical encompassment by the *yakas* and *bhuta*. Also important, it
held off their "attraction," their "sight," and their "shadow," all three
of which are believed to play key roles in *yaka-* and *bhuta*-induced illnesses. As it was explained to me, the *yaka* or *bhuta*, attracted to a victim,
directs its sight upon him or her and then physically goes toward him or

her in such a way that its shadow forms a boundary around the victim, and this is how the *yakas* or *bhutas* can exert their strongest influence over the victim. Thus, it is this encompassment that the protection thread aims to block.

According to the *yakeduras,* the protection thread accomplished its objective in two overlapping ways: first, and explicit in its origin myth, the thread physically embodied the power of the Buddha's dhamma; second, as suggested by the same myth, the thread embodied the protective powers of the higher deities who act on behalf of the Buddha and dhamma. Both kinds of overlap may be more clearly understood from the following.

During the *yaktovil,* the patient held the protection thread on one end while the other end remained tied to the flower altar. As long as the patient held the protection thread, the protective power of the dhammaically oriented deities, and of the Buddha and dhamma, was said to flow from the flower altar to the patient. At the conclusion of the ceremony, the *yakeduras* untied the thread from the flower altar and used it to tie a rolled-up *yantra* (a protective design etched onto a copper sheet) around the patient's neck.

Ultimately, the protection thread purified the patient's body of any malevolent supernatural influence and then physically protected her from any further *yaka* or *bhuta* attack. Indeed, both Kadawara and the *bhuta* were said to fear the power of the protector deities, the Buddha, and the dhamma. They were also said to be unable to penetrate the newly established protective boundary even if they wanted, above all because the protection thread itself derived its efficacy from the power of the moral ethos of the Buddha and dhamma.

Concluding Remarks: A Brief Historical Perspective

Enough has been described to demonstrate the pervasive presence and pragmatic function of the Buddha and dhamma in the *yaktovil.* It is significant that these pragmatic uses of the Buddha and dhamma are attempts to permeate the *yaktovil* with the power and efficacy of Theravada soteriology—a soteriology that is ultimately believed to show one how to break free from all forms of suffering. Indeed, the very power and efficacy of the *yaktovil* is seen in crucial ways to depend upon the nature of the Buddha and dhamma, both of which represent, embody, and exemplify Theravada soteriology.

There are many possible reasons why *yakeduras* have incorporated certain Theravada soteriological symbols into *yaktovil* practice. Three stand out in particular. One reason is that the *yakeduras* simply perceive the soteriological symbols to be efficacious in combating malevolent supernaturals and also in bringing about patient cure. A second is that Sinhala Buddhist cultural pressure and prestige may prompt *yakeduras* to accept the social and cultural authority of Theravada soteriology and thus to legitimate their practices in terms of that soteriology. A third is that Theravada soteriological legitimization of a particular religious practice (such as *yaktovil*) may actually happen, so to speak, by default. As John Holt points out, religious practices, if they are perceived to be efficacious for everyday existential concerns and not directly opposed to Theravada soteriology, will be legitimated in terms of that soteriology. These three possibilities have, in all likelihood, occurred and will continue to occur.

However, my presentation of the presence and function of the Buddha and dhamma in the *yaktovil* are intended to show that the first possibility is crucial. The linking of the *yaktovil* with Theravada soteriology does not occur outside the context of the ways in which *yakeduras* understand the symbols to have, or to be capable of having, certain power. In other words, how and if the soteriological symbols can practically function in regard to an immediate existential concern (patient cure) determines their incorporation in the *yaktovil*.

The incorporation and synthesis of particular Theravada symbols in the *yaktovil* itself serve to legitimate the authority of Theravada soteriology. The *yaktovil* performance casts Theravada soteriology as a repository of power and knowledge that can be drawn on for the assuagement of everyday problems (such as illness). Indeed, in the *yaktovil*, the Buddha and dhamma come to morally and physically encompass and pervade the entire cosmos, from the realm of the highest deities to the level of the individual mind and body of the patient. It should be stressed that this constitutes a significant contribution to the construction of a larger social and cultural drive to maintain the Theravada meditative ethos and thus the institution (the sangha) that sustains that ethos. If the social and cultural prestige of Theravada soteriology does play a part in prompting *yakeduras* to incorporate the Buddha and dhamma into the *yaktovil* practice, one must certainly understand the *yaktovil* as itself (re)productive of such authority.

Popular religious practice (in the present study, exemplified by the *yaktovil*) and Theravada soteriology are thus engaged in a mutually interactive process of legitimation. The Theravada soteriology provides a

source from which particular symbols may be drawn and used to legitimate and substantiate not only the immediate power and efficacy of the
yaktovil but its social and cultural status and prestige as well. At the
same time, the *yaktovil,* with its incorporation of such symbols, legiti-
mates both the Theravada soteriology and the institution that preserves
that soteriology as repositories of authoritative meaning and knowledge
necessary not only for a patient's health and harmony but also for the
health and harmony of society at large. The contemporary presence of
the Theravada tradition in South Asia, and presumably in Southeast Asia,
derives in great part from the ways in which people have creatively and
actively used the symbols of the Buddha and dhamma to solve the problems of everyday living. Indeed, a Sinhala Buddhist curative practice has
given the Buddha himself an enduring life, a life rooted in the continuing human drive to transform life itself.

Figure 13. A Japanese monk prepares to conduct a ritual at a shrine. Photograph by Michel Strickmann.

CHAPTER 13

Devotional Rituals: Recent Innovations (Sri Lanka)

Devotion is a dimension of religious expression that has been intrinsic to Buddhism since the very earliest strata of Buddhist tradition that we can discern. The term *bhagavan* ("blessed one"), which has strong devotional connotations, was one of the earliest ways of referring to the Gautama Buddha. As Buddhism developed, various other Buddhas and bodhisattvas also became objects of devotion. Devotional practices were perennially prominent among Buddhist renunciants and perhaps even more important among members of the Buddhist laity.

Though the Theravada school of Sri Lanka and Southeast Asia has sometimes been identified as a Buddhist school in which devotion has been severely if not completely muted, this is clearly not the case. The fact is that devotion, particularly devotion to the Gautama Buddha, played a prominent role in early Theravada contexts, and it came increasingly to the fore in an important corpus of Theravada literature produced in Sri Lanka in the early centuries of the second millennium C.E. The significant role of devotion has strongly persisted there and in other Theravada contexts up to the present day.

As Theravadins (and other Buddhists as well) have searched for new modes of religious expression and experience that resonate with people living in the late twentieth century, new experiments in the cultivation of devotional practice have been undertaken. The following essay by Richard Gombrich describes a fascinating liturgical experiment of this

The essay in this chapter is an abbreviated form of Richard Gombrich, "A New Theravadin Liturgy," *Journal of the Pali Text Society* 9 (1981): 47–73. Copyright © 1981 by Richard Gombrich. Used by permission.

kind: a new Theravada liturgy in Sri Lanka. Gombrich supplements his description with a translation of the devotional words actually employed in the ritual process.

A NEW THERAVADIN LITURGY

Richard Gombrich

We shall here present a text acquired orally, though we have also made use of printed pamphlets. Theravada Buddhist liturgical texts are few, and those used in Sri Lanka have hitherto been entirely in Pali. The text presented here is partly in Pali, partly in Sinhala. In content there is nothing radically new, but the religious service at which this text is used has a distinctive flavour which ever larger numbers of Sinhalese Buddhists find appealing.

The service has been invented and the text assembled, and in part composed, by a young monk called Panadure Ariyadhamma. The service he calls an *Atavisi Buddha Puja* ("Worship of the Twenty-eight Buddhas"), or simply a *Buddha Puja,* has become popularly known as a *Bodhi Puja,* and we shall see that this reflects a misunderstanding. So far most of the public performances of this *Buddha puja* have either been conducted by the Ven. Ariyadhamma himself or have used tape recordings of him, so that it is not yet possible to say whether the service can become popular without his participation as its leader. Not only does he have a most pleasing appearance and personal presence; his voice is extremely mellifluous and he chants in a musical way which contrasts strikingly with the usual clerical drone. When you mention the Ven. Ariyadhamma to people, his voice is usually the first thing they talk of. Those who know him personally, however, are devoted to him for more solid reasons: he radiates calm and kindness, and appears in his conduct to come as close as possible to the Buddhist ideal. He does not collect possessions, and every month when he has been conducting *Buddha puja* and the congregations in homage have presented him with masses of goods (mainly sets of the eight requisites, the conventional offering to a monk on such an occasion) he gives it all away to other monks. He does not even own proprietary rights in any monastery. He devotes himself to the religious life, both to preaching and to meditation (necessarily concentrating on the two activities in alternating periods), but without losing sympathy for other people and interest in their problems. In contrast to most modern monks who are in the public eye, he keeps himself totally apart from secular public affairs: when we asked him whether he took any interest in politics he replied that his lack of involvement in politics was so complete that that he did not even want to say he was against politics. He says that he is completely free of lay responsibilities, and now fills a frame he made for himself.

When we interviewed him, in September 1978, he explained that he does not normally give interviews and tries not to receive personal publicity. But he does not object to the publication of a few factual details. He conceived the desire to become a monk when quite young, but at first his parents did not approve of the idea and it took some time to bring them round to it. Before that, he had a job as clerk with the Anuradhapura Preservation Board, which looks after the ancient capital. He studied Buddhism both at school and at Buddhist Sunday school, and began to learn Pali. He also took up meditation while still a layman; he studied it at the famous meditation centre at Kanduboda.

The greatest day of his life arrived on 22 December 1966, when he finally entered the Order in the presence of all his relations and 39 monks at a meditation centre in a Colombo suburb. He was ordained into the Amarapura Nikaya by the Ven. Kudavalle Vangisa Nayaka Thero. The happiness he felt on that occasion was past all description. His higher ordination took place at Kanduboda with its incumbent, the Ven. Kahatapitiye Sumatipala, acting as sponsor at the ceremony and the Ven. Kudavalle Vangisa as tutor. After that he went and stayed, practising meditation in a cave by himself, at a forest hermitage, Kaludiyapokuna Arannasthana, at Mihintale near Anuradhapura.[1] He still goes there for periods of meditation. But in so far as he has any permanent base it is in a village monastery at Jaltara, near Hanvalla in the Low Country of south-western Ceylon.

He first evolved his distinctive form of *Buddha puja* around 1972, and celebrated it quietly with a few people in Jaltara. But its fame quickly spread. He conducts isolated services, like the one in honour of a monk's birthday which we have here recorded; but what are famous are the series of services held daily for a fortnight or a month at about 6 P.M. This time coincides with the traditional hour for the evening offering to the Buddha, but it is presumably chosen because it is convenient for people who have to go to work. The Ven. Ariyadhamma conducted such a series of *Buddha puja* successively at Divulapitiya, in Kandy, Negombo,

---

1. Editors' note: Mihintale and Anuradhapura are sacred places connected with the arrival and subsequent development of Buddhism on the island. They are located in the north central region.

Chilaw, Nuwara Eliya, Matale, and Galle. From Kandy on, these are all fair-sized towns, and the services were held not at monasteries but at Buddhist "centres," such as the Y.M.B.A., or even at normally secular premises.[2] This was necessary to accommodate the increasing crowds which assembled, despite the Ven. Ariyadhamma's avoidance of newspaper publicity. (He does not allow his sermons to be advertised in advance in the daily papers, as are others likely to be of wide interest.) At Matale in 1977 the crowds reached fifty or sixty thousand; at Galle in 1978 the month-long series drew crowds which the police finally estimated at a hundred thousand.

It is time now to characterize the service, and in so doing to justify the use of the word "service" and to explain its popularity. Traditional Theravada Buddhism has certain set ritual forms for the clergy such as the higher ordination ceremony and corporate fortnightly confession, but nothing remotely analogous for the laity. An ordinary *Buddha puja* is an offering to the Buddha made by an individual. At every temple the incumbent is responsible for seeing to it that it is made thrice daily. The individual making the offering usually recites (murmurs) certain Pali verses. If others are present, they are supposed to participate in spirit; they empathize, and thus gain merit. But their empathy takes no liturgical form. When monks and laity come together for religious purposes, their roles are complementary. Thus, when people come to the temple to hear a sermon, the monk preaches and the laity listen, participating only by occasional exclamations of "Sadhu!" (which is often shortened to "Sa!"). The monk administers the five precepts to the laity by having the laity repeat them after him; he faces the laity, is seated on a higher level, and is treated with the greatest formal respect.

Against this background, the new *Buddha puja* has four striking features. First and foremost, there is constant active participation by the congregation, for they chant or recite the entire liturgy themselves, in unison, either with the monk conducting the service or after him. In the former case, of course, the monk temporarily appears but as a member of the congregation, and this is the second striking feature: the monk conducting the service sits as a member of the congregation, like them facing the Buddha image in an attitude of humility. Before the Buddha he thus appears merely as *primus inter pares. A fortiori* the same position is adopted by any other monks present, so that they simply participate

2. Editors' note: The Y.M.B.A. is the Young Men's Buddhist Association, patterned after the Young Men's Christian Association introduced by Western missionaries.

as members of the congregation, whereas if any other monks besides the preacher attend a traditional sermon they sit on the higher level facing the laity and do nothing at all.

The third feature of this *Buddha puja* is that not all of it is in Pali; it includes Sinhala. And the final feature to which we draw attention is the heightened dramatic content and emotional tone. Few preachers ever make the slightest effort to involve their audiences emotionally (unless it be to instill in them fear of the consequences of wrong-doing), and indeed one could well argue that since Buddhism stresses the danger of the emotions and the necessity for their careful control, it is absolutely appropriate for Buddhist events to take place in an atmosphere of calm, even flatness. But the Ven. Ariyadhamma is not at all afraid of emotion. He told us that when Maha Pajapati, the Buddha's stepmother, became a nun, she said to him: "You are now my Buddha mother and give me the milk of immortality"; the story makes him weep with emotion. The words which are constantly on his lips, as well as featuring prominently in his service, are such words as loving-kindness, compassion, pity, and above all comfort, consolation. He also frequently mentions evenness of temperament, both as a quality of the Buddha and as a condition for others to aspire to. But it is perhaps his peculiar genius to realize that between the layman walking in off the street and this ideal state of calm there lies a gap which requires some emotional bridge. Not innovating, but bringing into unusual prominence an element from the tradition, the Ven. Ariyadhamma stresses loving-kindness, both the parental love which the Buddha felt for all creatures and which we may legitimately still project onto him, and the love, of the same quality, which we in our turn must cultivate. In recalling these qualities of the Buddha, he said to us, people's thoughts become broader and open out like a flower blossoming. The main message of the sermon we heard was that everyone should meditate daily on the qualities of the Buddha and practise loving-kindness. The climax of his *Buddha puja* likewise expresses the receiving of consolation and the giving of love. The sermon leads into a pair of Sinhala verses, chanted three times, saying that the one consolation for life's troubles lies in the Buddha and ultimately in nirvana. In the first of the verses the word *sanasilla*, "consolation," is anaphorically repeated in each line of the quatrain; the second verse culminates in the word *sanasima*, "consolation" again. Immediately after this the leading monk expresses in the most concise way possible, with four words of Sinhala prose, the essence of Buddhist loving-kindness: "May all beings be happy!" The congregation repeats the words. The monk, with superb histrionic insight, repeats them three more times, each time more quietly, and each time the congregation's response is more muted. The murmur of the fourth repetition is followed by profound silence, as everyone attempts to suffuse his own thoughts, and thence the whole world, with loving-kindness. The silence is finally broken, on the monk's cue, with a loud exclamation of "Sa!" and everyone breaks into a loud, fast repetition in a monotone of the *Metta Sutta,* the scriptural and thus the traditional liturgical form given to the same sentiments. Reciting the *Metta Sutta* in a monotone is a return to comparative banality, but after the deep emotion which preceded it the tone sounds triumphant and represents a return to the daily round with new vigour and confidence.

The first salient feature of the *Buddha puja,* the large part played in it by the congregation, is what impels us to call it a "service," using a term with an originally Christian denotation. When we see the officiating monk facing the altar and merely heading the congregation, rather than addressing them *de haut en bas,* we are again reminded of the Christian form. The switch from the ancient language to the vernacular can remind us of Protestant Christianity, and indeed of Roman Catholicism since Vatican Two. And if we are set on such comparisons, we could even find analogues in Christianity to the heightened emotional tone. But the Ven. Ariyadhamma assures us, convincingly, that there has been no direct Christian influence. He has never attended a Christian service and does not know what they are like. But in them, he says, people sing hymns to music, whereas he does not consider that in his service there is any music. The importance of this point for him presumably resides in the fact that music is forbidden to monks. He told us that in forest hermitages it is common for the monks to chant in unison, and he has merely extended the practice. We may comment that for monks in a hermitage to ignore status differences is quite another matter from giving such equality ritual expression when it comes to interaction between monks and laity; but that is a dimension with which he is not concerned. The use of Sinhala he likewise does not see as at all radical, perhaps with more justification, since Buddhism has no ideological opposition to the use of vernacular languages—quite the contrary. The attempt to bring religion nearer to the people, and especially to respond to demands by an educated urban middle class for more participation in the religion to which they are nominally affiliated has everywhere produced the same result. Finally, scrutiny of the text will show that its sentiments are indeed truly and distinctively Buddhist and that the Ven. Ariyadhamma has merely chosen, notably in the Sinhala verses he has composed, to stress that side of the tradition which seems to him (no doubt rightly) to be most accessible to lay religiosity.

The service lasts two to three hours, but the set part (given below) takes up only about an hour. Most of the rest of the time is taken by the sermon proper, which always occurs at the same point in the service and ends by leading into the climax of the service mentioned above. Even during the sermon the monk maintains his untraditional position facing the Buddha image(s) with his back to the laity. The rest of the time is accounted for by other little speeches the monk makes. The main one of these comes after the first section of the service, the taking of the three refuges and eight precepts (though not the usual eight); in it the monk speaks about the occasion for the service and dedicates the merit accruing from it. A similar speech very near the end of the service distributes the merit to all participants and those connected with them, as is customary; it has the function of a kind of valedictory blessing.

It remains to comment on two points. The interest of the first resides in its illustrating an important principle of scientific method: that you cannot find what you are not looking for. This *Buddha puja,* as its full title indicates, is strictly for all the 28 Buddhas recognized in the Pali tradition. This multiplicity has no importance for the text or message of the service, and the Ven. Ariyadhamma himself said that philosophically all the Buddhas were the same. When one of these *Buddha puja* is held, 28 pictures of the Buddha are put up in a row over a long flower altar; devotees queue up to offer flowers on this altar just before the service starts; and even so long an altar can barely hold all the offerings. Thus the multiplication is useful in the ritual. But this was not its origin. We were told by lay supporters that making offerings to the 28 Buddhas was an old custom. In our research in the Up Country we had come across offerings only to the 24 Buddhas, never the 28. We asked scholarly Sinhalese friends, and they too knew of no such old custom. We then met a monk who was conducting an *Atavisi Buddha puja* on the Ven. Ariyadhamma's instructions. He too asserted that the 28 Buddhas were traditionally worshipped, and to corroborate this he said that very day at midday when food is offered before the Tooth Relic at the Temple of the Tooth in Kandy it is offered in 32 parts, for the 28 Buddhas plus the 4 Buddhas so far born in our eon (who thus figure twice). We had just read H. L. Seneviratne's admirable book, *Rituals of the Kandyan State,* which gives a minutely detailed account of those very offerings but makes no mention of the 28 Buddhas or 32 parts; we were accordingly sceptical. But we were able to go to Kandy and ask the official in charge of the daily offerings. The monk was right. Every day 32 measures of rice are cooked for the morning and midday offerings, and 32 curries prepared. Seneviratne could not see 32 portions because no doubt the figure is purely conceptual and rarely or never empirically observable. In our ritual too the number is essentially conceptual: despite what has been said above, at the first *Buddha puja* we attended there was restricted space for the flower altar and we counted only 12 Buddha images; at the second there were 29—28 pictures (identical prints) plus the main image (a statue).

The second point concerns the widespread misunderstanding which somewhat irks the Ven. Ariyadhamma. Some of his Sinhala verses express the traditional worship of the Bo or Bodhi tree which stands in the compound of nearly every Buddhist temple, often adorned with little pennants. The tree, being of the kind under which the Buddha attained Enlightenment, symbolizes that Enlightenment. The popularity of his verses about it has led some people to infer that he is laying stress on the cult of the tree. Not only have they misnamed his service *Bodhi puja*, i.e. "worship of the Bo tree"; they have revived such extravagant customs as watering the tree with perfumed milk. For example, a layman whom we met at the house where the Ven. Ariyadhamma was passing the rains retreat in 1978 told us that his mother had seen in his sister's horoscope that the sister was about to pass through an unlucky period, so every day for a week she had watered a Bo tree with cow's milk with saffron and sandal in it and given the merit to her daughter, and all had passed off well. Watering the Bo tree was most meritorious in the dry season, when the tree most needed it, he added. Rather more sophisticated, a monk present on the same occasion said that these popular customs were beside the point, but the merit from this service was particularly offered to the deity living in the Bo tree. (Every major tree is thus inhabited by a spirit.) But the Ven. Ariyadhamma assured us that he envisaged no such special regard for the Bo tree deity; his attitude to all the gods is that there must be mutual respect, but he asks no favours of them and merely follows the normal custom of offering merit to all of them without distinction. As for watering the tree, he remarked that our respect is due to the Knowledge, not the Tree.

We have in our possession two somewhat different printed versions of this service, neither of them published commercially. One is a small pamphlet that says on the back that it has been produced in accordance with the Ven. Ariyadhamma's instructions. The second pamphlet has a cover that says that it contains the form of service used by the Ven. Ariyadhamma on the occasion of the birthday of the Ven. Pategama Vimalasiri of the Jetavana Pirivena (monastic college), Colombo, and is produced by those who supported that event. It is this latter pamphlet which contains the form of the service closer to the one we heard, though there were some deviations from its text too. We attended two of these *Buddha puja*. The first, on 16 September 1978, was conducted at a house in southern Sri Lanka by another monk who was deputizing for the Ven. Ariyadhamma that day. There were extra prayers for the Ven. Ariyadhamma, and at the end the merit of the service was transferred to him.

The version given here comes from our tape recording of a service conducted by the Ven. Ariyadhamma on 23 September 1978 at the International Buddhist Centre, Wellawatte, Colombo 6, on the occasion of the 79th birthday of the incumbent, who was unfortunately not well enough to attend.

Abbreviations

M—monk, i.e. spoken by the monk (here Ariyadhamma) only

C—congregation, i.e. spoken by the congregation only

U—unison, i.e. spoken by monk and congregation together

R—responses, i.e. spoken first by the monk, then repeated by the congregation

S—Sinhala

P—Pali

n—normal tone, i.e. with the cadence of normal speech

c—chanted in a melody pattern

m—monotonous chant[3]

Summary translation

MSn   Say "Sadhu."
          All do so.

---

3. This last set of distinctions (n, c, m) is only roughly indicative, and refers primarily to the monk.

MSn   Say "Namo . . ."

CPc   Homage to the Blessed worthy, the fully enlightened Buddha.

Twice repeated.

MSn   May the venerable incumbent and the other venerable members of the great Order accord their gracious permission.

RPc   I take refuge in the Buddha / the Doctrine / the Order (*three times each*).

MPc   The taking of the three refuges is completed.

CPc   Yes, venerable sir.

RPc   I undertake the rule to abstain from taking life / from taking what is not given / from sexual misconduct / from lying / from malicious speech / from harsh speech / from idle chatter / from wrong livelihood.

RSc   May these eight moral principles, ending with that of livelihood, with the triple refuge, cause us to enter the paths, attain the results, and see nirvana.

MPc   Keep the eight moral principles, ending with that of livelihood, with the triple refuge, fully and well, and with full attention achieve it.[4]

There is a pause and Ariyadhamma gives a 6½–minute address on the occasion; he praises the incumbent and especially dedicates the merit of this service to him and to another monk of the same temple who has recently died.

UPc   He broke through the tangle of defilements and their roots by the power of the unlimited perfections He attained, and by that He acquired worthiness and is called "Worthy" (*araho*); placing Him in my heart I worship the immaculate Buddha.

UPm   Homage to the Blessed worthy, the fully enlightened Buddha.

Twice repeated.

Thus is the Blessed worthy, the fully enlightened Buddha, perfect in wisdom and conduct, well, knower of the world, supreme charioteer of men, who have to be broken in, teacher of gods and men, Buddha, Blessed. I take refuge in the Buddha for life, till I attain nirvana.

---

4. " . . . with full attention achieve it." These last two words in the Pali echo the last words of the Buddha. Their meaning is very general, but in context the reference is to achieving nirvana.

Well stated by the Blessed one is the Doctrine, plainly apparent, timeless, a thing to come and see, conducive, possible for the intelligent to realize themselves.

I take refuge in the Doctrine for life, till I attain nirvana.

Of good conduct is the Blessed one's Order of disciples, of upright conduct, of proper conduct, of straight conduct; the four pairs of men, the eight individuals, they are the Blessed one's Order of disciples; fit to be called upon, to be invited, to be given gifts, to be worshipped in gesture, the supreme field of merit for the world.

I take refuge in the Order for life, till I attain nirvana.

The Buddha's knowledge is knowledge of ill / of the arising of ill / of the annihilation of ill / of the path leading to the annihilation of ill / of penetration of the truth / of penetration of the Doctrine / of penetration of etymologies / of penetration of realization / of the level of others' spiritual attainments / of latent tendencies / of the miracle of the pairs / of the attainment of great compassion / of omniscience / without impediment. I bow my head to the fully enlightened Buddha who has these Buddha-knowledges.

That Blessed one is thus worthy; worthy indeed is that Blessed one. I take refuge with the worthy one; I bow my head to the worthy one.

This formula is repeated for each of the Buddha's qualities; for "worthy" substitute in turn the fully enlightened Buddha; perfect in wisdom and conduct; well; knower of the world; supreme charioteer of men, who have to be broken in; teacher of gods and men; Buddha; Blessed.

RSc   My lord, the reverend king Buddha, was remote from defilements. He did no sin even in secret. He was free from all sins. He was worthy of all offerings, both objects and acts, made by all the world's inhabitants. The great wonder is the quality of the reverend king Buddha's compassion. Though one mass together the compassion of a million mothers and a million fathers, one can make no comparison with the compassion of the reverend king Buddha. Thus infinite, possessing measureless qualities, unequalled, equal to the unequalled, god to the gods, to me the lord, my own Buddha mother, my own Buddha father, the orb of dawn to the darkness of delusion, a great raincloud to the fire of the defilements, peaceful in His movements, restrained in His conduct, protector to the unprotected, refuge to those without refuge, to the reverend king Buddha, from the reverend king Buddha called Tanhamkara to the reverend king Buddha called Gautama, thus to the twenty-eight reverend king Buddhas I make this offering of lamps—may it be offered. I make this offering of fragrant smoke / of fragrant flowers / of five items ending with puffed rice[5] / of cool water / of evening refreshment / of four sweets / of betel leaves / of medicine—may it be offered. Aspiring to the peace of nirvana and liberation from the ill of worldly existence I make all these offerings to the twenty-eight reverend king Buddhas. (*Three times:*) May they be offered.

UPc   I bow to the good Buddha, senior in the world, bull among men.

I bow to the good Doctrine, leading out of the world, well taught.

I bow to the good Order, supreme field of merit.

I bow to the good Enlightenment tree,[6] fig tree worshipped by the world.

Free of craving, free of hatred, free of delusion, without defilement, I worship the clever Enlightened one, who taught in many a way.

I worship every stupa, wherever it may be established, the corporeal relics, the great Bo tree, every image of the Buddha always.

Seated at whose foot the Teacher defeated all His foes and attained omniscience, that Bo tree I worship.

Here are these great Bo trees, worshipped by the world protector; I too will bow to them: king Bo tree, worship be to you!

MSn   Out of veneration for the glorious great reverend king Bo tree at Anuradhapura:

USc   The Bo tree bearing golden leaf buds,

The Bo tree bearing dark leaves,

The Bo tree which supported the back of Gautama, lord of seers,

Let us too worship the glorious great Bo tree.

The Bo tree which sprang up on India's soil,

The Bo tree sent to blessed Ceylon,

The Bo tree which supported the back of Gautama, lord of seers,

---

5. The other four items are mustard seed, arrow-grass, broken rice, and jasmine buds.

6. The conventional "English" translation for *Bodhi* is "Bo tree" rather than "Enlightenment tree," but it is good to be reminded of the metonymy. We revert to "Bo tree" below because "Enlightenment tree" is too cumbrous.

Let us too worship the glorious great Bo tree.

The Bo tree which sprang up on India's soil,
The Bo tree the Elder Sanghamitta brought with her,
The Bo tree which supported . . .
Let us too . . .

The Bo tree which sprang up on India's soil,
The Bo tree planted in great Meghavana park,
The Bo tree which supported . . .
Let us too . . .

The Bo tree which sprang . . .
The Bo tree planted . . .
The Bo tree visible within the golden fence,
Let us too . . .

The Bo tree which sprang . . .
The Bo tree planted . . .
The Bo tree worshipped by thousands of people,
Let us too . . .

I pass to and fro on this enclosure,
I tread on the roots and leaves of the Bo tree;
Forgiving me, it does away with my sin;
The king Bo tree grants me permission.

The king Bo tree lives on the top level;
On the second level gleam flowers and lamps;
On the level of the sand worships a great crowd;
In the future we shall see nirvana.

UPc   With lamp kindled with camphor, destroying darkness, I worship the Enlightened one, lamp to the triple world, dispeller of darkness.

With fragrant perfume, I worship the one who is Thus, fragrant of body and face, fragrant with infinite virtues.

At the blessed lotus feet of the lord of seers I offer this colourful, fragrant heap of flowers.

May the reverend one accept the water we have prepared; out of compassion may He receive the best.

This verse is repeated in turn for evening refreshment / medicine / betel leaves.

Forgive me my transgressions committed through carelessness in body, word or thought, O Tathagata of great wisdom.

This verse is repeated, addressing in turn O Doctrine plainly apparent, timeless *and* O Order of good conduct, supreme.

RSc   For all the faults which have occurred through the three doors of my mind, body, and speech, from infinitely remote worldly existence until this moment, from the jewel of the Buddha, the jewel of the Doctrine, and the jewel of the Order may I receive pardon. For the second time, may I receive pardon. For the third time, may I receive pardon.

RPc   May this merit of mine bring about the destruction of my defiling impulses.

RSc   May all the elements of merit I have accumulated—keeping the moral principles, worshipping in gesture, making offerings to the Buddha, worshipping the Bo tree, contemplating the virtues of the twenty-four Buddhas—accrue to my parents, my teachers, my elders, to all. And I empathize with all the elements of merit from everyone, with respectful veneration, with respectful devotion. And may there come to me through the power of all this merit release from decay, death, and all the sorrows of worldly existence, and realization of the very bliss of nirvana. May I see nirvana.

MSn   Say "Sadhu."
       All do so.

Here follows the sermon. It begins with a unison chanting of the three refuges, first in Pali and then in a close Sinhala paraphrase; however, this does not form a set part of the service, so we omit it. The sermon concluded with a close Sinhala prose paraphrase of the following two verses, and their recitation follows without any break.

RSc   To see the Lord Buddha's image is consolation to the eyes;
       To bow before the Lord Buddha is consolation to the limbs;
       To think of the Lord Buddha's virtues is consolation to the mind;
       To take the path the Lord took is consolation for becoming.

       In life there is truly trouble every day,
       And to death we approach ever a little closer;
       Only doing good is at least some palliative;
       Nirvana it is that is the comfort for us all.
       Twice repeated.

RSc   May all beings be happy *Thrice repeated.*

MSn   Say "Sadhu."
       All do so. Then follows the Metta Sutta.

UPm   By this statement of truth may you always fare well; by this statement of truth may the world always be happy; by this statement of truth may the Teaching long endure. May there be every blessing; may all the deities afford protection; by the power of all the Buddhas may you always fare well.

This verse is twice repeated, substituting for "Buddhas" *first* "Doctrine," *then* "Order."

By checking evil influences of constellations, devils, and ghosts by the power of protective texts, may they lay low your misfortunes.

May all living creatures who are ill be free from ill, who are fearful be free from fear, who are grieving be free from grief.

May they give gifts with trust, may they always observe the moral principles, may they take delight in developing their minds, at their passing may they become deities.

I bind comprehensive protection[7] by the power of all the Buddhas, who attained power, of the Isolated Buddhas, and the worthies.

May the gods of the sky and earth and the nagas of great power empathize with the merit and long protect the Teaching.

This verse is twice repeated, substituting for "Teaching" *first* "instruction," *then* "me and others."

Ariyadhamma distributes the merit accruing from the occasion to all participants and their relatives and wishes that all may attain nirvana; all assent with a loud "Sa."

MPc   If one habitually makes respectful salutation and always waits on one's elders, four things increase: one's length of life, good looks, happiness, and strength.

By this may you successfully achieve long life, health, heaven, and finally nirvana.[8]

C   Amen!

---

7. The rest of the service is a normal conclusion to a *pinkama* (merit ceremony) especially to a *pirit* (protection) ceremony, to which some of the verses specifically refer. For example, *rakkham bandhami*, "I bind protection," refers to tying thread on one's wrist as an amulet after the monks have recited the protective texts over it. The text from here on is not in the pamphlets, and one could argue that it is not part of the *Buddha puja* proper; but some such conclusion to round off the occasion is indispensable.

8. These verses are commonly recited by monks to acknowledge any act of homage to them by the laity; all the monks present joined in its recitation, the only point at which there was a general monk/lay distinction.

Figure 14. Stone images representing Bodhisattva Jizo and aborted infants at Purple Cloud Temple, Chichibu, Japan. Photograph by William R. LaFleur.

CHAPTER 14

Death and Beyond (Japan)

In many Asian cultures in which Buddhism has held sway, it has coexisted and interacted with other religious elements that have played crucial roles in many areas of communal and individual life. However, in practically all such situations, Buddhism has assumed the primary role in matters that concern dying, death, and the fate of the deceased. Even in situations in which Buddhism has not been the primary religious force (for example, in many East Asian contexts), Buddhist communities have often provided the religious officiants—usually monks—who preside over funerary activities. Most important, these Buddhist officiants have mediated the beliefs and practices that enable people to deal with the crises posed by death. These crises include especially the human hopes and fears about what is "beyond" for the departed and the living alike.

Buddhists over the centuries have developed many different beliefs and practices associated with death and its aftermath. As we have seen in chapter 9, special funerary ceremonies have been deployed for highly respected monks. And different rituals have also been used for older laypeople who die natural deaths on the one hand and for members of the community who die in tragic or violent circumstances on the other. Typically, however, Buddhist funerary practices for lay members tend to deal with the issues of attachment and desire in a much more central way

The essay in this chapter was taken and adapted from William R. LaFleur, *Liquid Life: Abortion and Buddhism in Japan* (Princeton: Princeton University Press, 1992), 3–10, 44, 172, 221–23. Copyright © 1992 by Princeton University Press. Reprinted by permission of Princeton University Press.

than do funerals for monks, which tend to focus most explicitly on making merit. In general, Buddhists assume that members of the laity are markedly more attached than monks and that the worldly desires of a dying (lay) person do not end with his or her death. Indeed, in the Buddhist perspective, death may be the occasion for such attachments and desires to intensify, thereby causing adverse karmic consequences for the deceased and bringing misfortune on the living. This is one reason why, in some Buddhist cultures, the dying are exhorted to make their last thoughts fall on the life and virtues of the Buddha or on Buddhist exemplars.

In modern Japan, where abortion has become a widespread practice since the end of World War II, a very distinctive pattern of death-related beliefs and practices has emerged. Traditional notions concerning unnatural death have been taken up and adapted in Buddhist contexts, and new rituals have been generated through which guilt and grief can be assuaged. In the following piece, William LaFleur focuses on some of these rituals that, the reader should be aware, have raised a great deal of public controversy among contemporary Japanese, Buddhists and non-Buddhists alike.

MEMORIALIZING ONE'S MIZUKO

William R. LaFleur

The Crowd Out Back

The quiet, hill-nestled, seaside city of Kamakura, only two hours from Tokyo by train, is a natural stop for tourists. It combines beauty with history. During the thirteenth and much of the fourteenth centuries, it served as the de facto headquarters of the Japanese government, precisely at a time when a new wave of Buddhist influence from China was having a profound religious, aesthetic, and architectural impact on Japan. The beautiful temples of Kamakura are well maintained and remarkably intact. They, as well as a number of important Shinto shrines in Kamakura, can be reached on a walking tour—although most tourists nowadays make their visits by piling in and out of buses that make the temple rounds.

Tourists in Kamakura, both Japanese and foreign, are virtually certain to stop to see what is commonly referred to as the "Great Buddha" at Kotokuin, a 37.7-foot high cast-iron image of Amida Buddha seated outdoors in a pose of tranquil contemplation. A good number of people are invariably found there—strolling the enclosed plaza to admire the image, squeezing through a narrow door into the interior of the icon for an inside view, and taking snapshots of individuals or groups in front of the very photogenic, always accommodating, giant figure in seated meditation. The Great Buddha of Kamakura is, many would claim, one of the "wonders" of East Asia, and for that reason it is on the itinerary of most Europeans and Americans touring Japan.

Only two blocks away, however, is a Buddhist site that relatively few non-Japanese will include on their guided tours. Having once seen the Great Buddha, you must follow a back street to find it, a temple named Hase-dera. Like much in Kamakura, it has a history reaching back to the medieval period. Japanese with a special interest in medieval history or art go there to see the wooden image of Kannon, the figure who is considered by Buddhists to be a cosmic source of compassion.[1] The wooden Kannon at Hase-dera Temple is an image about which a good deal of lore has accumulated over the centuries, much of it of historical interest to some tourists.

If you are not Japanese, you will probably never get beyond the Great Buddha, and in the event you do go down the side street to see Hase-dera, you will more than likely return after a quick view of its Kannon. But that is unfortunate because, as a matter of fact, one of the most interesting and revealing scenes in today's Japan consists of what is taking place in the cemetery that is "out back," behind the Kannon of Hase-dera. The Buddhist cemetery there stretches in tiers up the slope of the hill behind the temple. And the careful observer will note that it is to that cemetery, not the Kannon image, that the majority of Japanese visitors to Hase-dera now throng. Many of them will spend more time there than anywhere else in Kamakura—in spite of the fact that tour books and guides make only a passing reference to the cemetery.

In 1990 one could obtain a small leaflet of information about the Hase-dera in English. Bearing a 1983 date, it tells about the Kannon image, tries to correct the impression—easily gained from the image itself—that Kannon is female, and gives a fair amount of legendary de-

---

1. Kannon, a figure originally known in India as Avalokitesvara, was initially male. In eastern Asia its iconography underwent a progressive feminization, so that in Japan today many think of it as the Buddhist "Goddess" of mercy.

tail about its history. Then, in what is little more than a note appended at the end, there is reference to activities taking place in the temple's cemetery. It reads:

Mizuko Jizo

The Kannon is a Buddhist deity whose special task is to help raise healthy children. Many people come and set up small statues, representing their children, so that he can watch over them. More recently, parents have set up statues for miscarried, aborted or dead-born babies, for the Kannon to protect. These are called Mizuko-jizo and in the Hase-dera there are about 50,000 such Jizos. Mothers and fathers often visit the Mizuko-jizo to pray for the souls of the children they have lost.

It is this casual, almost passing, reference to "aborted babies" that tells why there is a constant stream of people to the cemetery tucked behind a temple that is itself much less well-known than the nearby Great Buddha.

At one time, what was remembered here were mostly miscarried or stillborn infants; now, however, it is certain that the vast majority are the results of intentionally terminated pregnancies. At Hase-dera in 1983 the tally of the miscarried, stillborn, and aborted was already about fifty thousand; since then it has risen much higher.

Hase-dera, however, is only one of a growing number of Buddhist temples in Japan that offer such services. Many of these temples began by offering other kinds of services to their parishioners. In recent years, with the rise in the number of abortions, their priests found that more and more people were looking for some kind of religious service specifically attuned to the needs of parents who had had abortions, such religious service being a rite through which such people obviously seek to assuage the guilt or alleviate the distress they are feeling about abortion. These temples have responded with the provision of *mizuko kuyo*, the now common name for such rituals, which have recently shown phenomenal numerical growth. For temples such as Hase-dera, it appears that the provision of rites for aborted fetuses was an additional service that was at least initially subordinate to the more traditional rituals of the temple. In recent years, however, this augmentation has progressively become a major service of the temple, and people come from all over the greater Tokyo metropolitan area to Hase-dera because they feel somehow compelled, rightly or wrongly, to "do something" about the abortions they have had. The mizuko kuyo of Hase-dera meet a certain public demand.

Purple Cloud Temple

There is another kind of temple, however, for which the mizuko kuyo
is the original and only reason for the temple's existence. Such temples
are relative newcomers to the scene and have been the object of most of
the public criticism of mizuko kuyo in Japan. There are some striking
differences. Unlike Hase-dera, the place described below began its existence as a memorial park to provide rites almost exclusively for delib-
erately aborted fetuses. It occupies ground dedicated for that purpose,
advertises itself as such in the public media, and provides no other
observable public service.

A good example of this kind of institution is a place named Shiun-zan
Jizo-ji, on the outskirts of the city of Chichibu in Saitama Prefecture,
approximately two hours from Tokyo by train. Its name rendered into
English is "The Temple of Jizo on the Mountain of the Purple Cloud." [2]
This institution also has a branch office in the city of Tokyo. The main
temple in the Chichibu mountains—here abbreviated to "Purple Cloud
Temple"—can best be understood if I describe what I saw on my own
visit there.

Although a bus passes by it, the temple is most easily reached from the
city of Chichibu by car or taxi—approximately a thirty- or forty-minute
drive. There is no mistaking the place once it has been reached. It occupies a sequence of adjacent hillsides, all of which are carefully tiered
and set with narrow walking paths and row upon row of nearly identical,
small, stone images—statues of Jizo. These are very similar to the ones
seen in the cemetery at Hase-dera, except that virtually all those at Purple
Cloud Temple are newly chiseled and carefully installed. Their gray granite is still precise in outline and shiny on the surface, not worn down by
the elements—that is, they do not have the Buddhist image's famed reputation for showing the attractive signs of great age or antiquity.

There is something very striking about the scene—but also perplex-
ing, perhaps even disturbing, to someone who does not know exactly
what is going on there. Unlike most Buddhist institutions which have a

2. Jizo is central to the Japanese Buddhist way of handling the human pain and moral
conflicts associated with abortion. A more complete appellation is "Jizo Bosatsu," a phrase
meaning "The Earth Store Bodhisattva," although many Japanese familiarly refer to him
as "Jizo-Sama" or "Mr. Jizo." He is considered to be a special protector of deceased infants and children and is known, along with Kannon, for demonstrations of compassion
and altruistic help to others.

prominent, architecturally impressive temple building as the center of focus, the "temple" on this site is a diminutive, modern building and almost insignificant in the midst of the carefully honed hills with their
multitude of Jizo images. Inasmuch as the images constitute a "cemetery," it is clear that here the ordinary pattern for temples has been re-
versed. That is, although in most Buddhist institutions—Hase-dera, for
instance—the temple building itself stands forth prominently and has a
cemetery "out back," Purple Cloud Temple immediately presents itself
as in fact a cemetery, and its "temple," by contrast, serves much more
as a kind of business and promotion office. Although it calls itself a
"temple," in layout and architecture it is really what the Japanese call a
mountain *bochi*—a cemetery or memorial park.

Also striking to the first-time visitor is the uniformity of the stone Jizo
images on this site. Row upon row upon row—they are the same in basic shape. They differ only very slightly in size; most are approximately
two feet in height. The stone is cut so as to suggest that each image
wears the foot-length robes of a Buddhist monk, who is also tonsured.
There is no cut in the stone to suggest even a hint of a hairline or hair;
these figures are perfectly bald. Their eyes are almost completely shut,
in the manner found in most Buddhist images, a manner that denotes the
meditation and tranquility into which the figure has become absorbed.
To anyone able to recognize the signs, there can be no doubt that these
figures are, at least in some sense, monks who are aspirants to the highest
goals of Buddhism. The robes, the tonsure, and the eyes closed in meditation all combine to make this clear.

At the same time, however, something else comes quickly to mind.
These are diminutive figures—child-sized. The visage they present,
while that of tranquility, could also be seen as one of perfect innocence.
And even their lack of hair connotes something of childhood, if not
infancy. The statue which on first sight may have suggested a monk now
prompts something of a double take; the monk is really a child. More
precisely, it is *also* a child.

The figure's accoutrements make this certain. Virtually every one of
the stone Jizo images wears a large red bib—of the type usually worn
by an infant or a young child. Then, as if to push the identification with
childhood beyond doubt, Jizo images are frequently provided with toys.
Whole rows of them at Purple Cloud Temple are provided with pin-
wheels, whose brightly colored spokes spin audibly in the wind. But individual statues are given individual toys as well—for instance, the kind
of miniature piano a child might play with. For some of the images,

sweaters or even more elaborately knitted garments and hats are provided. And, of course, flowers are placed by each one.

The double-take effect—seeing in the figures both monk and child
simultaneously—is important, because the image is meant to represent
two realities at the same time. For the visitor to Purple Cloud Temple
who does not understand such things, there is a readily available brochure, which says:

A Jizo image can do double service. On the one hand it can represent the
soul of the mizuko [deceased child or fetus] for parents who are doing rites
of apology to it. At the same time, however, the Jizo is also the one to whom
can be made an appeal or prayer to guide the child or fetus through the realm
of departed souls.

Jizo is quite remarkable in that it is a stand-in for *both* the dead infant
and the savior figure who supposedly takes care of it in its otherworld
journey. The double-take effect—one moment a child and the next a
Buddhist savior in monkish robes—is intentional.

Visits to places such as the temple at Purple Cloud are in no way limited to adults. In fact, one finds there a surprisingly large number of children. They join their mothers—and sometimes fathers or grandmoth-
ers—in putting flowers in front of the Jizo images, in washing down the
granite stone with water carried over from a nearby faucet, and in saying
simple prayers before the sculptured stones. At Purple Cloud Temple
there is even a small playground in the middle of the cemetery where
children can be seen enjoying themselves.

To note the presence and play of these children is also to call attention
to the relatively "happy" mood in this kind of place. The atmosphere is
far from lugubrious. The red-bibbed images on the hills, the gentle
whirring sound and bright appearance of the thousands of upright pin-
wheels, the presence and play of well-dressed children—all these combine to provide a lightness of feeling that would probably be totally unknown, even incongruous, in the cemeteries of Europe and America. In
the garb provided for some of the images, in the toys they are given, and
in the pins and medallions attached to them there is a playfulness—even
a gentle levity. In fact, the notion that Jizo is a savior who very much
enjoys playing with children goes back some centuries in Japan's religious history.

The non-Japanese who might chance to visit such a place would probably at first have their perplexity compounded with the feeling that all
of this is a type of religious kitsch or, at least, is rather "inappropriate"

for a place dedicated to memorializing the departed dead. An hour spent walking around the stones and carefully observing the Japanese and their activities might, however, bring the visitor to quite different conclusions—especially if the intent of the activities were explained.

The sense of kitsch arises because two things are conflated here that we in the West usually want to separate as much as possible—that is, the cemetery and the nursery. But such temples are, after all, cemeteries not for adults but for children—children who, even though dead, are assumed to be, in ways explained below, still "alive" and related to this place. Consequently, a sense of play is deemed entirely appropriate, as are the toys that make that possible. These cemeteries are the concrete embodiment of human imagination directing its attention to beings who, while no longer in the same world with us as they once were, still are present in our memories and projections. In the minds of most Japanese, the cemetery is the place par excellence that links this world with the "other" world; it is the mode of contact between the metaphysical and the physical. And when it is the departed children or aborted fetuses that are being remembered, it is the Jizo image and cemeteries such as these that provide such a tangible, empirical contact point with the "other" world in which they are thought to reside.

Levity, it is worth noting, is not altogether absent from the cemeteries of the West. The inscriptions on occasional tombstones and even the designs of some memorial architecture show that clearly. However, what reinforces the tendency of the Japanese to make their Jizo cemeteries places of lightness and play is the sense that the deceased children "on the other side" are, if anything, eager to enjoy a few happy moments with the family members who come out from their otherwise busy lives to visit them. The promotional literature provided by the Purple Cloud Temple makes it clear that most of the time spent by such children in the "other world" is far from happy; since they are quite miserable there, the visit from their families is especially appreciated. Thus, the whole experience is modeled after that of reunion rather than separation and, as such, the proper thing is to demonstrate the joy rather than the sorrow of the occasion. Loving attention to the dead is shown by washing down the memorial image—an ancient Buddhist practice—providing fresh flowers, and bringing the occasional new toy or garment. These activities and the recitation of simple prayers are expected. But beyond these there is the sense of an active *communication*, emotional if not verbal, between the living family and the departed child.

Loving communication is a part of the dynamics involved in the mizuko kuyo ritual. But other dynamics exist as well—dynamics that can be discerned in the full text of the brochure that is made available at the Purple Cloud Temple. Entitled "The Way to Memorialize One's Mizuko," the full text reads as follows:[3]

1. The mizuko resulting from a terminated pregnancy is a child existing in the realm of darkness. The principal things that have to be done for its sake are the making of a full apology and the making of amends to such a child.

In contrast to the child in darkness because of an ordinary miscarriage or by natural death after being born, the child here discussed is in its present location because its parents took active steps to prevent it from being born alive in our world. If the parents merely carry out ordinary memorial rites but fail to make a full apology to their child, their mizuko will never be able to accept their act.

Think for a moment how even birds and beasts, when about to be killed, show a good deal of anger and distress. Then how much more must be the shock and hurt felt by a fetus when its parent or parents have decided to abort it? And on top of that it does not even yet have a voice with which to make complaint about what is happening.

It often happens that the living children of persons who have repeatedly had abortions will in the middle of the night cry out: "Father, help!" or "Help me, Mommy!" because of nightmares. Uncontrollable weeping or cries of "I'm scared! I'm scared!" on the part of children are really caused by dreams through which their aborted siblings deep in the realm of darkness give expression to their own distress and anger. Persons who are not satisfied with this explanation would do well to have a look at two publications of the Purple Cloud Villa; these are entitled *Mizuko Jizo-ji's Collection of the Experiences of Departed Souls* and *The Medical Dictionary of Life*.

2. The next thing to do in remembering the mizuko is to set up an image of Jizo on the Buddhist altar in one's own home. That will serve as a substitute for a memorial tablet for the mizuko. Such a Jizo can do double service. On the one hand it can represent the soul of the mizuko for parents doing rites of apology to it. Simultaneously, however, the Jizo is the one to whom can be made an appeal in prayer to guide the fetus through the realm of departed souls. Such Jizo images for home use can be obtained from the Purple Cloud Villa but can also be purchased at any shop specializing in Buddhist art and implements. As long as one performs this worship with a pure heart it is bound to have a positive effect.

Some prices follow. Jizo images made of metal are either 3,000 yen for silver ones or 4,000 yen for gold. Add 1,100 yen to the price of either of these if home delivery is desired. These are prices as of September 1984.

3. Inasmuch as the Jizo image on the Buddhist altar also does double duty

---

3. Editors' note: This paragraph introducing the text of the brochure has been inserted by us.

as a memorial tablet for a terminated fetus, it is allowable—after asking permission of the Jizo—to give it a place on the altar lower than the memorial tablets for one's parents and ancestors. Also it does not matter greatly whether it is to the right or the left on the altar.

4. The next thing of importance is to set up a stone Jizo image either in the cemetery of the Mizuko Jizo Temple or at one's own family temple. Such will serve as substitute for a grave-stone for the aborted child and will constitute an eternal, ongoing ritual of apology and remembrance. Such action will undoubtedly have a good effect—a fact shown in things published in our monthly periodical "The Purple Cloud." The expenses involved in setting up a stone Jizo Buddha at our place are fully detailed in our publication "Concerning the 10,000 Jizos." If requested, we will be pleased to send it.

5. The following pertains to the number of images needed if a person is the parent of more than one mizuko. One of each on the home altar and in the cemetery will suffice if all the mizuko were produced by a single couple—whether married or not. If, however, the father of a later mizuko was different than an earlier one—and, of course, also had a different family registry—separate Jizo images will be required. An exception to this could be made if a woman were to discuss this candidly with her second husband and get his permission. Then it would be just as in the case of a woman bringing along into her second marriage the children begotten in an earlier one. In such as case if she requests that the deceased ancestors understand the situation, it is allowable for all her mizukos to be collectively remembered with a single image.

6. When at your home altar you are giving a daily portion of rice and water offering to your deceased ancestors be sure to include the mizuko too—and let them know of their inclusion. Also pray for the well-being of your mizuko in the other world. Do this by standing before the Buddhas there and reciting either the Heart Sutra[4] or the Psalm to Jizo used at the Jizo cemetery in Chichibu. In addition to that, if as an ongoing remembrance of your mizuko you write out in longhand a copy of the Heart Sutra once a day, you will at some point along the way receive the assurance that your child has most certainly reached Buddhahood. Until you receive such an assurance you should continue to perform these rites of apology and remembrance.

7. To make amends for the fact that you never had to pay anything for the upbringing and education of a mizuko you should give to the Buddha every day an offering of 100 yen for each of your mizuko. However, if you have had as many as ten terminated pregnancies, there may be hardship in laying out 1,000 yen every day; in such cases it is permissible to give only 300 or 500 yen—or even to give more or less depending on one's income. This is an expression of apology to the child for not having given it a love-

---

4. Editors' note: The Heart Sutra is a very concise rendition of a Mahayana teaching on Emptiness and the Perfection of Wisdom. Versions of it have been historically significant in many parts of Asia.

filled upbringing. Therefore, you should put your love into these acts of remembrance, not being stingy with your time and resources. Once you get into the habit of thinking how much easier it would be simply to make a 10,000 yen contribution once a month, you are missing the whole point. It is far better to put a daily offering on the altar table every day and then on a special, designated day pay a visit to the Jizo Temple at Chichibu and make a contribution to the temple. Alternatively, you could do it while making the 88-temple pilgrimage on the island of Shikoku or the pilgrimage to the 100 Kannon sites in western Japan.

8. When a person has awakened to the value and importance of remembering mizuko, one gains a much deeper faith and makes efforts to live as a bodhisattva, setting one's mind to performing at least one act of goodness each day. Also vowing to go on pilgrimage to Shikoku or the Kannon sites is an excellent way to be total and thoroughgoing in one's act of apologizing to and remembering the mizuko. It is important to be of a mind to do more than enough; to be of the opinion that one has already done plenty is just the kind of attitude that evokes a bad effect.

9. Children that are miscarried, born dead, or die shortly after being born differ, of course, from those whose lives are cut short by being terminated by their parents. Nevertheless, they too are mizuko and, when one gives consideration to his or her responsibility for the fact that these too did not enter life successfully, it would seem good to provide them too with mizuko rites as one would in the case of aborted fetuses.

10. Households whose members think about the seriousness of karmic laws related to abortion are also households which can take advantage of such occasions in order to deepen the faith of those within them. By continuing to perform adequate rites of apology and memorial, such persons later are blessed with the birth of fine, healthy children. Or, as an extension of good fortune, there are many instances of people really thriving. Some persons find that their own severe heart diseases are cured or that the rebelliousness of children or neuroses go away. When on top of all that there is increased prosperity in the family business, there is good cause for lots of happiness.

Why not find out more about this by simply paying a visit to the Jizo Temple in Chichibu?

This brochure makes no mention of the extenuating circumstances of life that may have necessitated the abortion. It makes no attempt to present any sympathy for the plight of parents. Instead all the emphasis is on the fact that those parents have *willfully* sent such a child into the nether realm where it now languishes. The text simply assumes that the fetus, at no matter what stage it was aborted, had sufficient presence of mind to feel anger at its parents and somehow now has the full consciousness of a child able to comprehend and even mull over such things—to the point of feeling resentment. Also the text makes much of the fact that what occurred in the act of abortion is *unnatural*. Great stress is placed on that.

This is so because it taps into one of the oldest patterns of Japanese cultural life. Rich documentation, from historical and literary sources, as well as from the notes of anthropologists and sociologists working in Japan, gives abundant evidence that the concept and cultural role of *tatari* (the exacting of revenge or a penalty by a god, spirit, or deceased person who has been wronged by living humans) is old and probably antedates all the written records we have. What such materials suggest—and the point of special importance here—is that from early times in Japanese culture there was a deep sense that persons who had died "unnatural" deaths were virtually certain to feel tremendous resentment vis-à-vis the living and would, unless somehow pacified, wreak havoc on the living.

The mizuko-related activities that the brochure recommends are obviously designed to placate, through remembrance and apology, the presumed resentment of the aborted child and the danger of retribution that it poses. But it is also clear that the activities recommended by the brochure are designed to achieve this first purpose in ways that will at the same time deepen the Buddhist commitment of the parents and siblings, improve their lives, and encourage their practice of the bodhisattva path.[5]

5. Editors' note: This final paragraph is a concise restatement by us of points made in a more extended way by the original author.

PART IV

Buddhism in the West

Figure 15. **Zazen** at the Santa Monica Zen Center, California. Photograph by Don Farber.

CHAPTER 15

An American Example

It is perhaps most appropriate to end this collection by focusing on a theme that has been implicitly embedded in the preceding essays. This theme—a perennial one from early in the history of Buddhism—is the transmission of Buddhist traditions to new lands and peoples. Indeed, the preservation and spread of Buddhism has largely depended upon the degree to which it has been adapted artistically, conceptually, and ritually to new cultural and social contexts. A concluding point that we wish to make, then, is a basic but fundamental one: To understand why Buddhism has a "life" at all, we must consider and reflect seriously on the fact that many Buddhists—monks, nuns, and laypeople alike—have been deeply committed to preserving the integrity of their vision of the Buddhist dharma, while making it accessible and accountable to a community with its own distinctive (and often contrary) cultural sensibilities.

For instance, early and medieval Chinese Buddhism was involved in a great deal of controversy surrounding the ethos of the monastic life itself. Many Chinese who opposed Buddhism contended that Buddhist renunciation was a foreign tradition that eroded the traditional Chinese family by trivializing or negating any concern for filial piety. Against this accusation, Chinese Buddhist monks and apologists advanced the argu-

The essay in this chapter was taken from Philip Kapleau, *Zen: Dawn in the West* (Garden City, NY: Anchor Press/Doubleday, 1979), 171–83. Copyright © 1979 by Zen Center, Inc. Used by permission of Doubleday, a division of Bantam Doubleday Dell Publishing Group, Inc.

ment that renunciation was actually the highest and best form of filial piety: Despite the fact that renunication removed the son or daughter from certain familial obligations, it provided an opportunity for the monk or nun to generate a great deal of merit and to dedicate that merit to the ultimate well-being of his or her parents. Clearly, these apologists sought to sustain their vision of Buddhism while at the same time making Buddhist traditions accessible and accountable in the new Chinese context.

Let us consider an example historically and culturally less distant than the early and medieval Chinese one: the transmission of Buddhist traditions to the West over the past century or two. While radically different in time and place from the transmission of Buddhism to early and medieval China, this transmission to the contemporary West has been equally complicated and problematic. The process has involved communities of people from many Asian nations who have brought with them their Buddhist traditions and practices.[1] And it has also involved the "conversion" of many Western natives. Both the immigrants and the converts have had to contend with the problems that English and other Western languages have posed for doctrinal and textual transmission. Further, issues associated with the Enlightenment and modernity, which have challenged Buddhism in many Asian lands, have also conditioned the expansion and appeal of Buddhism in the West.

The following excerpt, which is much more confessional and apologetic than any of our previous selections, represents one moment in the expansion of Buddhism to a native Western population, more specifically, to one in the United States. Written by a very influential convert to Buddhism who founded the Rochester Zen Center in New York State, this presentation of Zen chanting seeks to transmit the author's vision of the dharma in a form that preserves its religious integrity yet remains both palatable and accountable in the American cultural setting. Obviously, the author's tradition and approach varies from those of other Buddhists, but he provides explicit insight into some of the complexities and problems that arise when transmitting, transforming, and yet preserving the Buddhist tradition to which he is committed. His essay highlights crucial processes in which many other Buddhists have also engaged: making certain religious claims and arguments, searching for

1. Unfortunately, good scholarly discussions of immigrant Buddhist communities in the West are few and far between. Perhaps the best book presently available is Paul David Numrich, *Old Wisdom in the New World: Americanization in Two Immigrant Theravada Buddhist Temples* (Knoxville: University of Tennessee Press, 1996).

evidence from the tradition, and, most important, engaging in active and creative communication with others.

TRANSMITTING THE DHARMA

Philip Kapleau

There are many who, having been exposed to Zen only through academia, find themselves after entering a Zen center gaping in confusion at the buddha and bodhisattva figures, the chanting and the rituals. Zazen, yes, they tell themselves, that is to be expected—but this?[2] Yet the twenty-five-hundred-year-old living and growing discipline called Zen Buddhism is a full-bodied spiritual tradition in which such devotions play a vital role. Indeed, it is artificial to speak of Zen devotions as separate from zazen. Bowing with hands together upon entering and leaving the zendo (the place where Zen practice is carried on), doing prostrations before buddhas and bodhisattvas and making offerings to them, taking part in regular confession and repentance ceremonies—these acts when performed no-mindedly refine the emotions and purify the mind, gradually softening the sharp corners and rigid outlines of the personality. And because they all serve to "prune" the ego-I, they hasten awakening. Sincere devotional practices also help to liberate our inherent compassion so that it may work freely in everyday life.

Ceremonies performed for centuries in traditional Buddhist countries have now taken root on American soil. At the Zen Center these observances have been adapted to our Western culture through a process of natural evolution. In addition to rites of passage—funerals, weddings, and ordinations—the calendar of ceremonies includes the Buddha's birthday, death day, and day of enlightenment; Bodhidharma's death day;[3] Founder's Day; New Year's Day; and, each month, a confession-repentance ceremony and a ceremony dedicated to the aid of starving people throughout the world. Equally significant are the celebrations held each year at Thanksgiving—celebrations that, because they are a deep expression of gratitude, fit ideally into Zen devotions and add substance to a home-grown American Buddhist holiday.

2. Editors' note: *Zazen* is a form of meditation that is an important practice in many Zen traditions.

3. Editors' note: Bodhidharma (ca. 480–520) is considered the founder of the Zen tradition.

At a time when many followers of traditional Western religions appear to have no significant understanding of or relationship to rites and ceremonies, it is well to remember that formality need not be an empty shell. For where gratitude, reverence, and other genuine spiritual feelings are present they can be deepened and made more significant when expressed through a formal pattern, just as movement can be made more meaningful when turned into dance, or sound into music.

No element of Zen devotions occupies a more central role than chanting. There is hardly a Zen temple or center where men and women do not assemble in the main hall at least once a day and chant sutras and the words of the masters who have realized the highest truth. Chanting forms the focal ground on which every ritual, ceremony, and rite of passage is performed, setting a tone through which participants acquire a heightened awareness of and receptivity to what is being enacted.

Each day at dawn the thunderous beat of the large standing drum breaks the zazen silence to signal sitters to file into the main zendo for chanting. After this initial, booming call, the drum player sweeps his wooden sticks over the brass beads along the drum's rim, producing a deep, rushing sound. Then the sharp strikes to the wooden rim itself— "clackety clack, clackety clack"—building in tempo before leading into a final rhythm on the face of the drum.

After the drum ends, with no gap the large *keisu* (pronounced "kay-su"), or bowl-shaped gong, is struck, its deep resonance filling the zendo. The keisu player sits poised before it, deftly holding a large padded cylindrical striker in both hands to intone the introductions to the different chants and to punctuate the chanting after all have joined in. He "drops" the heavy striker onto the rim of the gong, aware that contact which is either too hard or too soft, or aimed at either the incorrect angle or the wrong point on the keisu, will fail to release the full and rich body of tones coiled within the instrument. In Zen it is said, "Don't strike the instrument; let it be struck."

After each chant has been introduced, the wooden-fish drum comes in. It begins slowly, "thump . . . thump . . . thump," gradually building in speed, like a departing train, as the individual voices blend into a single sonorous drone. As with the keisu, the drum player with his padded stick does not "beat" the instrument but rather, by handling the striker lightly, simply guides it, with the effect that the instrument in a sense "plays itself." The sound of this fish-shaped, hollowed-out drum is deep enough to ride underneath the vocal chanting, thus setting a cadence that can be followed by all.

A chanting service blends a wide range of diverse elements. The strong, clear voice of the lead chanter is heard alone to introduce the chants, evoking a response in the full "chorus" of between fifty and three hundred chanters. The pulselike throb of the wooden drum offers a counterpoint to the vibrant ring of the bowl-gong even as they mesh to contrast and harmonize with the drone of chanting.

During chanting the whole body is relaxed. The energy for the chanting comes from the lower belly with the sound resonating in the head cavities. In Zen there is no swaying or rocking during the chanting; it is carried on in an erect and stable posture with the hands in the lap.

Each chanter takes his or her own lowest natural pitch—a note in the lowest part of one's range that can be maintained easily without strain—while at the same time blending in with the dominant pitch to form a harmonious unity. The particular words of the chants emerge from one's basic pitch; thus the words flow together into a drone issuing from the hara (the lower abdomen). The pitch does not rise and fall in a singsongy way. Zen chanting is a unique way of engaging the deepest level of mind. It circumvents the intellect to awaken understanding and energetically expresses feeling without emotionality.

Broadly speaking, there are two types of chants: sutras and *dharani*. In the category of sutras, which are the purported words of the Buddha, may be included the words of the masters. The advantage of chanting these in one's own language is that when repeated regularly the truth of the words is hammered home to the subconscious mind, thereby instilling greater understanding and faith. No conscious effort need be made to grasp the meaning, for it is absorbed spontaneously, unchecked by the rational mind. The mind state created by the chanting—involvement to the point of self-transcendence—is of primary importance.

A dharani is an extended mantra, a rhythmic sequence of sounds that expresses, through its unique spiritual vibrations, the essential truth transcending all duality. The power of such a formula to evoke unseen forces when chanted wholeheartedly depends to an extent on the sound itself, but even more on the mind state of the chanter. Thus a dharani will carry greater potency when uttered by one pure in faith, concentrated in mind, and responsive in heart. The structure of a dharani is not insignificant; it must be rhythmic, melodious, and the outgrowth of genuine religious experience. Since no one yet has managed the difficult task of making suitable English chanting versions of them, no mantra or dharani is presented here except for the mantra at the end of the Heart of Perfect Wisdom sutra.

Chanting must be distinguished from reciting. The latter may be nothing more than repetition of an account or passage. Chanting, however, is generated deep in the belly, and when performed egolessly has the power to penetrate visible and invisible worlds. Mind is unlimited; energetic chanting done with a pure mind, with single-minded involvement, is another form of zazen, another mode of learning the buddha-truth in a direct, nonconceptual way. Performed in this manner, chanting is also a means of strengthening samadhi power and of helping to bring about awakening.[4]

At the Rochester Zen Center most of the chants are in English; the most well-known are The Four Bodhisattvic Vows, Heart of Perfect Wisdom, Chant in Praise of Zazen, and Affirming Faith in Mind. These chants are set forth to open this section on devotions. While there are other English translations of these works, what distinguishes those that appear here is that they were adapted specifically for chanting, rendered with an ear for euphony and cadence.

The Four Bodhisattvic Vows

The Four Great Vows of a bodhisattva comprise the most widely recited chant in Mahayana Buddhism:

> All beings, without number, I vow to liberate.
> Endless blind passions I vow to uproot.
> Dharma gates, beyond measure, I vow to penetrate.
> The Great Way of Buddha I vow to attain.

The content of these chanted vows commonly poses difficulties for Western students, who over the years have expressed two main objections. Students of Christian background complain that, having left Christianity and its missionary spirit, the last thing they want in Zen is more of what they misconstrue in the first of the Four Vows as "saving." Others ask, "How can I vow to liberate all beings when I haven't yet liberated myself? And if I do liberate myself, how would it be possible to liberate *all other* beings?" One serious aspirant put it this way in a letter:

"What troubles me about the Four Vows is that I cannot *honestly* commit myself to them. To myself I have to add, 'as far as the limitations and weaknesses within me permit,' which destroys the value of saying the

---

4. Editors' note: *Samadhi* is a state of intense meditative concentration that is an essential component in many forms of Buddhist meditation.

Four Vows. I would like to be able to affirm these vows, but in all sincerity I cannot."

The problem behind both of these objections is that of seeing the Four Vows as an external formula that must be learned and somehow, against all odds and reason, lived up to. In the first of the Four Vows, that which is traditionally translated "to save" is chanted as "to liberate" at the Rochester Center. This difference of expression avoids the moralistic and un-Buddhistic implication of redemption from sin, and more truly reflects the spirit of the original. Understood correctly, this vow is a statement of the purpose and scope of one's practice, an affirmation that one's zazen is not for oneself alone but for all humanity. The remaining three vows outline the mind state by which one is empowered to aid the numberless beings through countless realms.

The expression "all beings" is not hyperbole. Zen awakening reveals unmistakably that all is one—oneself—and that oneself is all. Whatever happens to any one being inevitably affects every other being. Thus when one awakens, everything is charged with the same awakening. This was affirmed by Zen master Dogen (1200–1253) when he said: "Without enlightening others there is no self-enlightenment."

In Zen a bodhisattva is anyone who has vowed, out of his great compassion, not to enter nirvana until all beings have entered—that is to say, he naturally puts the welfare of others before his own. He does continue to develop himself, however, for no one who needs help himself can truly help another. The vow stresses that having dedicated himself to those in need, he will not turn back.

The bodhisattvic vows, then, are far more than mere positive thinking. In the same sense that the peach stone vows to become a peach, the acorn an oak, the infant a man, the man a buddha, the Four Vows are a reaffirmation of our innate vow to become what we intrinsically are— whole and complete. Seen in this light they are nothing less than a call to Self-awakening, to Self-liberation.

Heart of Perfect Wisdom

The Heart of Perfect Wisdom, chanted daily in Buddhist monasteries and centers throughout the world, is considered the most potent for piercing the delusive mind. It is the kernel, or core, of the Buddha's teaching, the condensed message of the wisdom sutras he gave over the course of twenty-two years. Also referred to as the Heart sutra, it is to be grasped not through the intellect but with the heart—that is, through one's own deepest intuitive experience. Thus "perfect wisdom" here means transcendental wisdom, as well as the path leading to the attainment of this wisdom and the text of the teaching conducive to its realization.

In the Heart sutra the Buddha is speaking to Sariputra, a chief disciple noted for his wisdom. The Buddha recounts how the Bodhisattva of Compassion realized through deep samadhi that the human personality is merely the product of five *skandhas* (literally "aggregates")—form, feeling, perception, tendencies, and consciousness—that are fundamentally empty of real substance. The Buddha then discloses the illusory nature of the eighteen realms of sense, made up of the six sense organs, the corresponding six types of sense data, and the six acts of sensing; the twelve links in the chain of causation; the Four Noble Truths; and even the dualistic conception of nirvana and *samsara.*

The Sanskrit mantra at the end of the sutra may be rendered into English as follows:

Gone, gone
gone beyond,
fully beyond.
Awake: rejoice!

It is difficult to translate the word *svaha* exactly; it is a word of exultation, meaning "hail."

The Sanskrit mantra at the end is pronounced:

Gǒ-tay, gǒ-tay
Pah-rah gǒ-tay
Pah-rah som gǒ-tay
Bod-hi sva-ha

[An upside-down *e*, ǒ, is pronounced like the *u* in fun.]

Heart of Perfect Wisdom

The Bodhisattva of Compassion
from the depths of prajna wisdom [5]
saw the emptiness of all five
skandhas and sundered the bonds
that cause him suffering.

---

5. Editors' note: *Prajna wisdom* refers to the highest form of wisdom that constitutes the content of enlightenment as understood in the Zen tradition.

Know then:
Form here is only emptiness,[6]
emptiness only form.
Form is no other than emptiness,
emptiness no other than form.

Feeling, thought, and choice,
consciousness itself,
are the same as this.

Dharmas here are empty,[7]
all are the primal void.
None are born or die.
Nor are they stained or pure,
nor do they wax or wane.

So in emptiness no form,
no feeling, thought or choice
nor is there consciousness.

No eye, ear, nose,
tongue, body, mind;
no color, sound, smell,
taste, touch, or what
the mind takes hold of,
nor even act of sensing.

No ignorance nor end of it
nor all that comes of ignorance:
no withering, no death,
no end of them.

Nor is there pain or cause of pain
or cease in pain or noble path
to lead from pain,
not even wisdom to attain,
attainment too is emptiness.

So know that the bodhisattva
holding to nothing whatever
but dwelling in prajna wisdom
is freed of delusive hindrance,
rid of the fear bred by it,
and reaches clearest nirvana.

6. *Here* refers to the level of transcendental wisdom.
7. Editors' note: *Dharmas* refer to the constituent elements into which all reality can
be analyzed.

All buddhas of past and present,
buddhas of future time
through faith in prajna wisdom
come to full enlightenment.

Know, then, the great dharani
the radiant, peerless mantra,
the supreme, unfailing mantra,
the Prajna Paramita,[8]
whose words allay all pain.
This is the highest wisdom
true beyond all doubt,
know and proclaim its truth:

> Gate, gate
> para gate
> para sam gate
> bodhi, *svaha!*

Heart of perfect wisdom.

Master Hakuin's Chant in Praise of Zazen

One of the great lights of Japanese Buddhism is Zen master Hakuin (1686–1769). Although his teaching stands in the tradition of the old masters of China, he effectively adapted it to Japanese culture, creating a living Zen that was accessible to laymen even while it was rooted in the pure heritage of his own monastic orientation. Hakuin is perhaps best known for his revitalization of the koan system and for the koan he himself devised, still widely used in training: "What is the Sound of One Hand?"[9]

Even in his own day Hakuin was widely respected and beloved, especially by the common people, whose lot in the feudal society of his day was a bitter one. They came to him in great numbers seeking relief from their heavy burdens of poverty and oppression.

High government officials also received his teaching, and in his bold and colorful replies to letters from them we find him inveighing against proponents of an adulterated mass-appeal Zen[10] and "dead sitting and silent illumination."

---

8. Editors' note: *Prajna Paramita* is usually translated as "perfection of wisdom."
9. Editors' note: A *koan* is a kind of riddle developed and used in the Zen tradition to vex the rational mind and to evoke a mental breakthrough along the path to enlightenment.
10. "Adulterated mass-appeal Zen" refers to the practice of combining the koan with the reciting of the Pure Land formula, or *nembutsu:* "I put my trust in the Buddha Amida."

Hakuin's chief concern, naturally, was the training of his monks and disciples and the development of qualified successors. He himself says in one of his letters that he seldom had less than five hundred monks and laymen training under him.

A man of extraordinary versatility and inexhaustible energy, Hakuin was not only a vivid and powerful writer, he was also a respected painter and calligrapher and an accomplished poet and sculptor. Brilliant Zen master, Renaissance man—this is the author of the "Chant in Praise of Zazen," still regularly intoned in Zen temples in Japan, at the Zen Center in Rochester, and elsewhere. Perhaps nowhere else is there to be found so spirited and eloquent a testimony to the power of zazen.

Zen Master Hakuin's Chant in Praise of Zazen

From the beginning all beings are buddha.
Like water and ice,
without water no ice,
outside us no buddhas.
How near the truth
yet how far we seek,
like one in water crying "I thirst!"
Like the son of a rich man wand'ring poor on this earth,
we endlessly circle the six worlds.
The cause of our sorrow is ego delusion.
From dark path to dark path we've wandered in darkness—
how can we be free from the wheel of samsara?
The gateway to freedom is zazen samadhi;
beyond exaltation, beyond all our praises,
the pure Mahayana.
Observing the precepts, repentance, and giving,
the countless good deeds, and the way of right living
all come from zazen.
Thus one true samadhi extinguishes evils;
it purifies karma, dissolves obstructions.
Then where are the dark paths to lead us astray?
The pure lotus land is not far away.
Hearing this truth, heart humble and grateful,
to praise and embrace it, to practice its wisdom,
brings unending blessings, brings mountains of merit.
And if we turn inward and prove our True-nature—
that True-self is no-self,
our own Self is no-self—
we go beyond ego and past clever words.
Then the gate to the oneness of cause-and-effect

is thrown open.
Not two and not three, straight ahead runs the Way.
Our form now being no-form,
in going and returning we never leave home.
Our thought now being no-thought,
our dancing and songs are the voice of the dharma.
How vast is the heaven of boundless samadhi!
How bright and transparent the moonlight of wisdom!
What is there outside us,
what is there we lack?
Nirvana is openly shown to our eyes.
This earth where we stand is the Pure Lotus Land,
and this very body the body of buddha.

Bibliography

Overviews

Cabezon, Jose Ignacio, ed. *Buddhism, Sexuality, and Gender*. Albany: State University of New York Press, 1992. A collection of essays critically addressing issues of sexuality and gender as they relate to Buddhist history, culture, texts, and symbols.

Kitagawa, Joseph M., and Mark D. Cummings, eds. *Buddhism and Asian History*. New York: Macmillan, 1989. A collection of essays on Buddhist history and culture. Of particular importance are the first two essays of the collection, both by Frank Reynolds and Charles Hallisey. One essay, "Buddhist Religion, Culture, and Civilization," offers a useful threefold periodization of Buddhist history: Buddhism as a sectarian religion, Buddhism as a civilizational religion, and Buddhism as a cultural religion. The other essay, entitled "The Buddha," discusses various conceptions and representations of the Buddha, Buddhas, and Buddhahood. All of the essays in *Buddhism and Asian History* are also available in Mircea Eliade, ed. *The Encyclopedia of Religion*. New York: Macmillan, 1987.

Robinson, Richard H., and Willard L. Johnson. *The Buddhist Religion*. 4th ed. Belmont, CA: Wadsworth, 1996. A useful historical introduction.

Strong, John S., ed. *The Experience of Buddhism: Sources and Interpretations*. Belmont, CA: Wadsworth, 1995. An anthology of textual materials that innovatively integrates a large number of Buddhist historical and cultural developments. Strong's selections cover such areas as myth, history, doctrine, daily practices, notions of community, and religious experience.

Other Important Secondary Sources

Bantly, Francisca Cho. *Embracing Illusion: Truth and Fiction in the Dream of the Nine Clouds*. Albany: State University of New York Press, 1996. A study of a Korean novel that deals creatively with Buddhist notions of reality and illusion.

Bartholomeusz, Tessa J. *Women under the Bo Tree.* New York: Cambridge University Press, 1994. Discusses aspects of the history and identity of Buddhist nuns in Sri Lanka.

Collins, Steven. *Selfless Persons: Imagery and Thought in Theravada Buddhism.* Cambridge: Cambridge University Press, 1982. A systematic exploration of the doctrine of "not-self" (*anatta*), and of the related issues of personality and continuity, as found in the Theravada tradition.

————. *Nirvana and Other Buddhist Felicities.* Cambridge: Cambridge University Press, 1998. An important study that investigates the nature and meaning of nirvana and other good things in what the author identifies as the Pali imaginaire.

Dobbins, James C. *Jodo Shinshu.* Bloomington: Indiana University Press, 1989. Studies dimensions of the history and development of Pure Land Buddhism in medieval Japan.

Faure, Bernard. *The Rhetoric of Immediacy: A Cultural Critique of Chan/Zen Buddhism.* Princeton: Princeton University Press, 1991. Explores the dynamics of the Ch'an tradition with a special focus on the relation between its rhetoric and practice.

————. *Visions of Power: Imagining Medieval Japanese Buddhism.* Princeton: Princeton University Press, 1996. An investigation of the thought world— the "imaginaire"—of the medieval Japanese Soto Zen master Keizan Jokin (1268–1325).

Goldstein, Melvyn C., and Matthew T. Kapstein, eds. *Buddhism in Contemporary Tibet: Religious Revival and Cultural Identity.* Berkeley: University of California Press, 1998. A series of essays that explore certain dimensions of the Buddhist revival in Tibet following the imposition of Chinese rule and the destruction suffered during the Cultural Revolution.

Gombrich, Richard F. *Theravada Buddhism.* London and New York: Routledge & Kegan Paul, 1988. An introductory text tracing the social history of Buddhism in India and Sri Lanka.

Gross, Rita M. *Buddhism after Patriarchy.* Albany: State University of New York Press, 1993. A discussion that proposes a feminist history, analysis, and reconstruction of Buddhism.

Holt, John Clifford. *Buddha in the Crown.* New York: Oxford University Press, 1991. A study and analysis of the transitions and transformations of the bodhisattva Avalokitesvara in the Buddhist traditions of Sri Lanka.

————. *The Religious World of Kirti Sri.* New York: Oxford University Press, 1996. Examines the role of paradigmatic discourses, art, and "visual liturgy" in the religio-political activity of an important eighteenth-century Sri Lankan king.

Kasulis, T. P. *Zen Action, Zen Person.* Honolulu: University of Hawaii Press, 1981. An accessible introduction to Zen Buddhism.

Ketelaar, James Edward. *Of Heretics and Martyrs in Meiji Japan.* Princeton: Princeton University Press, 1990. Investigates dimensions of the religio-political persecution of Buddhism in Japan during the late nineteenth and early twentieth centuries.

Kieschnick, John. *The Eminent Monk*. Honolulu: University of Hawaii Press, 1997. A discussion of monastic behavioral norms present in medieval Chinese Buddhist hagiography.

Klein, Anne C. *Meeting the Great Bliss Queen*. Boston: Beacon Press, 1995. A cross-cultural exploration focusing on Buddhist and feminist notions of the self.

LaFleur, William R. *The Karma of Words*. Berkeley and Los Angeles: University of California Press, 1983. Analyzes the interaction between Buddhism and the literary arts in medieval Japan. In the process, LaFleur develops an interpretation of what he calls the medieval Japanese "episteme."

Lopez, Donald S., ed. *Curators of the Buddha: The Study of Buddhism under Colonialism*. Chicago: University of Chicago Press, 1995. A collection of essays offering critical approaches to the cultural history of Buddhist studies in the West.

————. *Prisoners of Shangri-La: Tibetan Buddhism and the West*. Chicago: University of Chicago Press, 1998. Interrogates constructions of Tibetan Buddhist culture and identity that have emerged during the course of interactions with the West.

Malandra, Geri H. *Unfolding a Mandala: The Buddhist Cave Temples at Ellora*. Albany: State University of New York Press, 1993. A study of architectural and iconographic elements that developed roughly between the early seventh and early eighth centuries at an important site in western India.

Numrich, Paul David. *Old Wisdom in the New World: Americanization in Two Immigrant Theravada Buddhist Temples*. Knoxville: University of Tennessee Press, 1996. A sociological analysis identifying and analyzing important problems and possibilities associated with the growth of Theravada Buddhist communities in the United States.

Orzech, Charles D. *Politics and Transcendent Wisdom: The Scripture for Humane Kings in the Creation of Chinese Buddhism*. University Park: Pennsylvania State University Press, 1998. A critical examination of the relations among religion, politics, and cosmology in the period from the fifth to the eighth centuries in China.

Ray, Reginald A. *Buddhist Saints in India: A Study in Buddhist Values and Orientations*. New York: Oxford University Press, 1994. Probes certain images and functions of forest saints and their traditions in the development of the Buddhist community in India.

Schopen, Gregory. *Bones, Stones, and Buddhist Monks*. Honolulu: University of Hawaii Press, 1997. A collection of essays highlighting the importance of material remains for any attempt to reconstruct the history and culture of Buddhism in South Asia.

Streng, Frederick J. *Emptiness: A Study in Religious Meaning*. Nashville: Abingdon Press, 1967. An exploration of the concept of emptiness as it was employed by the Mahayana Buddhist philosopher Nagarjuna (second century C.E.). The author uses Nagarjuna's notion of emptiness to problematize and offer a perspective on the relationship between religious awareness and conceptual or symbolic expression.

Strong, John S. *The Legend and Cult of Upagupta*. Princeton: Princeton University Press, 1992. A work that draws on historical, ethnographic, and literary sources dealing with the Buddhist saint Upagupta to survey the presence and life of a Sanskrit tradition in South and Southeast Asia.

Swearer, Donald K. *The Buddhist World of Southeast Asia*. Albany: State University of New York Press, 1995. An introduction to cultural and social dimensions of Theravada Buddhism in Southeast Asia. The author's survey gives particular attention to the structure and dynamics of popular religion, of political legitimation and integration, and of urbanization and modernization.

Tambiah, Stanley Jeyaraja. *The Buddhist Saints of the Forest and the Cult of Amulets*. Cambridge: Cambridge University Press, 1984. An examination of the cultural and social dynamics relating to the forest saint tradition as it is found in parts of South and Southeast Asia (especially Thailand).

Teiser, Stephen F. *The Ghost Festival in Medieval China*. Princeton: Princeton University Press, 1988. Explores cultural values and orientations in a widespread Buddhist ritual practice in medieval China.

———. *The Scripture of the Ten Kings*. Honolulu: University of Hawaii Press, 1994. A study of the production and life of a noncanonical text that highlights medieval Chinese Buddhist attitudes and practices concerning purgatory.

Trainor, Kevin. *Relics, Ritual, and Representation in Buddhism: Rematerializing the Sri Lankan Theravada Tradition*. Cambridge: Cambridge University Press, 1997. A practice-oriented historical study that explores the relation between relic veneration and the "presence" of the Buddha.

Williams, Paul. *Mahayana Buddhism: The Doctrinal Foundations*. London: Routledge, 1989. Examines doctrinal features of the Mahayana tradition associated with the themes of wisdom and compassion.

Wilson, Liz. *Charming Cadavers*. Chicago: University of Chicago Press, 1996. Analyzes South Asian Buddhist stories that tell how monks eradicated desire through encounters with disfigured female bodies.

Introductions to and Translations of Primary Sources

Carter, John Ross, and Mahinda Palihawadana. *The Dhammapada*. New York: Oxford University Press, 1998, paperback edition. An important Pali text and its commentary.

Cone, Margaret, and Richard F. Gombrich. *The Perfect Generosity of Prince Vessantara: A Buddhist Epic*. Oxford: Clarendon Press, 1977. The story of the Buddha's penultimate birth as it is preserved in the Pali Theravada tradition.

Crosby, Kate, and Andrew Skilton. *The Bodhicaryavatara*. Oxford: Oxford University Press, 1996. A work by the seventh- to eighth-century Buddhist poet-scholastic Santideva focusing on the nature and meaning of the bodhisattva and the bodhisattva path.

Garfield, Jay L. *The Fundamental Wisdom of the Middle Way*. New York: Oxford University Press, 1995. A translation of and commentary on a Tibetan version of a highly influential work written by the Mahayana Buddhist philosopher Nagarjuna (second century C.E.).

Gomez, Luis O. *The Land of Bliss: The Paradise of the Buddha of Measureless*

Light. Honolulu: University of Hawaii Press, 1996. Sanskrit and Chinese versions of the shorter and longer Sukhavativyuha Sutras, which are sacred texts of the Mahayana tradition.

Hakeda, Yoshito S. *Kukai: Major Works*. New York: Columbia University Press, 1972. Eight major works of an important Japanese Buddhist monk who lived during the eighth and ninth centuries.

Khoroche, Peter. *Once the Buddha Was a Monkey*. Chicago: University of Chicago Press, 1989. The Jatakamala, a Sanskrit telling of previous lives of the Gautama Buddha.

Leighton, Taigan Daniel, and Shohaku Okumura. *Dogen's Pure Standards for the Zen Community*. Albany: State University of New York Press, 1996. Treatises on monastic life and practice written by the Japanese Zen master Dogen (1200–1253).

Lhalungpa, Lobsang P. *The Life of Milarepa*. New York: Viking Penguin Books, 1992. The biography of a popular Tibetan Buddhist saint who lived during the eleventh and twelfth centuries.

Lopez, Donald S., ed. *Buddhism in Practice*. Princeton: Princeton University Press, 1995. A large selection of translated texts representing a cross-section of practices from several Buddhist contexts.

Obeyesekere, Rajini. *Jewels of the Doctrine: Stories of the Saddharma Ratnavaliya*. Albany: State University of New York Press, 1991. Fifteen stories from a Sinhala work written in the thirteenth century by a Sri Lankan monk.

Olson, Grant A. *Buddhadhamma: Natural Laws and Values for Life*. Albany: State University of New York Press, 1995. A rendition of central teachings in the Pali canon written by the contemporary Thai monk Prayudh Payutto.

Reynolds, Frank E., and Mani B. Reynolds. *Three Worlds according to King Ruang*. Berkeley: Asian Humanities Press, 1982. A royal text from Thailand that focuses on cosmology.

Strong, John S. *The Legend of King Asoka*. Princeton: Princeton University Press, 1983. A study and translation of the Asokavadana, a second-century Buddhist narrative from northwest India that records a version of the life and religious activities of King Asoka.

Thurman, Robert A. F. *The Tibetan Book of the Dead*. New York: Bantam Books, 1993. A manual for negotiating the travails of dying, death, and transmigration.

Tsai, Kathryn Ann. *Lives of the Nuns*. Honolulu: University of Hawaii Press, 1994. A collection of biographies of Chinese Buddhist nuns from the fourth to sixth centuries.

Watson, Burton. *The Lotus Sutra*. New York: Columbia University Press, 1993. A Mahayana text that has played a prominent role in East Asian Buddhist history and culture.

———. *The Vimalakirti Sutra*. New York: Columbia University Press, 1997. A popular Mahayana text, especially in East Asian traditions, that deals with the activities of a lay exemplar.

Yampolsky, Philip. *The Platform Sutra of the Sixth Patriarch*. New York: Columbia University Press, 1967. A text that claims to be the teachings of Hui-neng, an important figure in the Chinese Ch'an and Japanese Zen traditions.

Contributors

Robert E. Buswell is professor of East Asian languages and cultures at the University of California, Los Angeles. His contributions to Buddhist studies include *Paths to Liberation: The Marga and its Transformations in Buddhist Thought,* coedited with Robert M. Gimello (Honolulu: University of Hawaii Press, 1992).

Jason A. Carbine is an advanced graduate student in the history of religions program at the University of Chicago Divinity School. His contributions to Buddhist studies include "Discord and Concord in Buddhist Perspective," coauthored with Robert A. Yelle and Frank E. Reynolds in Joseph B. Gittler, ed., *Ideas of Concord and Discord in Selected World Religions* (Stamford, CT: JAI Press, expected 2000).

Rebecca Redwood French is associate professor of law at the University of Colorado at Boulder. Her contributions to Buddhist studies include *The Golden Yoke: The Legal Cosmology of Buddhist Tibet* (Ithaca, NY: Cornell University Press, 1995).

Richard Gombrich is professor of Sanskrit at Oxford University. His contributions to Buddhist studies include *The Perfect Generosity of Prince Vessantara: A Buddhist Epic,* translated with Margaret Cone (Oxford: Clarendon Press, 1977).

Hanna Havnevik is associate professor of history of religion in the Department of Culture Studies, University of Oslo. Her contributions to Buddhist studies include *Tibetan Buddhist Nuns: History, Cultural Norms, and Social Reality* (Oslo: Norwegian University Press, 1989).

Philip Kapleau is now retired and living at the Rochester Zen Center in New York. His contributions to Buddhist studies include *The Three Pillars of Zen,* which has been published in a number of editions.

Hiroko Kawanami is lecturer in religious studies at Lancaster University. Her contributions to Buddhist studies include a work in progress, *Worldly Sanctity: The Life of Burmese Buddhist Nuns.*

Charles F. Keyes is professor of anthropology at the University of Washington. His contributions to Buddhist studies include *Thailand: Buddhist Kingdom as Modern Nation-State* (Boulder, CO: Westview Press, 1987).

William R. LaFleur is professor of Japanese studies in the Department of Asian and Middle Eastern Studies at the University of Pennsylvania. His contributions to Buddhist studies include *The Karma of Words: Buddhism and the Literary Arts in Medieval Japan* (Berkeley and Los Angeles: University of California Press, 1983).

James Bissett Pratt (d. 1944) taught at Williams College, where he became professor of intellectual and moral philosophy. *The Pilgrimage of Buddhism and a Buddhist Pilgrimage* (New York: Macmillan, 1928) constitutes his major contribution to Buddhist studies.

Frank E. Reynolds is professor of history of religions and Buddhist studies at the University of Chicago. His contributions to Buddhist studies include *Three Worlds According to King Ruang: A Thai Buddhist Cosmology,* cotranslated with Mani Reynolds (Berkeley: Asian Humanities Press, 1982).

Juliane Schober is associate professor in the Department of Religious Studies at Arizona State University. Her contributions to Buddhist studies include her edited volume, *Sacred Biography in the Buddhist Traditions of South and Southeast Asia* (Honolulu: University of Hawaii Press, 1997).

Donald K. Swearer is professor of religion at Swarthmore College. His contributions to Buddhist studies include *Ethics, Wealth, and Salvation: A Study in Buddhist Social Ethics,* coedited with Russell F. Sizemore (Columbia: University of South Carolina Press, 1990).

S. J. Tambiah is professor of anthropology at Harvard University. His contributions to Buddhist studies include a trilogy on Buddhism in Thailand: *Buddhism and the Spirit Cults in North-East Thailand* (1970), *World Conqueror and World Renouncer* (1976), and *The Buddhist Saints of the Forest and the Cult of Amulets* (1984), all published by Cambridge University Press.

Holmes Welch (d. 1981) taught at Harvard University, where he became a lecturer in Chinese studies. His contributions to Buddhist studies include a trilogy on Buddhism in China: *The Practice of Chinese Buddhism, 1900–1950* (1967), *The Buddhist Revival in China* (1968), and *Buddhism Under Mao* (1972), all published by Harvard University Press.

Taiko Yamasaki is a professor in the Department of Esoteric Buddhist studies at Shuchi-in University in Kyoto, Japan. His contributions to Buddhist studies include *Shingon: Japanese Esoteric Buddhism* (Boston: Shambhala, 1988).

Index